Hi Tau Whincup.

from One Legend too Another legend

CHUBBY LAID BARE

Published in hardback in 2021 by Sixth Element Publishing on behalf of George Proudman and Roy Chubby Brown.

Sixth Element Publishing
Arthur Robinson House
13-14 The Green
Billingham TS23 1EU
www.6epublishing.net

© George Proudman and Roy Chubby Brown 2021

ISBN 978-1-914170-18-8

British Library Cataloguing in Publication Data. A catalogue record for this book is available from the British Library.

All rights reserved. No part of this publication may be reproduced, stored in a retrieval system or transmitted, in any form or by any means, electronic, mechanical, photocopying, recording and/or otherwise without the prior written permission of the publishers. This book may not be lent, resold, hired out or disposed of by way of trade in any form, binding or cover other than that in which it is published without the prior written consent of the publishers.

George Proudman and Roy Chubby Brown assert the moral right to be identified as the authors of this work.

Printed in Great Britain.

CHUBBY LAID BARE

GEORGE PROUDMAN
FOREWORD BY ROY CHUBBY BROWN

FOREWORD

My old school teacher used to say to me, 'Do you know, Vasey, you're wired up all wrong? Your brain differs from everyone else's. One thing you'll never need to improve on though is your personality 'cos you're always laughing.' Other kids used to be told, 'You'd be good at running or you'd be good at football.' My dad just used to say, 'You'd be good for nothing.'

How I got into show business has to be classed as a minor miracle, because my attitude always was, 'What effect am I going to have on people? We're all going to die anyway.' Wired up wrong, see?

I'd always admired lots of different styles of entertainers including Spike Milligan, Alexei Sayle, Ken Dodd and John Cleese amongst others, but generally all of them funny men. I quite quickly came to the conclusion that all comics are fiercely possessive about their originality, all having their own way of making people laugh and sticking to it.

I needed a bit of that, I needed to find my own niche in the entertainment world, so I became a blue comedian. There were plenty of 'clean' comics around, I was one of them, regularly passing the same jokes around between ourselves, but I was constantly ransacking my brain trying to come up with new funny lines. I still do that now. I was determined to stand out from the crowd, make people sit up and take notice. Everything I've ever done in my career has been done to make people laugh, not to offend.

I've caused some massive shocks even to myself when performing in such a huge variety of venues including The London Palladium, a circus tent, luxury liners and the roughest pub on any council estate with the same result of making them all laugh. It's the greatest feeling in the world, wherever it may be.

I've met and worked with some fantastic people along the way, not all pop stars but down to earth people who have all played a massive part in my life. George, who has written this book, is one and we've been great friends since meeting over fifty years ago. I can't imagine

George having an enemy in the world, he's so trustworthy… quite frankly, it's sickening. Even after all these years he makes me laugh every day with his observations on people. Yes, he's a right nosey old sod.

It's a very special thing to have your life chronicled for all to see, but even more so when other people have given their precious time to help, and I can assure you that you're in very safe hands when fingering through this book, having witnessed for myself the dedication from George to bring to you the real life story of myself… Roy Chubby Brown.

'Life's for living', hope you enjoy reading about mine.

Thanks to you all, love you.
Chubbs xxx

INTRODUCTION

'Chubby Laid Bare… The Roy Chubby Brown Story' cannot be described as an autobiography because a lot has been told by the people who have known him best throughout his rise to stardom, namely Roy's own family and those who have been lucky enough to have worked or been associated with him throughout his show-business career. Much has had to be told by the man himself, especially the early years, so we could actually call it a semi-autobiography… if there is such a thing.

It tells of how the streetwise Roy Vasey, a young lad who was never far away from landing himself in a whole load of trouble, turned into the hard-working comedy genius Roy Chubby Brown who we know today. Also known these days as Britain's King of Comedy, Roy has to be one of the hardest-working funny men to have trod the boards of theatre and clubland this country has ever seen.

Roy and I go back a long way. We used to go to limbo dancing classes together in the seventies. I first came across Roy Vasey back in 1970 BC (Before Chubby) when he was drumming with the band Pipeline. I joined the band as rhythm guitarist/lead singer in 1971, after which we performed together under various guises culminating with the Allcock and Brown act which gave Roy his adopted Brown surname.

The stories you'll read have developed from my conversations with a mixture of artistes, club acts, musicians, technicians, roadies, in fact most who have had a connection with Roy over his working life, as well as Roy's family, and of course the main man himself. You will learn a bit about their background and how they came to meet Roy and were, or still are, associated with him. You will read many stories that have never been told previously, plus a few that might be familiar.

We are going to cover seventy six years plus, from the day baby Roy took his first breath, through a time when getting on stage was all just a bit of fun, right up to the present era when Roy has fans stretching the length and breadth of the British Isles as well as all around the globe, while still classing it all as a bit of fun… 'We're just having a laugh, aren't we?'

We'll visit those years that have seen Roy face up to the same traumas that occur in many other people's lives too, as well as one's we wouldn't wish on our worst enemies, while still endeavouring to perfect his talent and vocation to make us all laugh our socks off. We are going to take you on the ride of a lifetime from Roy's impoverished early life as a child, through his troublesome teen years into adulthood and give you an insight as to how this extraordinary comedy machine came about.

You will experience all the lives he has touched and changed on his way to the top of his profession and his endless charity work, something that hasn't always been a well-known Roy Chubby Brown fact. You'll read that most who spent time working with Roy would end up regarding him more like a family member than a work colleague, and I make no excuses for repeating it in the book whenever I'm told.

Roy has dedicated his whole adult life to making us all laugh, and, as you've probably already gathered, it's been no cakewalk, even though there has been plenty of cake on the way. Roy himself is the first to admit that it took him thirty years to grow up, so we are going to try to show you how this extraordinary man swapped punch ups for punchlines.

As said, much of what you are about to read aren't only Roy's stories but stories from people who have played a big part in Roy's working, social and family life, so if anyone is going to be interested, excited and often surprised by the content it could be Roy himself. Events are remembered to the finest detail with some quite impossible to forget, but because the majority of us, including Roy, are old fogies now, when they actually took place can be a bit of a blur so please accept that we could be a year or two out on occasion.

The last fifty or so years have fittingly, for someone often referred to as 'Mr Blackpool', been something of a rollercoaster ride, so please fasten your seat belts, adjust your goggles and hold on to your helmets, while we enjoy a bumpy ride on 'The Big One' that is 'Chubby Laid Bare... The Roy Chubby Brown Story.'

Hope you get as much out of reading it as we've all had living it with him.

1

It seemed a normal night like any other, but noticeable was the bright red aura lighting the sky as if making a biblical statement of a forthcoming 'happening'. The reality of it was that the furnace at the local iron and steel works had just belched out its regular thunderous emission, filling the air with smoke and dust while turning the night into daylight engulfing the streets of Grangetown. Hard to call it normal though after six long hard years of war that still hadn't ended… nobody knew what normal was anymore.

Instead of the constant murmur and regular bursts of ear-splitting noise keeping residents awake, it was received as a reassuring sound like the sweetness of a lullaby giving the impression to all around that everything in the world was good. The works overlooked the surrounding area with the domination akin of a mysterious ancient god who would mumble and groan with occasional outburst to remind the good folk of Grangetown that he was still there looking after them. It was like a comfort blanket that allowed everyone to sleep safe and peaceful at night.

But this was no ordinary night. The bright red glow coming from the blast furnace appeared to be hovering, if not pointing toward a particular property in the town. That property was 78 Broadway, where Amy and Colin Vasey lived together with their five year old daughter Barbara. Even though there were no wise men available and not a virgin in sight, unbeknown to anyone else in the area, a star was being born.

The child – a boy, and born at home which was not an unusual occurrence – was immediately rushed into hospital with complications, having been found to be struggling for his little life with appendicitis and a twisted bowel. He was taken to Normanby Hospital only a few miles away, affectionately known locally as 'Titty Bottle Hospital' because it was directly opposite 'Titty Bottle Park' where young mothers would walk their newly born babies in their prams. After a worrying short stay, with a couple of delicate operations to put things right, the grit and determination that was to follow this tiny being through the whole of his life kicked in and the doctors decided that baby was fit enough to return home with his parents.

The homecoming was rightly celebrated, with the whole family being delighted at the birth of a baby boy, since mam Amy had suffered the tragedy of a stillborn boy before elder sister Barbara had been born... he would have been called Colin, after his dad.

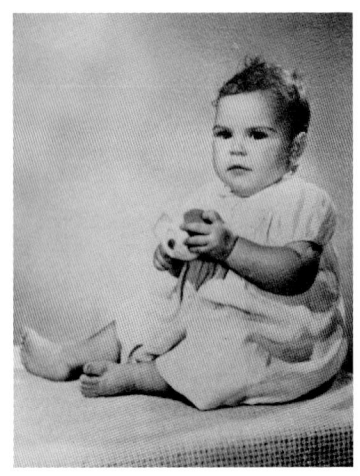

Yes, Chubby was a baby once!

This time though the name Royston was chosen after Colin's favourite actor, Roy Rogers, who was also a country and western singer famous for his hit record 'My Four Legged Friend', which was about his horse and not a freak who should have been in a circus. Royston quickly became known as Roy by Amy and Colin's extended family, only ever being given his full title over his youthful years on a Sunday or whenever he was in trouble.

Roy's Aunty Alice told him later that his mam thought that the name Royston was a bit too posh for Grangetown and after a heated family discussion she went back to the registry office and changed Royston to plain Roy. The change of name caused ructions between Amy and Colin, with her accusing him of wanting to posh Roy's name up to impress his golfing pals. Roy's still not sure what it says on his birth certificate, being certain he's seen it as both on different certificates. Royston Chubby Brown doesn't trip off the tongue as well as Royston Vasey does so we'll just have to accept the fact that it could be either.

Roy was a war baby... when his mam had originally told his dad she was pregnant there was fucking war, because having babies at that time was just a side effect of getting your leg over and no more. Now the birth had arrived, dad was just as elated and proud as the rest of the family. Roy was born 3rd February 1945, just before the end of World War Two. Roy's dad had done his bit for his country with Roy saying, 'Me dad fought with Mountbatten in Burma and Montgomery in Africa... couldn't get on with no bastard, me dad couldn't.'

Being born in 1945 meant that Roy missed out on being one of the 'Baby Boomers' who were born post war between mid 1946 and 1964. It seems Colin wasn't prepared to wait until the end of hostilities to have his end away.

As many of Roy's followers will already be aware, his early childhood years were spent at the family home in Grangetown, just a few miles south of Middlesbrough. Grangetown's main claim to fame by then had been the supplying of the materials for the building of the Sydney Harbour Bridge, the iron and steel having been produced at the giant Dorman Long Iron and Steel Works, later to become British Steel, which dwarfed the whole town. If anyone had been crazy enough to imagine that the new baby Roy would eventually perform on stage within a stone's throw of that famous bridge they would have marched them off to the nearest nut-house.

What Grangetown didn't yet know, as it wouldn't become apparent until years later, was that it had just become famous again in providing this lovely country of ours with one of the funniest men we'd ever encounter in our lives, someone who would eventually turn the entertainment business on its head, sending shockwaves through club and theatre land with his no nonsense, no holds barred style of comedy.

The Teesside area has never been known for its accent… being very much in the middle ground when it came to dishing out dialects. So without the ringing tones of the Geordie, Welsh, Brummie, Scottish, Scouse or Peter Kay's Bolton twang, the many famous vocalist/musicians, such as Chris Rea, Paul Rodgers of Free, David Coverdale of Whitesnake and more recently James Arthur, would have had to work extremely hard at creating their own melodic sounds.

Having said that, these industrial towns still had their own language – Grangetown being no different – that appeared to emerge from the back of the throat instead of the depths of the diaphragm. Together with regularly dropped aitches, the local slang sounded a bit like, 'Mr Stert went to werk in his best perple shert', instead of 'Mr Sturt went to work in his best purple shirt,' as they would have pronounced it on the BBC.

Typically, Grangetown was one of those grey industrial towns of the day with thick smoke belching from its blast furnaces at the steel works, blocking out the sun for much of the surrounding area. You certainly wouldn't have needed fake tan if you 'werked down the werks' as every pore of your exposed body would be ingrained with coal dust and soot. If you had a clean face and no muck under your nails, it probably meant you were on the dole.

Expectations were built on survival rather than ambition, which were generally to follow your father and the rest of your male family members into the monotony of werking your balls off at Dorman's to put food on the table, with the hope that there might be enough left over for a few pints in the club. In many homes, it was often the other way round with the club coming first and the food on the table a disappointing second, so much so that what often happened was that wifey would be waiting at Dorman's gate on a Friday after work to collect her hubby's just received pay-packet, in order to pay the household bills before it was all handed over the bar at the local Unity Club.

The Vasey family lived in a council house which was so damp they once caught a fish in a mousetrap and Roy's sister got rickets in her wooden leg. Even though Roy's dad had a good job 'down the werks' he liked his nights in the club, so Roy's mam had to be extra frugal when making purchases for the home, often buying second hand. Roy reckons their furniture was so old even then that it could now be a prime exhibit in the National History Museum. The eiderdown on his bed had two arms and two large pockets, being a well-used RAF overcoat his mam had managed to acquire from the local Army and Navy surplus shop.

Roy's dad went out to work while his mam stayed at home to look after the family. There was always something hot on the table for tea and a meal keeping warm for dad in the oven at the side of the large iron fireplace in the kitchen for when he came in from work. The kitchen was the main living room in those days, with most houses having a back kitchen where the cooking and washing up was done, and a parlour at the front of the house which was only ever used if you had visitors and wanted to make an impression.

Colin was ten years older than Amy and was a keen sportsman, enjoying the likes of tennis, cricket and snooker as well as golf, which Amy always thought made him look a bit snooty. It would have been the snooker though that introduced him to the social club life which he came to enjoy at the local Unity Club, becoming one of the committee and eventually Concert Secretary who would be responsible for arranging entertainment as well as other club-related functions.

Colin was a handy man, Roy remembers with a tear in his eye. 'He made my first pram, there was no bottom in it so I could walk before I could talk.' He'd been part of the Home Guard during the war and, according to Roy, one of his sayings was 'Always fight fire with fire!' which Roy thinks is why they kicked him out of the Fire Brigade. Colin made a windy-up gramophone out of an old orange box for the family and Barbara and her friends would sit baby Roy on the turntable, wind it up and then watch him spin round at 78rpm.

Roy, Mam and Barbara

Amy came from a big family, the Taylors. Roy recalls grandad Tommy, who worked at Smith's Dock on the River Tees, and Nanna Sarah, bringing up a whole host of aunties and uncles; in all they raised three boys and five sisters. The Taylor family lived on the same Broadway Road only at the opposite end, apart from Roy's Aunty Alice who actually lived just next door.

They were a close-knit family and, especially the girls, would often call in at the Vasey household to visit Amy and catch up on the local gossip. Although the two households were at opposite ends of the same road, it was still just a short walk away. Aunty Alice, living next door, was the most regular to call in, and it was one such visit that proved to be timely to say the least.

Amy was epileptic and prone to taking fits without warning,

often completely blacking out. On this particular day while she was bathing baby Roy in the tin bath on the floor in front of the fireplace, it happened. Amy had a fit, losing total control and falling forward onto Roy's tiny body, pinning him down in the bath water. She was lying across the bath as though lifeless, not moving at all, when thankfully the front door opened and in walked Aunty Alice; a timeless intervention if ever there was one.

Aunty Alice simply wandered into the kitchen, having popped in to borrow a cup of sugar, unaware of what was to greet her, getting the shock of her life at seeing Amy prostrate across the tin bath. Aunty Alice had seen Amy like this before so she knew what to do straightaway but had no idea how long she'd been in this position, and with no sign of Roy, after hearing a weak cry, she realised where he must be. Using all of her strength, she pulled Amy away from the bath to gain access to her baby nephew and lift him from the water.

As Amy was being unceremoniously manhandled, she started to come round at the same time as little baby Roy gave out a splutter and a loud cry. Aunty Alice took the frightened little boy out of the bath and calmed him down by wrapping him in a towel before handing him back to his mam who by this time had fully recovered from her fit and was sitting in an armchair next to the glowing fire. Both shaken from what had happened, it was now time to put the kettle on. Amazing what relief a good cuppa can give, but it hardly bears thinking about the consequences that could have occurred if Aunty Alice hadn't had a sweet tooth and couldn't face the prospect of drinking her tea without any sugar in it.

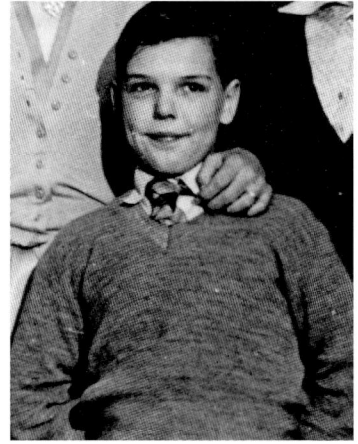

The Vaseys and the Taylors were quite religious, with the whole family, including Roy – or Royston as he still got called on a Sunday – attending the local Methodist church every week. From that it might be hard to believe that Roy would quite soon become one of those children your mam might say you shouldn't play with. It was one of those Sundays, when Roy was dressed in his Sunday best, which we all had in those days, religious or not, when he decided to sneak off on the way back from church with some of his mates to play at the local beck.

It was a popular spot with a Tarzan rope swing fastened to a tree branch that swung out over the beck. On a fine day there would generally be a queue waiting to take turns to see who could swing out the furthest, with the lucky ones still hanging on to it when it swung back. Roy and his mates would regularly go to the local Lyric cinema to watch Johnny Weissmuller as Tarzan and would always be looking forward to emulating his tree swinging antics on the local 'Tarzie' swing whenever they could.

On this day, dressed in his finery, Roy wasn't one of the lucky ones and, you've guessed it, whilst in full flow, his grip failed and he came plummeting down into the torrent below. There wasn't much water running through the beck really, just enough to turn it into a muddy mess, but, having landed upright, Roy knew he'd be in big trouble if he went home with his Sunday shoes soaked in mud.

Never one to be beaten, Roy decided that he could use his vest to clean himself up as no one would see it hidden under his shirt. Roy stripped down, taking off his vest and soaking it with the cleanest bit of water he could find then started to scrape and wash his shoes the best he could, eventually getting a reasonable result that he thought he could get away with. Unfortunately by now Roy's vest was so badly soiled and wet that it wasn't worth putting back on so he just threw it in the beck and left it there, putting the rest of his clothes back on and setting off home where nothing was noticed for the rest of the day.

Sunday was bath night ready for school the next morning and Roy's mam would do the honours, undressing and bathing him as most mothers would do for their young kids. After removing Roy's shirt, she blasted, 'Where's your vest, our Royston?' 'I... I... did'nt put one on this morning, mam,' came the reply. 'You bloody well did, I put it on you myself, CORRRRLIN!!!' at the top of her voice, 'Our Roy's come home without his vest, he's lost his bloody vest, I put one on him this morning!' At which point Roy's dad entered the room, glaring menacingly in the direction of the vest-less child.

'Some boys j-jumped on me, p-pinned me down and s-stole my vest, h-h-honest, dad,' whimpered Roy. But there was only one thing on his dad's mind and Roy braced himself for what was to come. Quite silently, without any real fuss, his dad's bony hand swung around and whacked him clean round the back of the head, after which his dad walked back out of the room, job done. Roy says, 'There was no talk about the vest after that. I'd had my fucking punishment so everything was forgotten about, but it wasn't the first clout around the lug I'd had and certainly wasn't going to be the fucking last.'

2

The family home on Broadway was part of the busy main trunk road between Middlesbrough and Redcar, but rather than get knocked down by a car, you would have been more likely to slip up on some horse shit left over by the milkman or the coalman's means of transport. That's if it hadn't already been shovelled up and placed in a bucket to be put on granddad's rhubarb (prefer custard meself). The kids in the area used to play a game called 'chicken' where they would lay in the road with the last one to get out of the way when a car came along being crowned as the winner; problem was they could all still be lying there a fortnight later waiting for a car to appear.

Broadway, being the main thoroughfare, was not an ideal place to bring up a young family who would want to play out in the street with their friends, as was the way back then. Health and safety as we know it today didn't really exist, having gone clean out of the window during the war years when anything metal and surplus to requirements – such as protective fencing surrounding school playgrounds and busy main roads – had been melted down to turn into munitions.

Some of Roy's earliest memories are of waking up in the morning to the smell of burning rent books, which helped to disguise the usual pong that followed him around. He says, 'I pissed the bed when I was a kid, went on for much longer than most kids. In fact I pissed the bed for so long that I learnt how to swim before I learnt how to walk… I could swim a full length of the bed before I was two. There was a permanent rainbow stretching from wall to wall in my bedroom, and I think I probably invented the very first fucking water bed.'

Roy's mam had placed a bucket at the side of his bed so she could lift him out for a wee before retiring herself… not that it made any difference. 'Me mam couldn't get me out of bed on a morning and I never had time for much of a wash so I usually ended up going to school stinking of dried piss,' says Roy. 'Still, the lad who sat next to me never had any problems with his sinuses.'

Roy's first day at school, aged five, could probably be seen as an insight of what was to come thereafter. Having been registered and met his new classmates and teacher, they were all given instruction as to what to do if they needed anything. 'Just put your hand up in the air and ask to go to the toilet if you need to,' explained teacher. Roy didn't need telling twice and shortly afterwards he put his hand up and asked if he could go. His request was granted so off he went unaccompanied out of the building to the toilet which was in the open air at the other end of the playground.

The playground was wide open to the streets outside with the metal railings having been removed for the war effort, so when Roy came back out of the toilet he took full advantage and just walked out of school and headed off home not really thinking he was doing anything wrong. On arriving home, he found the front door locked and no one in. Aunty Alice who still lived next door was in her front garden and spotted young Roy, who had decided to sit down on the doorstep. She told him that his mam had just nipped out to the shops and took him into her house to wait for her.

Needless to say that when his mam came back, Roy got a right rollicking and was frogmarched all the way back to school just in time for his dinner. No, Roy didn't get the best of starts to his schooling life and it became obvious very quickly that academia was never going to be his thing. Roy and school just weren't really going to hit it off at all. He does say though, 'There was nothing wrong with my school, it was approved.' That, I'm sorry to say, would be an experience he would endure in the not so very distant future.

Generally Roy looks back on his childhood in Grangetown with great fondness. Times were hard and people had to be tough but they were also an honest bunch who would always look out for each other regardless of what it took. Having said that, Roy still finds it hard to explain a certain incident that took place while his mam was out at the shops.

Roy takes up the story. 'There was one day me mam had put a stew on the stove to be ready for tea later on, then decided she had enough time to do her shopping whilst it was simmering away. During the short time she was out at the shops, the house got broken into and ransacked… wallpaper was ripped off the wall, the settee and chairs were torn, then one of the dirty bastards went and shit in me mam's stew!' Roy says. 'It was awful, we had to throw most of it away, well, two turds anyway.' *Great gag, Roy, but it's supposed to be a serious book about your life.*

These houses, mostly built after the war, had a huge black fireplace in the middle of the kitchen, and as a small kid Roy always found it quite frightening. The family, minus dad who was always at the club, would huddle around the fire on a cold night often listening to the radio, the only form of electrical entertainment there was. Maybe it was the fact that there was nowt else to do that contributed to the forthcoming 'baby boom'.

There was a song the kids used to sing about the big black oven; songs haven't always been lovey-dovey about boy falling in love with girl, boy falling out with girl then boy making back up with girl, you know. Roy remembers singing along to *'You push the damper in and you pull the damper out'* without an innuendo in sight. Apparently 'the damper' was state of the art technology of the time that helped keep the fire going.

'In the winter near Xmas, we would place chestnuts on a shovel and rest the shovel on the open hot coals until they were done.' Roy's licking his lips as he tells me. 'A real treat but I always burnt my fucking fingers taking the hot shells off, then everyone would laugh like fuck when I put the still red hot chestnut in my mouth, scorching my cheeks while flipping it from side to side in a desperate attempt to cool it down. It still didn't stop me wanting to have another one though. Those were some of the very few times that the family all laughed together… club must have been shut.'

Alongside and attached to the fireplace was a large oven. In fact the fire and the oven were one single unit, the oven being kept warm by the fire. Roy's mam would make an evening meal then having fed the kids, Barbara and Roy, she would put the remainder on a plate and place it in the big black oven to keep warm for Roy's dad coming in from work.

There was one teatime Roy remembers with a bit of a grimace. 'It was a Monday and a cold winter's evening. Mam had made a pie for our tea. Mam wasn't a great cook by any standard, but she did a decent enough meat and potato pie. Barbara and I had already eaten so dad's piece of pie, always much bigger than our share might I add, was left for him as usual in the oven. When dad came in from work he would always go into the back kitchen and wash the filthy work muck off his hands before sitting down to his tea.'

'Mam shouted, 'Get your dad's pie out of the oven, Roy.' It was always my job to retrieve dad's meal from the dark cauldron that always reminded me of the scary kid's stories we'd be told at school. I opened it slowly as I always did, it creaked quite loudly like a door opening on a horror movie and I never told anyone that I nearly shit myself every time had to go near it. I opened the door… screeeeech… always closing my eyes at this point. I knew when it was fully open 'cos I would hear a loud clunk as it dropped down on its hinges. I slightly opened one eye, searching into the black abyss in order to get my bearings to reach in and lift out me dad's tea. This time as I lifted the plate out I got the shock of my life. Draped across the pie were dad's work socks and a pair of badly stained long-johns. Monday was always wash day but because of the bad weather me mam had put dad's socks and undies in the oven to dry after washing them. She didn't give a shit that she'd had to rest them on me dad's tea, then I thought, Yuck! I've just had a piece of that pie. Still,' Roy admits, 'it certainly hasn't put me off eating pies. I love pies, me.'

Roy would have been about seven or eight, he's not sure, when the family moved house. They had been on the council list to move for quite a while, wanting to get away from the busy main road and finally got their wish, staying in Grangetown but moving to 30 Essex Avenue, with three bedrooms and a front and rear garden.

Life hadn't been easy for the Vaseys, with Amy and Colin leading very separate lives. It had taken its toll on their already extremely strained relationship, so Essex Avenue was intended to be a new start for everyone. Problem was that Essex Avenue was just around the corner from the Unity Club which was regarded as Colin's first home, not his second, with the reality being that, on the marital front, things were destined to go from bad to even worse.

3

Roy is the first to admit that his mam and dad were two very different people.

'One was a bloke and one was a women,' he cracks.

They were two very different personalities and didn't socialise as a couple very often at all.

'The only thing I ever saw me mam and dad do together was fucking argue,' quips Roy.

Amy and Colin had a volatile relationship, with Roy often wondering how they'd managed to form a close enough liaison long enough to produce both Barbara and himself. There's half a smile on his face as he recollects, 'We hardly had any crockery left in our house, most of the cups had no handles, having been used as missiles during numerous household bust-ups between them, with neither being much of a shot.'

There would be many a time when both Barbara and Roy found themselves in the middle of what often appeared to be a copy of the gunfight at the OK Corral with household objects being the ammunition instead of bullets.

The battles between Roy's mam and dad continued throughout his young life with both himself and his sister Barbara doing their best not to be caught up in them. They were usually confined to after the kids' bedtime when Colin came home from the club, though it was pretty obvious what was going on downstairs as they didn't make any effort to keep the noise down.

Amy would have liked to have gone out occasionally, see a movie at the cinema or dancing at the scout hut on Birchington Avenue. One night a week would have been enough for her but that wasn't possible. Colin was a club man and would visit the Unity Club on a nightly basis, going out about half past six and not coming in until closing time after ten thirty. Amy never went anywhere. All she had for company was the radio. Television was still relatively new and not affordable to most families. She would tune in to the radio, listening to The Archers each day as a form of escapism from the real world around her. The Archers was the forerunner of TV soaps such as Coronation Street, Emmerdale and Eastenders, and is still running to this day.

'There weren't many people who had a car in our street,' says Roy, 'not like now with cars parked along the side of the road, and there was only one house with a TV set, the Speakmans who lived further along. In 1953, the Queen's Coronation was televised on the BBC and just about everyone in the street huddled round their front window to watch it on the telly. They opened the windows so everyone could see. There was a street party with sarnies, cakes and fizzy drinks, and I can remember stuffing my face 'til I almost burst.'

A few years after that, in 1956 the Queen visited the giant ICI Chemicals complex which was just outside Grangetown, on the way to Redcar. 'She had to pass the end of our street, coming along the Trunk Road, so I went and stood on the bridge with other onlookers to get a glimpse of her as she went past. We all had small Union Flag sticks to wave.' Roy smiles. 'It was a beautiful sunny day and as the Queen's car reached to where I was standing, I'll swear she looked me straight in the eye and waved back at me. She probably dug Prince Philip in the ribs with her elbow and said, 'Phil, look there's Chubby,' with Prince Philip replying, 'So it is, the Fat Bastard."

On rare occasions there would be a family card night at Roy's house, when aunties and uncles would come round for a game of Chase the Ace. Being good Methodist churchgoers, there was never any foul language used on those nights. One time when all of the cards had been dealt out, Roy noticed that he'd been dealt the only ace left in the pack with the others having been removed as part of the game. At the age of eight or nine, Roy wasn't always sure what was going on but enjoyed joining in as it wasn't that often the whole family sat round the table together. Aunties and uncles were taking it very seriously, betting with pennies and halfpennies and going round the table in turn. It came to Roy's turn when one of the aunties quizzed, 'I wonder what our Roy's got.' Then quite excitedly, not realising he should be keeping it to himself, Roy blurted out, 'I've got the arse of spades!' Well, his dad, who was sat right next to him, whacked him so hard that he knocked him off his chair on to the floor. Roy still doesn't know to this day what made him say 'arse' instead of 'ace'. The aunties and uncles evidently found it hilarious and couldn't stop laughing for ages.

Even with tension at home being fraught, there were happier times to remember when Colin always made sure the family enjoyed an annual holiday… generally Scarborough, Whitby, anywhere that you could get to quite easily on the train. Those were the times that Roy and Barbara would look forward to but always with increasing trepidation as each year their mam and dad's relationship appeared to be deteriorating right in front of their very eyes.

'Opposite Peasholm Park in Scarborough was an open air swimming pool,' recalls Roy. 'We'd regularly go in for a swim and a play on the diving boards, but it was always fucking freezing. I'd be about seven or eight so we're talking early fifties, and me mam had knitted me a swimming costume which wrapped round my bollocks like clingfilm making them feel even colder than they actually were. I was just glad she hadn't been to the Army and Navy surplus store like she usually did or I would have been going in for a dip wearing a rusty old frogman's suit. Our one week away each year was a bit like entering into another world. We'd stay in a bed and breakfast and there was always plenty to do during the day, leaving less time for me mam and dad to fight with each other. On an evening though, when it was time for me and Barbara to go to bed, me dad, who never went anywhere without his CIU club card, which was his pass into any Social or Workmen's Club in the country, would leave us kids and me mam and bugger off to the nearest workies for a few pints. Me mam never said fuck all, it was regarded as par for the course and by now she was quite used to it. I'm now sure she put up with it for the whole week just for the sake of giving us kids a good time.'

Back to reality in Grangetown, the marital relationship was to hit such a low point that Colin would ask other men to take Amy out for the day. Roy says, 'Me dad was so not bothered at the time that one day he asked his boss at work, a fellow called Ted Bridges, if he was doing anything the next day. When Ted said that he wasn't, Colin asked if he'd take Amy out in his car maybe to the seaside, Redcar being just up the road.' Roy continues, 'It was as if me dad was trying to get rid of me mam. Ted was only one of three or four blokes me dad would ask to take me mam out for a few hours.'

Roy thinks his dad was at the end of his tether, with his mam having such a short temper, it was as if his dad couldn't cope anymore and just wanted shot of her. The scraps between the two of them were becoming more regular and of epic proportion, screaming at the top of their voices with his mam often yelling to his dad not to shout so loud in front of the kids and his dad retaliating, threatening to 'batter her!'... which he often did. Roy thinks, even now, that in those days the violent behaviour between husband and wife would regularly finish up with the husband giving the wife a thump, which was rarely talked about, just accepted as the norm.

Colin continued to play cupid, lining up suitors to accompany Amy on day trips in an effort to keep her happy but also, Roy is certain of, in an attempt to get one of them to take her off his hands. Eventually one day during Roy's first year at the senior school, Sir William Worsley's, on arriving home he found Barbara sat in the kitchen with a note in her hand.

'It's from our mam,' said Barbara, 'she's gone.'

With the wind taken out of his sales, Roy sat down while Barbara read their mam's letter.

It was short and not so sweet. 'I love you both very much,' read Barbara, 'and I'm going to miss you but I can't live with your father anymore and I've gone away. I'll get in touch with you when I can.' Roy explains that the fights between his mam and dad were usually six of one and half a dozen of the other, his mam having a terrible temper but also having to endure regular wallops from his dad during many of their arguments.

The end result was that Amy went off with one of Colin's friends, Norman, someone that he'd paired her off with for days out. It appears from what Roy says that his dad's original plan, if there ever was one, had actually worked with Amy disappearing out of his life forever.

Grown up... Barbara and Roy

It meant Barbara had to suddenly become the lady of the house at the tender age of sixteen, looking after both Roy and their dad, cooking, cleaning and general household duties which would have been attended to by their mam.

'Mr and Mrs Robinson – Jenny and Harry – lived next door to us at number 28 with their daughter Joy,' says Roy. 'They appeared to have a marriage made in heaven, total contrast to our house, never heard them argue though I'm sure they must have in their own four walls. Unlike my mam and dad's angry tirades where the whole street would be able to listen in as though it was an episode of The Archers. I often used to wish my own house could be like Jenny and Harry's, you know… cups with handles.'

Joy was in the same class as Roy at school and Mrs Robinson asked Roy to look after her. They would go off to school together hand in hand with all of Roy's mates teasing them calling out 'Joy and Roy, Joy and Roy' and laughing, as though they were boyfriend and girlfriend.

It was Mrs Robinson who said to Roy that she couldn't understand his mam going off like that because she absolutely adored him and thought the sun shone out of Roy's arse.

Barbara continued with her new life as main cook and bottle washer, eventually escaping after meeting a boy and moving out of the house to make a home with him. This left Roy at home with his dad, and with dad working every hour he could before spending the rest of the day in the club, it became up to Roy to keep the house in order. Roy would get his main meal at school which he remembers with a not so pleasing look on his face.

'Some things were alright, but I never liked to eat greens, cabbage and stuff, and every meal was served with something I couldn't stand, salad with cucumber, I hate cucumber even now. Then bugger me, they'd bring out a bowl of fucking frogspawn for afters, yuck! I would have been happier with a fishcake and some beans.'

Roy's dad would get fed in the works canteen at Dorman's, having breakfast early on and lunch at mid-day. Teatime sorted itself out. Roy says, 'There was always someone in the street, sometimes Mrs Robinson from next door, or it could be anyone, who said, 'Here's a pie to warm up for your dad when he comes in from work, Roy,' or, 'There's some chips and a couple of eggs for tea when your dad comes in.' Everyone wanted to look after us.'

Sometimes Roy would cook for them both but it couldn't have

Roy with his Dad on holiday in Blackpool

been that appetising because Roy's always said that he's the only person he knows that burns salad.

Roy was now a latchkey kid, coming home from school to let himself in to an empty house. With his dad coming in from work, having his tea and then going off to the club, it allowed Roy plenty of unsupervised time to get up to whatever he wanted to. We are talking age eleven, twelve, not even quite a teenager and, with so much delinquency around him from his mates, it was probably inevitable, with his destiny in his own hands, that he would follow in their footsteps.

Even then, Roy was always up for a laugh. His mates loved it and were always egging him on… not that he needed egging on, by the way. Fearless Roy would make his pals laugh by always being the first one to volunteer if there was a mischievous or even dangerous prank to be performed. If anyone said, 'Let's smash a window,' as a joke, Roy would be the one to do it.

He says, 'It's the sort of thing kids got up to if they didn't have a loving mother and father at home. It's been said before that comedians crave the attention because they're looking for love. I suppose that would have been the same for me, acting the fool at every given opportunity.'

The lads would regularly nick bottles of milk off people's

doorsteps, but that would be classed as mild entertainment just to keep their hand in, if you like. Sweetshops would be their main target, the smaller shops were tight little units, quite dingy and dark with narrow aisles that snaked around in order to cram as much produce in as possible. Consequently this left many hidden areas around the shop out of view of the shopkeeper just begging for the likes of Roy and his mates to fill their pockets with whatever they wanted.

Roy's lack of fear, which would hold him in great stead later on in life as he conquered the trials and tribulations to become the country's King of Comedy, was at this age threatening to get him into more and more trouble as he grew into his teens.

Again, the fear factor was missing as Roy mastered the art of pilfering whatever he wanted without having to pay. Sadly the slippery slope that was to shape Roy's existence for the next ten years or so had well and truly reared its ugly head, and he would find it an extremely difficult platform to resist or break away from.

4

This was post war Britain and although we are more aware of Post Traumatic Stress Disorder (PTSD) today, it's hard to imagine what state of mind the soldiers might have been in on their return to Civvy Street, or the things that could trigger off unusual or even violent behaviour. Grangetown would certainly not have been on its own coping with the mental and physical problems that followed such a catastrophic event as World War Two yet this would be the atmosphere that the likes of Roy Vasey and his peers would experience during their formative years, moulding the personalities that they would take with them for the rest of their lives.

The fifties was also a time of great change and experiment, especially for the younger generation. Mam and dad had been used to going to the cinema to see Fred Astaire with Ginger Rogers, Bing Crosby, or maybe our own Gracie Fields and George Formby. Now it was the kids' time, the revolution came along with James Dean and glamorous Hollywood actresses like Jayne Mansfield and Gina Lollobrigida which resulted in testosterone levels going through the roof.

Then along came Elvis and all hell let loose… just about every hot-blooded young male wanted to be like him with his slick black hair, quiff and sideburns. If any old geezer of our age tells you he didn't stand in front of the mirror with 'tapoline', tap water to you, on his hair, miming Elvis records into his mam's hairbrush, he's probably lying through his back teeth… if he still has any.

All that was missing were the clothes, then boom… it was time for the Teddy Boy. Teddy Boys got their name from the clothes they wore, being partly inspired by the styles worn by dandies in the Edwardian period. Teddy Boys also came with a reputation of being unruly, cheeky, off-hand, rebellious and totally out of control. With the introduction of the rock 'n' roll sound from America and the films – such as Rock Around the Clock – to go with it, Teddy

Boys, or Teds as they came to be known, would slash seats, let off fireworks or throw bottles… scenes you would never have seen at a showing of The Wizard of Oz.

Roy wanted to be a Teddy Boy, but he was still only a young lad with no money coming in. He'd had a paper round but got the sack for putting all of his papers in the nearest bin instead of delivering them. He used to supplement his paper round wages by nicking ice cream and lollies out of the shop's fridge after he realised it was out of sight of the shop keeper, then selling them on, so it hadn't been a total waste of time.

Teds would have a quiff style haircut plastered with Brylcreem and long sideburns, adorning themselves with drainpipe trousers and chunky soled leather shoes, together with a velvet collared knee length jacket. Being penniless, Roy was unable to afford all the gear that he needed to become a genuine Ted, so without telling anyone, he decided to borrow one of his dad's work coats which stretched down around his knees, then soaked his hair in tap water and went off to join his mates, looking about as menacing as a bloke who was about to start a shift down the werks.

Roy's pals – Nanda Bassett, Swet Parfitt and Gandi Jarret – couldn't stop laughing but, still only aged twelve, Roy was deadly serious about becoming Grangetown's first Teddy Boy so it was decided that he would get the outfit to go with it by hook or by crook… with crook being the usual way Roy managed to acquire things by then.

Visits to Burton's the Tailors, Freeman Hardy Willis for shoes and finally the barber did the trick (with only the haircut being paid for, by the way). Roy was finally a Ted. These clothes shops were always very busy at that time with everyone wanting to keep up with the latest trendy gear, copying what they'd seen on the telly coming from Carnaby Street in London, so sneaking out with something tucked under your arm was no problem to well established tea leaves like Roy and his mates; just think of the Artful Dodger from 'Oliver!'

By this time, Roy's behaviour had become more unruly, getting into trouble at school and in the community, leaving him at risk of turning into a delinquent. This was much to the disappointment of his dad, who had led a very staid life so far, going to church, minding his own business, even training Alsatian Dogs for the local Police Force. But Roy was now a Ted, and his world was becoming more criminalised by the day, and he wouldn't be able to resist shoving something in his pocket whilst walking around a shop, whether he needed it or not.

Roy was also getting a reputation as someone you wouldn't pick a fight with, although Ged Luker, who lived behind Roy then in Robert Avenue, remembers, 'Roy wasn't the kind you would ever feel threatened by, not someone you had to avoid. You never felt that it would be safer to cross the road if he was coming towards you in the street, though there were plenty of other boys that you would keep out of the way of in Grangetown. He wasn't one of those lads that would start a fight for no reason, in fact you would often see him stepping in if he thought someone was being given a hard time, getting bullied or tormented.' Problem was that whenever that happened there'd always be someone who would call the police and by the time they had arrived Roy would be in the thick of it, so it was always Roy who got carted off to the police station on an all too regular basis.

The Luker family and the Vasey family lived back to back with an adjoining fence at the bottom of both gardens. Ged and Roy still meet up after all these years, often talking about how they survived the Grangetown fifties lifestyle when they were back door neighbours.

Something that has stayed in Ged's memory all these years gives enlightenment to what life might have been like for anyone in 1950s Grangetown. 'Next door to Mr and Mrs Robinson were the Flanagans, they would be Roy's next door but one neighbours,' recalls Ged. 'Margaret Flanagan was a good friend of me mothers. I never knew Mr Flanagan's first name 'cos he always got called Bud after Bud Flanagan of The Crazy Gang. They were a strong catholic family and one Christmas Eve Mr Flanagan was at midnight mass in the St Mary's catholic church when someone came in and unprovoked knocked fuck out of him with a hammer. He survived but turned into a recluse after that and never went out.'

'What was it over? Did you ever find out?' asks Roy.

'No, I never knew, I think it was just someone coming home from the pub pissed but it looked like he'd singled Mr Flanagan out on purpose.'

Folk had got used to aggressive behaviour being a regular occurrence in the streets of Grangetown, but even that would have shocked everyone to the core.

With that sort of thing able to happen at the drop of a hat, it's no surprise that Roy and his pals had to grow up really fast and make sure they were able to look after themselves in a tight corner. Roy had noticed that they were giving martial arts classes for free at his local boys club, quite unusual for those days, so he enrolled and got taught how to kickbox. Roy says, 'They showed me how to knock someone out with me bare feet, then one night while I was walking home from the boys club I got jumped on by two lads who knocked shit out of me while I was getting me shoes and socks off.'

A few years later, Joy, Mr and Mrs Robinson's daughter from next door married a submariner. Ged says, 'He would go off to sea in his submarine and no sooner had he gone but he was back again. Me dad used to say, 'Is he back already? How long do submarines submerge for these days? I can hold me bloody breath longer.' Ged continues, 'He was a bit of a wrong 'un, he treated Joy really bad.'

Ged tells of the time Mrs Robinson came into Roy's house looking quite glum and Roy asked why. Mrs Robinson answered, 'That lad's been knocking our Joy about. I wondered if you'd go and have a word with him, Roy.'

'Have a word?' Roy was still very protective towards Joy. 'Have a word? I'll knock his fucking head off!'

Ged knows all of theses tales and he carries on, 'You went round and as soon as he opened the door, you just panned him there and then, didn't you?'

Roy says, 'I gave him one hell of a fucking whack! I said, 'If you fucking touch her again I'll come round here and fucking kill you!' I loved Joy to bits, but we never went out together, even though the lads at school used to put two and two together and make five… we were all fucking useless at maths in our class.'

One of the main focal points in the area was The Lyric cinema, people would queue round the block to get in to see the latest films. There'd usually be a scrap or two going on in the queue with one of the Grangetown hard knocks thinking he could just walk straight to the front while six other lads jumped him to remind him that he couldn't and that 'he wasn't as fucking hard as he actually thought he was anyway'.

Both Roy and Ged have memories of arranged meetings with girls before going in to miss most of the big picture being too busy groping in the back seats. Cinema was in its hey-day with South Bank just up the road having three picture houses: The Empire, Majestic and Hippodrome where Paul Daniels' dad was the projectionist, Paul being a Slaggy Islander (from South Bank).

Roy remembers seeing Elvis in his first film, Love me Tender, at the South Bank Hippodrome. With everyone having only seen the King on photos and billboards at first, nobody knew which one on the screen was him. 'We want Elvis!' shouted Roy at the top of his voice, only for old Jack the doorman to come along, shine his torch in his face and threaten to kick him out. Jack obviously didn't know just how close he was to getting his torch rammed so far up his wrinkly old arse that it would be beaming out of his not so shiny blue eyes. Roy concludes, 'When I look back, weren't bouncers old and skinny in those days?'

The Hippodrome had a corrugated iron roof and if it rained while you were watching a film you couldn't hear the actors speaking. Roy tells of the time he went to see Gregory Peck in Moby Dick, a film about a giant whale. 'Just as the film came on, it started to rain, a proper downpour. It got heavier and heavier beating against the tin roof until, as they were chasing the whale through the rough seas on the screen, there was thunder and lightning too. Now I know it wasn't available then but I'll swear it was the very first film I ever heard in fucking surround sound. We were shitting ourselves by the end of the movie, thought the roof was going to cave in.'

The Forum was another cinema within a short trolley bus ride. It was in Normanby and one of Roy's mates had fixed him up with a blind date, it was arranged that they would meet outside. Roy had to get two buses, changing at South Bank, to get there. The trolley buses used to come along every ten minutes and the fare was only ever one or two old pennies to get to wherever you wanted to go.

The bus stopped directly outside the Forum cinema and as Roy got off he could see a young girl standing outside the front door as if she was waiting for someone. 'I won't go into a full description of what my 'mate' had fixed me up with,' says Roy, 'but as I got closer, well, let's just say she wasn't exactly my type. We introduced ourselves, I said I was Cary Grant, a heartthrob of the day, now I wasn't going to give her my real fucking name, was I? Hadn't got any plans of seeing her again. She had a nice name though, Marilyn Monroe. Then she said, 'I'll pay for myself.' I said, 'No, I'll pay.' I had a few bob in those days. We got in and she led me straight to the back row of seats, then as soon as we sat down she tightly grabbed hold of my hand. Before she could go any further, I said that I needed the toilet, but instead of going for a waz, I went straight out of the front door, onto the first trolley bus and fucked off home, a trick I'd picked up on my first day at school, leaving Marilyn Monroe sat in the flicks on her own.'

As kids though, The Lyric was the chosen cinematic venue, being virtually just around the corner in Grangetown. Ged is quick to back Roy up when he says, 'Saturday morning matinees were great. Our parents would give us the money to get in and another tanner to spend on ice cream or sweets. They were just glad to get rid of us all for a few hours. The Lyric was always packed to the rafters with unruly kids shouting at the top of their voices, throwing sweets and drinks at each other, but as the lights dimmed to start showing the movies, there'd be a loud cheer then silence for a while. We'd watch The Three Stooges, cartoons like Casper The Ghost, Mickey Mouse and Tom and Jerry. The matinee would always finish with a serial film that followed on each week, Zorro, Batman, maybe a cowboy. Then the lights would go back on, mayhem would return as everyone filed unceremoniously out through the side doors. Once we were in the street, we'd fasten our cardies round our neck to copy the heroes we'd just seen on the big screen like Batman, or fly around smacking our arse cheeks to make the sound of a horse galloping like the cowboys, then it was off down the beck to play on the Tarzie swing. We must have looked fucking stupid, but at seven, eight, or nine who really gave a shit?'

Roy and Ged reminisce about Grangetown being a great place to grow up in even with its rough edge. The seaside was just a few miles up the road and Eston Hills, on the edge of the North Yorkshire moors, only a short walk away. Kids were allowed a lot more freedom then and, as long as you were back in time for your tea, you could go off anywhere you wanted to, though Roy's home situation gave him more scope than others when it came time to being back at the ranch.

Roy and his mates would often go rambling to the top of Eston Hills, real name the Cleveland Hills, to reach The Nab which is a small monument marking the highest point. This gave them a view over their home territory which in those days would have been mostly obscured by the smoke bellowing out from the Dorman Long works. The lads would take with them bottles of water, jam sandwiches and anything else they could pilfer from the local shops on the way, spending hours exploring the extremely dangerous open shafts that had been left over from the iron ore mines that supplied the local iron and steel works.

    Parents were never sure what their kids were getting up to, not seeing them for most of the day, especially during school holidays. The bottom line being that Colin, Roy's dad, didn't have a clue what mischief his son could be engaged in while he was either at work or at the club. That would be until the local bobby knocked on the front door, with Roy in hand, having caught him involved in something less innocent than a jaunt up the hills or a visit to the seaside, which was happening with increasing regularity the older Roy got.

5

Roy loved to doodle, always fiddling around with a pencil, drawing anything he could think of instead of concentrating on lessons. We all learn how to scribble when we're tiny and then be encouraged to draw mam or dad with a big nose, one eye in the forehead and big floppy African elephant's ears. 'Looks just like you,' mam will say to dad.

Having moved on to senior school, Roy was about to realise he had a talent for drawing without initially thinking it was anything special. At first Roy would try and draw the Walt Disney and Looney Tunes characters he'd see on Saturday mornings at the Lyric cinema matinees, Donald Duck being his favourite. Then, with little interest in what teacher was saying, he would spend his class time drawing cartoon images of his friends and teachers at school, then pass them round the class. Once it got known, all of his classmates wanted a drawing of themselves to take home so Roy was always kept quite busy, but not with lessons, much to his teacher's dismay.

Roy remembers his teacher calling him out to the front of the class one day and asking, 'How many drawings have you done today, Roy?' 'Er… er… only about one or two, Miss.' 'Well, how come I've got ten or twelve in my hand? Have you not been taking notice of anything I've said today?' Then she screwed all of the drawings up, threw them in the bin and gave him a clip round the lug before sending him to stand in the corner of the room in disgrace.

Roy would always want to get involved if there was ever any redecorating being done at home, wallpapering or painting. He would ask his dad if he could help and get the same answer every time, 'No, son, you'll put the paint on upside down.'

'For years,' Roy says, 'I thought you could.'

Inspiration came from reading the newspaper his dad would bring home from work. Roy wasn't interested in what was going on in the outside world, it was the Andy Capp strip cartoon and the drawings in the joke section of the paper that were the focus of his attention. Andy Capp was drawn by Reg Smythe who, unbeknown to Roy at the time, originated from Hartlepool just the other side of the River Tees from where Roy lived in Grangetown.

The Andy Capp stories were usually about four or five frames long and were based around Andy's escapades in the pub or the bookies, with his long suffering wife Florrie waiting at home, standing behind the front door with a rolling pin in her hands, ready to give him a wallop as he walked in. Andy and Florrie's stories were always very funny, but also brilliantly drawn, and they probably reminded Roy of his own mam and dad. It was likely that you could walk into many households in the fifties and come across similar couples with dad sporting Andy's flat cap and mam adorned in Florries's flowery pinny.

Those cartoonists that Roy would see each day in the newspapers and on the cinema screen, even though not knowing who they were, became in Roy's world his own Picasso or Leonardo da Vinci. Roy would practise and practise, honing his own skills to make his cartoon drawings as near to theirs as he possibly could, becoming quite the expert himself at still a very young age.

Roy aged about 15 (note the Teddy Boy quiff)

Roy's drawing was something that would get him into trouble more than just at school though… once he let his mind wander, there was no stopping him. As well as the regular bother with his teacher, he also came a cropper when he thought he was helping out at home. Roy had decided that the bathroom at home was looking a bit drab and needed a bit of an overhaul. Taking the matter into his own hands, he decided that it could be massively improved with something a little bit more interesting on the walls.

Out came the coloured paints and Roy the decorator took over. 'Think we'll have an Andy Capp here overlooking the bath with Florrie staring menacingly toward him rolling pin in hand.' Roy's mind was going overboard. 'Tom at one side of the mirror above the sink chasing Jerry at the other side of the mirror.' Then standing back to admire what he'd already done, 'Now for my favourite Donald Duck standing proudly above the bog.'

Roy was absolutely delighted with the finished article. Not so his irate father when he came in from work. The first thing dad always did when he came in from work was go straight upstairs and sit on the toilet with his newspaper.

'ROYYYYSTON! ROYYYYSTON!' Roy's dad still gave him his full name when he was in trouble whether it was on his birth certificate or not. 'ROYSTON… get your bloody arse up these stairs right now. What the fucking hell have you done to my bathroom?' 'Er… er… I thought it needed decorating, dad.' 'Decorating? You call that decorating? I'll have my head between Tom and Jerry while I'm having a shave, threatened by Florrie Capp's rolling pin when I'm in the bath and bugger me, Donald Duck looking straight up the crack of my arse while I'm having a shit!'

'Er… er… thought you'd like it, dad.'

'Like it? Fucking like it? You've ruined the bathroom, I'll have to get some paint and cover it all up. Get out of my sight!'

'Strangely enough,' says Roy, 'I didn't get the usual smack round the back of the head.'

A few days later, Roy was in the front garden when next door neighbour Mrs Robinson came out. 'How are you, Roy? Is everything okay?' she always asked.

'Yes thanks, Mrs Robinson,' replied Roy, 'apart from our dad playing hell with me for drawing on the bathroom walls. Says he has to repaint them now.'

'Well, your dad's two-faced, Roy, that's all I can say.'

'Why do you say that, Mrs Robinson?'

' 'cos he's been bringing his mates around all week and taking them to your bathroom to show them your cartoons. He's actually as proud as punch and all of his mates love 'em.'

'It wasn't something you thought about in those days but I do wish I'd taken a photograph of the bathroom before me dad painted over them,' concludes a sullen Roy.

Roy's sketches started to draw attention and eventually around the age of fifteen, after first trying to carve a career out at Welford's Bakery, he secured himself a job at the local Evening Gazette in Middlesbrough, drawing caricatures of anyone who might be in the news. A dream job for someone who just loves drawing, you might think, but it only lasted four weeks when he was paid the measly sum of twelve bob for his efforts (twelve shillings which today is 60p). Twelve bob actually went quite a long way in those days but Roy's ex-school mates were raking it in werkin' down the werks, and he decided he fancied a bit of that.

Still only fifteen going on sixteen, Roy told his dad what he wanted to do. Roy's dad knew all that was going on down at Dorman's and said William Press, who were a contracting company working in Dorman's, were looking for labourers and to give them a try. Roy got a start straightaway, doing heavy digging work. He was a big lad and it didn't bother him because the money was good.

Roy hadn't been there very long, when one of the gaffers, Arthur Stairs, asked, 'Can anyone drive a dumper truck?' Roy said, 'I can.' Roy admits now, 'I'd never driven a dumper before but was told it was only two gears so what could wrong? It's got to be better than heavy digging all fucking day.'

Arthur said, 'Let's go and get the dumper.' Roy says, 'The dumper was parked up outside the hut where we had our cup of tea. Big orange thing it was. I climbed on board and started it up, slipping into first gear. It gave a bit of a shudder but I was alright, I was going forward.' Roy carries on, 'We went on to the site where a big ready mixed concrete wagon drove in. I had to edge my way very gently under the chute to let the liquidised concrete flow into the dumper bucket until it was full. Then I had to drive the dumper to a hole in the ground that was waiting to be concreted and tip it in. First day went without a hitch so, next day when I arrived at work, I asked, 'Am I back on the shovels today?" Arthur the foreman replied, 'No, you're on the dumper truck again, Roy. 'Great,' thought Roy. Driving the dumper truck was a doddle compared with the heavy digging he'd been doing before. Roy picked up the dumper then went off to where the ready mix concrete wagon was waiting to unload and got it filled.'

Roy explains, 'When the wet cement was in the dumper bucket it slopped around as you moved so, as I was reversing, the concrete was doing just that. I was to drop it into a large hole that had about a dozen lads at the bottom still digging it out. When I got there, Arthur shouted for me to come forward, which I did at first but then accidentally put the gears in reverse. As I did the whole dumper jerked with the wet cement gushing forward and out of the bucket, covering Arthur from head to toe.' Roy laughs. 'It looked like a scene from a Hollywood gangster movie where I'd just given someone a concrete jacket ready to drop them in the river. As I went back, I shit myself and quickly jammed it into first gear causing the dumper to lurch forward over the top of the hole and headfirst towards the bottom. There were about a ten or twelve lads down there still working. I'm screaming at the top of my voice for them to get out of the way. When I came to a stop, Arthur the foreman shouted, 'Is he down there? Is he alright?"

Roy with more hilarity, 'I had two pairs of trousers on and the top pair had a hole in the crotch area and as the dumper was falling I tried to jump off but my pants got caught on a hook or a screw on the dumper seat so it kept pulling me back. In the end, I was at the bottom of the hole still sat in the dumper. Everyone was okay, when Arthur shouted back down, 'Is he alright?' One of the lads replied, 'Yes, he's alright, boss.' Then an irate Arthur shouted back, 'Well, tell him he's fucking sacked!'

Roy would go on to find himself getting into even bigger 'holes' as he meandered through his teens desperately searching for the perfect job.

'With my tail between my legs, I went over to the blast furnaces where dad was working with his mates and he asked me how I was. When I told him I'd got the sack, all of his mates came over to hear what had happened, they all just laughed like fuck. I said, 'It's not fucking funny.' I could have killed someone, the hole was about ten feet deep and if I'd landed on anyone they'd have been fucked. Now I was out of work and looking for another job. Thankfully at that time you could literally walk out of one job straight into another, if you weren't too fussy what you did, that was.'

Roy's teenage working disasters were now becoming an adventure of their own and we'll hear more about his employment related experiences as we move on.

Although Roy had left his cartoon making career well behind him after leaving the Evening Gazette to chase 'The Big Bucks', he has continued with his drawings right up to the present day, from having covered one of our band vans with colourful flowers in the early seventies to auctioning his efforts off at theatre shows supporting his many charities. These days his subjects are a little bit more near the knuckle than his earlier Andy Capps and Donald Ducks and accompanied with the no-nonsense Roy Chubby Brown humour we've all come to love.

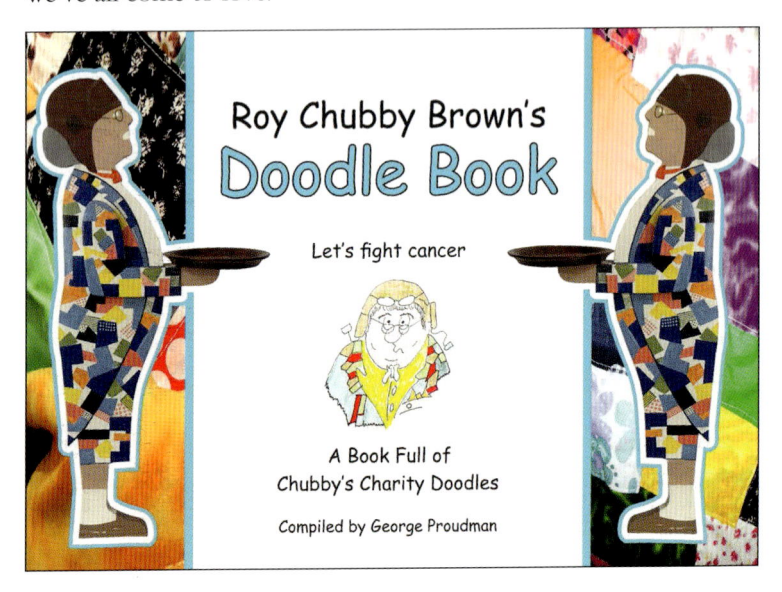

Roy Chubby Brown's Doodle Book

Let's fight cancer

A Book Full of Chubby's Charity Doodles

Compiled by George Proudman

You can get a taste of Roy's current expertise from a recent book called 'Roy Chubby Brown's Doodle Book'. It's a collection of drawings that have been auctioned for charity and presented to Chubby fans at various gigs over the years, with a boat load of gags thrown in. It's a great fun read.

6

Going back a bit, at the tender age of fifteen, which was the legal age of kicking kids out of school back then – with no idea how he managed to last that long – Roy stepped manfully into the world of full time employment. He had always been one who strove to provide for himself... yes, he did have a paper round for a while, but providing for himself in Roy's world generally meant sticky fingered pilfering.

Generally, each summer at the end of the school year, there would be an influx of young 'uns ready to take that wobbly first step out into the real world. Many would have been cosseted at home during their early existence in the bosom of a loving family with every need affectionately catered for, so, for these youngsters, leaving the nest as it were was very much of a 'one small step for man, one huge step for a spotty teenager' moment. Not our Roy though, even by then he'd been round the block more than just the once and back again.

Welford's Bakery was situated off the Trunk Road just past South Bank on the way to Middlesbrough. They baked everything... fancy cakes, buns, iced buns, biscuits and loaves of bread. Roy must have thought that this would be a great place to start earning a crust and got himself a job helping out on the delivery vans. Roy, as did all of his mates, left school without any qualifications but even he was surprised to find out that there were thirteen in a baker's dozen... he'd only just found out how many beans made five.

Roy says, 'I was employed as a van lad and each day I'd be with a different driver. There was one driver called John, he'd be in his forties, that seemed quite old to me then, who took a fancy to Jenny Robinson, our next door neighbour, Joy's mam. Jenny was around the same age as John and had striking blonde hair. Blondes always got likened to the glamorous movie stars of the day, Marilyn Monroe, Jane Mansfield and the like. Looking back, it's probably not a surprise that John had the hots for her. At the time they both seemed like old fogies, though now I can appreciate the attraction that John had towards her, the mucky old sod. When we were delivering to any of the smaller shops in Grangetown, I would ask him if he fancied a cup of tea at my house. He never said no 'cos he was always hoping that Jenny would be in so they could have a chat over the garden fence. He was like a dog on heat.'

Roy continues, 'When we got to our house, I'd go into the back garden and shout, 'Jenny, are you there, Jenny? John's here, he wants to speak to you.' Jenny would always come out, giving her hair a quick tweak and straightening her pinny with John wasting no time trying to charm her with his patter. They would be in the back garden for a good ten or fifteen minutes. On one occasion, while they were talking, I saw my opportunity to swipe some cakes, biscuits, buns, or loaves, whatever I could put my hands on. I managed to get loads out of the back of the van while John was being all starry eyed with Jenny and put them in our pantry. When dad came home from work, he said, 'Where did you get all of that lot from?' I said, 'Oh, they're rejects, dad, they were just going to throw them away so they said we could have 'em.' 'There's sixteen battenberg cakes here,' said me dad. I said, 'Take some to work and flog 'em to your mates, you should get a few bob for that lot, they're all fresh.' 'Thought you said they were rejects.' 'They are, just come out a bit wonky, that's all.' I had an answer for everything then.'

Welford's was only ever going to be a short term fix for Roy after he realised there wasn't much dough to be had from delivering bakery produce, and it was after leaving Welford's that he did his four week drawing stint at the Evening Gazette before going on to his dumper disaster down the werks.

We resume Roy's early work history from the point of being literally dumped out of his job with William Press and sheepishly walking over to see his dad with his P45 in hand. After first finding Roy's story quite amusing and enjoying a good laugh at it with his mates, his dad, being well respected for his work, managed to get him a start directly employed by Dorman's, working on the coke ovens.

This meant there were new workmates to meet for Roy, regular Dorman's lads who'd been there for ages, which wasn't going to be a problem for Roy as he always made friends easily.

On his first day though, Roy was told by one of his new pals to go to the stores for a long stand… this was a regular initiation for new young lads starting work straight out of school and the hardened workers, many of whom had spent most of their lives so far doing the same job, got great amusement from it. Needless to say that when, still green behind the ears, Roy got to the stores, he was left standing for a very long time by an only too pleased to accommodate storeman.

The next day it was a glass hammer Roy was sent to retrieve, then a bucket of steam and so on until the lads had exhausted their repertoire of young new worker-related pranks and decided that the recipient, Roy in this case, had earned his stripes and was now one of the lads.

Roy absolutely loved working in the coke ovens alongside the railway that brought coal in, and one of his tasks in his new employment was to clean out the huge boilers when they were shut down.

'I must say I've serviced a few old boilers in my time since those days,' says Roy.

The boilers could be filled with toxic fumes and had to be fumigated to purge out any poison before anyone could be allowed in. We are talking 1960 here and the antiquated method they used to make sure it was safe to enter was to lower a bird cage with a canary down into the depths of the boiler. If the canary was still alive when it was pulled back out then it was deemed safe enough for a human to enter.

'I think the canary was on forty fucking fags a day,' jokes Roy, 'so a few toxic fumes weren't going to do it any damage.'

Tragically though, not long after Roy started, there was an accident where three lads died after being poisoned by the fumes while cleaning inside the boilers and dad thought it was too dangerous so got Roy to leave and find another job. Roy was sad to go. He'd found that the smells of the trains, coal dust and especially petrol from the wagons quite intoxicating and missed them a lot after he left.

The jobs were coming thick and fast… the only qualifications you needed to do the work that Roy was being offered was that you had to be 'thick and fast'.

He was given a chance at the Calor Gas works in Haverton Hill on the other side of the River Tees from Middlesbrough. To get there, Roy would have to catch a bus from Grangetown, getting off in Middlesbrough town centre then walk down to the River Tees before crossing on the Transporter Bridge, leaving him a relatively short walk to the Calor Gas works.

'It wasn't long after I started when one of the bottles blew up and took a bloke's fucking head off,' recalls Roy. 'I think I'd been there about a week. I turned up for work one morning and there were police cars waiting at the gate. The accident had happened during the night shift, probably in the middle of a fag break. I thought, fuck this. I jacked it in straightaway. I was beginning to think I was a bit of a jinx. It seemed disaster had the habit of following me around and I'd still only just gone sixteen.'

After that Roy went down to Teesport and got a job with a Dutch firm called Blankenfaurts, whose job it was to dynamite the River Tees in order to stop it silting up and becoming too shallow for the large container ships that came in… dynamite …! phew…! wonder what's coming next.

'The money was great,' says Roy. 'On top of my wages, I got an extra £5 a shift, £5 danger money, £5 allowance for dinner. Although when I went to the canteen, it appeared that dinner allowance and danger money were very much the same. I was getting hundreds of pounds a week. That was fantastic for a sixteen year old lad, especially then. I was never away from the top clothes shops, buying all the latest gear… Teddy Boy jackets, modern trousers, winkle picker shoes. I looked a million dollars. The money I was getting was crazy. Then one morning, this is how unlucky I'd been, there was a shout upstairs while I was still in bed. It was me dad. 'There's been an accident at Blankenfaurts.' I said, 'You're fucking joking.' I went down to the dockside, where there were loads of ambulances. The fucking rig had blown up, and tragically four Redcar lads had been killed by the explosion.'

Roy's CV was starting to make very grim reading indeed. As to why he'd left his last three terms of employment, Roy thought he was becoming a bit of a Jonah. When asked why he'd left so many jobs in such a short time, he says, 'Well, some people got gassed, a chap had his head blown off and then there was an explosion'. If they'd been looking for someone to play the role of Frank Spencer at the time, they wouldn't have had to look much further than Roy.

Having been in such close proximity to yet another disaster, Roy moved on again, walking straight into another job at the Dorman Long works doing Red-Leading for a contracting company. Red-Lead was an anti-corrosive primer that was painted onto steel works, pipes, gutters, any kind of metal to protect it from deteriorating. It was a proper messy job applying it. Most lead-based paints were banned in 1992 so you probably can't get it now.

Roy says, 'I only lasted one fucking day. It was dead windy and the Red-Lead paint was blowing everywhere. I had red dots all over me, by the end of the day I looked like I'd got the fucking measles. That was it, I wasn't going back for the same the next day.'

By now Roy was going from job to job and unless we want to rewrite War and Peace – with less emphasis on the Peace – from now on we'll be concentrating on the edited highlights.

Roy was given a contract on the massive ICI chemicals complex of a company called Davenports. ICI was on the other side of the Trunk Road to Dorman Long so still only a short journey for Roy. In fact, he could have just about walked there. Davenports had been given the contract to paint the giant cooling towers that had just been built for the nylon works. The towers stood at the West Gate of the complex, which was on the edge of Grangetown, and were about one hundred metres tall, that's 328 feet. They towered over the neighbouring community... you could see them from miles around.

Roy says, 'There was a sign outside their portacabin offices saying 'Men Wanted, Rough Painters', and I thought, well, they don't come any rougher than me, so I went in. The boss man said, 'Have you got your cards with you?' I gave him my P45. 'Go and see Arthur,' was his first command. I said, 'Where is he?' He said, 'There he is,' and pointed upwards, he was about a hundred and fifty feet off the ground up the side of this whacking great cooling tower and I could feel my neck creaking as I looked up. I wasn't so sure, heights really aren't my thing. I'd been getting nosebleeds since buying a pair of thick crepe soled shoes to go with my Teddy Boy outfit. Arthur was up on the scaffolding, I could just barely make him out from where I was... he looked tiny. I had to climb up the ladders that were fixed to the side of the scaffolding, and when I got halfway up there, I looked down. It was freezing, windy, and I thought, fuck this for a lark, as one flew past me. I'm not fucking having this. Then I looked round and could see our house. I went straight back down to the boss's cabin. He said, 'Is there a problem, son?' I said, 'Can I have my P45 back? I've just realised I don't like heights.' He said, 'How did you feel?' I said, 'I felt fucking dizzy.' He said alright and gave me my P45 back. He didn't seem that surprised. It looked like I hadn't been the first to bottle it half way up the tower and come back down again. It was so easy to go from one job to another that six hundred yards away I noticed a bunch of lads working, so I went over and asked them if there were any jobs going. They were working for the

Darlington Insulation Company, lagging pipes throughout the ICI site. One of the lads said, 'Can you mix darbo?' I thought it can't be that fucking hard so I said I could. I was mixing vermiculite, that they would put it on the pipes to fireproof them. It was bloody hard work and I only had a small mixer. The problem was that the lads, who were all from Hartlepool, were on piecework where they were getting paid by the amount of work they did rather than by the hour. I'd give them a tray of darbo then they'd just slosh it on. I was feeding four laggers so they were all shouting over to me for more and more darbo. It was such hard work that I was going home on a night and just collapsing, but it was good money. I'd been there about two months, when one day we were in the cabin for tea, and two of the lads I'd been feeding darbo to were in as usual. One of them was a potential hard case, but I was also strong as an ox then. Every time I went in the cabin though he would spout out, 'Here he is, the fat cunt,' and I had to just put up with it. This one morning in particular, I think I must have got out of the wrong side of the bed 'cos as I walked in to the cabin, the lad shouted out 'Have you made the tea?' 'cos being the youngster they'd decided that was my job. I used to mix the darbo, wash the mixer down then I'd go into the cabin and put the kettle on. We had a tea urn with boiling water in. This time when he said, 'Is it ready, you fat cunt?' I said, 'Hey now, let's just cut it out.' He said, 'You what?' I said, 'Let's just cut all this fat cunt stuff out, I'm getting a bit sick of it, it's wearing a bit thin now.' He started shouting out to me, 'Oh, you big fat fucking Boro twat,' and all that sort of stuff. I was thinking that I didn't want to get the sack, so I controlled myself, but he went in the other room and when he came back in through the door I happened to be standing next to it holding it open. The lad was carrying two cups of red hot tea one in each hand, so I let go of the door which was on a spring and it knocked the scalding tea all over his hands. He went to attack me so I hit him, I only hit him once but he went right over the fucking table. His brother was the gaffer, and said to the lad, 'You fucking asked for that, he told you, he warned you once. I told you he's not a fucking idiot, he's not a soft shit.' It all went quiet after that and I apologised, I said I was sorry but that he'd asked for it. He just said, 'Get out of my face before I do something I'll regret.' He still thought he was a killer. About two weeks later we were playing cards, I can't remember what we were playing. The lad was an awful loser, hated losing at cards or anything, but I had a good hand and won. He just threw his cards at me with one of them hitting me in the face and causing a cut. Well, that was it. I must have hit him ten times, I fucking battered him and of course I got the sack. A few weeks later there were a couple of lads I knew from Hartlepool and one of them said to me, 'Hey, you fucking sorted him out, didn't you?' It had got round like wildfire what had happened 'cos the lad had a reputation in Hartlepool of being a real hard man and not many people would have had the nerve to confront him.'

Roy went from one job to another at the beginning of the sixties, moving on for whatever reason, more often than not falling out with some clever shite that would try it on taking the mick. One thing that was ringing out loud and clear though was that Roy was no slouch, prepared to do any hard work that came along to earn a living, but neither was he one to back out of an argument, especially if that someone thought they could bully the young Roy Vasey. No, Roy was never one to start a scrap but, without doubt, usually the one to finish it.

7

While Roy was spending his days doing any kind of rough work he could get, most of his evenings were spent hanging around the streets with his mates. 'We all had girlfriends,' Roy says, 'so we'd be looking for a shag up one of the alleyways where no one could see us. Dad had bought a telly. There were only black and white ones then, so I'd stop in some nights and watch my favourite programmes. It was still a bit of a novelty. I particularly liked the comedy programmes like The Army Game, which was a bit like the Carry On Films, and Hancock's Half Hour with Tony Hancock, one of my early comedy heroes. I used to like watching the snooker and I remember when colour TV had just come in and not many people had one, whispering Ted Lowe who used to do the snooker commentary once said, 'Just in case any of you are still watching in black and white, the pink ball is just behind the blue.' Now we were still watching in black and white so if we didn't know where the pink ball was we didn't know where the fucking blue ball was either.'

On the nights when Roy had enough energy left after working so hard, he'd wander off to the local boy's club which was just at the end of his street and on the other side of the Trunk Road. There he'd engage in a variety of sports. He liked to join in with whatever was going, boxing, basketball, football.

He says, 'I liked basketball and became quite good. I was okay at football but not brilliant. You know you're not absolutely crap if you're never the last one to be picked when the sides are being chosen. I think the lads picked me for their team so they wouldn't be the ones getting kicked up the arse if they ran past me with the ball. Middlesbrough Football Club came one time bringing with them a machine that measured the speed of a ball being kicked and I won with the hardest shot. I missed the goal by a fucking mile so they didn't sign me on, but it was still the hardest shot.'

It was during this period that Roy started to get into bother with the local police because it seemed that if there was ever a scrap going on, Roy was probably going to be slap bang in the middle of it. Roy's back door neighbour, Ged, has already told us that Roy wouldn't stand by if he saw someone being bullied but would usually get singled out when the police arrived and marched off to the nearest police station.

Roy got caught scrapping so many times with different lads that he got a reputation with the police and was labelled as something of a ring leader, a trouble causer, someone to keep an eye on… which resulted in several appearances in front of the Magistrate. His appearances in front of the beak weren't only for fighting though, Roy still had light fingers even when he was earning good money and was caught pilfering on more than one occasion.

A visit to Hamilton's Music Store in Middlesbrough brings a smile to Roy's face as he recollects, 'I was mooching around the store, which sold musical instruments upstairs, and I'd always fancied myself as a bit of a drummer so would regularly go there to see the drums. This day though I was wandering about the record section, which was downstairs, and while nobody was looking I shoved three LPs inside my coat and buttoned it up. Some nosey bastard must have been watching and snitched on me 'cos as I left the shop I was stopped on the pavement outside by the manager. Someone had already rang the police and they arrived quite quickly after I'd been taken back into the store. I was arrested and taken to South Bank Police Station, put into a room and left on my own to wait for an officer to come and question me. I still had the LPs inside my jacket, nobody had bothered to search me, so I thought if I got rid of them there would be no evidence… worth a try anyhow. There was a massive radiator on the wall just under the window, so I decided to hide the LPs behind it and managed to wedge all three of them between the wall and the radiator then sat back down. When the officer came in, I'd casually left my coat open, pleading my innocence that somebody must have been mistaken and the officer rather reluctantly had to let me go. Years later when I joined The Pipeline show group, Lee, my youngest cousin, was lead guitarist and was going out with Dotty. One night we had to pick him up from Dotty's house and while we were waiting I got talking to her mam. It only turned out that Dotty's mam was a cleaner at South Bank Police Station and I couldn't wait to tell her the tale. 'So it was you, was it?' she said. I said, 'What do you mean?' She said, 'Those LPs, they melted and dripped down the back of the radiator all over the floor below and set like concrete. It took two of us four hours on our knees to scrape it off the floor.' I couldn't help laughing. Thankfully she saw the funny side of it too.'

Pilfering and fighting was now the way Roy lived his life, whilst still acting the jolly joker with his pals… being the first to jump through Woollie's window if anyone thought it was a great idea. With his mam having left and dad either at work or the club, there was nobody giving him any guidance as to what was right and what was wrong. Roy didn't think about his unruly behaviour, he just thought that this was the way life was and didn't question it because he was surrounded by other lads who were up to the same antics.

Dramatically though, out of character as it may have seemed, that was about to change, or so Roy thought, when he had an idea about doing something in the hope of changing his lifestyle. After going from one job to another in such a short time while still only a kid, Roy felt his working life was going nowhere and that he'd like to join the Army… Coldstream Guards was what he'd been thinking. Without hesitation, which was how Roy had lived his life so far, he went off to the recruitment office in Grange Road in Middlesbrough. Roy and a bunch of about twelve other lads who wanted to join up were taken into a large room and given a written aptitude test to assess if they would be suitable Army recruits. Pretty basic stuff really but, for the not so academic Roy Vasey from Grangetown who'd skipped more days off school than he'd actually been, it turned out to be a bit of a tough ask, to put it mildly.

'The officer who took us in said, 'Fill in your details on the front page, then turn the page over and answer the questions.' I was okay with the first bit, I wrote Royston Vasey, my address, any jobs I'd already done – thankfully they didn't ask why I'd left them, people getting blown up and poisoned. Then it asked why I wanted to join the Army. I'd been told 'It'll make a man of you', mainly by people who were too shit scared to join the fucking Army themselves, so I put that down. I'd filled the front page without too much trouble and turned the page to find a list of questions like, 'What's the capital of South Africa?' 'What's the largest ocean?' 'What's the highest mountain?' 'What do they call the Queen's residence in London?', that sort of stuff. Jokingly, I'd always been a big joker, I put 'The Queen's residence is a big house with massive gates in the centre of London'. I couldn't remember that it was Buckingham Palace, and I answered most of the other questions in the same way. After we'd finished, they gave us all 3s 6d, old money, to go to a local store, Tower House, where there was a café. I got a sandwich, doughnut and a cup of tea. Us lads got talking, everyone saying where they thought they were going to go with the Army at the same time as pretending to fire an invisible Tommy gun at other people enjoying a cup of tea in the café. We were still just bits of kids, but very much the gun happy gangster branch who thought we were going to go to war and shoot someone as soon as we'd signed up. After we'd finished, we went back to the recruitment office and were ushered back into the room where we'd taken the test. A door opened and a rather important looking Army Officer called out 'Vasey?' I stood up. He said, 'Royston Vasey?' I said, 'Yes, sir.' He said, 'Can you come this way, please?' I thought fucking hell, I'm the only one who's passed here and when I walked in there were three officers sat behind what looked like a pasting table. The officer who was sat in the middle must have been the main man 'cos he said, 'Well, we've looked at your answers in the test and must admit that you're a very humorous man. This question about 'What is a logarithm', you've answered, 'Goes on the firerithm'. Well, I didn't know what a fucking logarithm was. I'd answered a lot of the questions like that, writing comedy answers down instead of just leaving the ones I didn't know blank. He carried on to say, 'Our advice to you is why don't you come back in a couple of years and try for the Green Howards. There was always competition between different Army Corps and these officers must have thought they'd palm this thicko off on to someone else. When I got home, me dad said, 'How did you get on, son?' 'Oh,' I said, 'I could have signed up there and then, but I'd have been ten years in Cyprus or fucking Malta. I don't want to do ten years, I just want to do three years or so.' 'Oh,' he said, 'you did right, son.' Thick as shit me dad was, so I pulled the wool over his eyes too.'

Roy had to resign himself to being back to square one, though now more determined than ever, he wasn't going to let the fact that he didn't know what a fucking logarithm was hold him back from making something more out of his life than a string of dead end jobs.

'The problem was,' says Roy, 'is where did I go from there?'

8

Having unfortunately been given his marching orders by the Army Recruitment Officers, Roy was still determined that his future lay in getting away from the humdrum of the casual labouring jobs he'd been doing since he left school. During his work in the dockland of the River Tees, he'd seen first hand lads coming ashore off ships from all over the world. Roy, thinking that those lads didn't look any different to himself, began to wonder if the Merchant Navy might be the answer to his wanderlust. He was still seeing his childhood sweetheart, Sandra, and it would be a wrench to have to leave her at home, but needs must and Roy made his mind up to give it a go.

Roy says, 'I found out where the Federation Building was in Middlesbrough, that's the office you had to apply to if you wanted to join the Merchant Navy. It was an old building that looked a bit like a library. I went along, filled in the usual forms and was sent off on a six week training course to Sharpness near Bristol with a bunch of other Boro lads. It was a long enough journey having to catch the train at Middlesbrough railway station and changing a few times, so by the time we got to Sharpness we sort of knew each other a little better. You know, Boro lads sticking together, just like anyone from most other towns would. These were hard young boys who were sure they could cope with whatever a life on the open seas would throw at them. On arriving at the training centre, we met up with more new starters just as hard and rough as the gang I'd travelled down with, all hoping to find their sea legs in the mostly landlocked port of Sharpness on the River Severn. We had to form a queue and were given our waterproof clothing, jacket, heavy lace up boots and the baggiest pair of trousers I'd ever seen. I'd just started wearing drainpipes, which were all the rage with the Teddy Boys, and now I had to swap them for trousers which were even wider than the one's me fucking dad wore. It wasn't like I'd imagined any training camp to be, only having seen them in the comedy films I'd watched at The Lyric cinema. I'd seen Carry On Sergeant and Norman Wisdom as a new Army recruit in The Square Peg, but there was definitely nothing funny about having to get up when the bugle was blown at six o'fucking clock for us all to line up on the parade ground then being marched around… all before breakfast was served. We attended different classes… one was how to tie various knots. I made a bit of a joke of it later on when I said, 'I used to be in the Navy and learnt three knots. I was trying to shag a girl in one of the ports when she said, 'You're not hard, you're not in, and you're not getting your money back.' There were hundreds of lads from all over the country on this training course, learning all sorts of different skills like taking guns to bits, cleaning them, putting them back together. All without ammunition, might I add. It was then that I realised I had a good memory when I was taught how to read a nautical compass, learning and remembering every point on it within one day. With so many lads from different backgrounds, who all thought they were hard as nails, there would be friction at times. We were discouraged from taking things into our own hands by the inclusion of a boxing night where, if you had a quarrel with anyone, you sorted it out between yourselves in the boxing ring on a Friday night. Everyone would turn up to watch. There was one huge lad called Fenwick who I got into a bit of an argument with over a sausage roll. I thought he'd put his hand on it and said, 'You fucking mauled that.' He said, 'Who are you fucking talking to? I'll knock your fucking head off.' I said, 'Alright, alright, Friday night,' which was unusual for me 'cos if anybody had come between me and a sausage roll before I'd have just put their fucking lights out there and then. I said, 'I'll meet you in the gym Friday and we'll sort this out. I put our names down on the list for Friday's bouts. There'd be up to twenty fights each week and the place would be packed with the rest of the trainees watching on. Friday night came and we were given these huge sixteen ounce gloves to wear. There was no way anyone was going to get really hurt with a clout from one of those floppy things which made it quite comical, a bit like Norman Wisdom after all. It was about three weeks into the course and I'd made quite a few friends who I'd been bragging to by saying, 'I'm going to make fucking mincemeat out of him.' Unbeknown to me, this lad I was about to climb into the ring with was only an ABA fucking boxing champion and when the bell went for the first round he must have hit me six fucking times before I realised my boot laces were still undone. There were three three minute rounds and I think I landed one punch. Anyway he was declared the winner. Afterwards I made a joke of it with the lads, saying that I was going to call myself Picasso 'cos I was always on the canvas and that I was glad I'd taken up boxing 'cos you don't have to walk back to the changing room, you get carried on a fucking stretcher. I heard that someone had spoken to this Fenwick guy after the fight and told him he should come over and apologise to me otherwise I'd have stabbed him 'cos I was staring daggers in his direction, but everyone knew from that night on that they were never to come between me and my sausage roll ever again.'

Roy only had one other Friday night encounter while he was there. He can't remember what it was about but as the weeks went on and tensions got higher it could have been for any daft thing.

'The second lad I fought wasn't much of a boxer but during the first round every time we clinched in the middle of the ring, he bit me. After one bite I said to him, 'Are you in love with me or something, get off me, you fucking ugly twat.' In the second round he was doing it again, then he stood on my foot. He knew what he was doing, he was a bit wiser than I was. In between rounds two and three, he was sat on his stool in his own corner talking and laughing with the two lads who were acting as his trainers. They were looking over in my direction at the same time, so when the bell went for the third round, I ran across the ring and smacked him across the head with my fucking stool. I got disqualified. I don't understand why 'cos I didn't hit him that hard. It was the talk of the training camp for the rest of our stay, but I'll tell you this, I didn't get bothered by anyone after that, they all kept well away from me and left me alone. There would be about five or six hundred lads and most of them wouldn't have a home life at all, having been rejected by their families. You aren't going to get all of those loose cannons confined together in the same place without getting into arguments and stuff, usually over nowt really. Looking back, it was probably very childish, but then we were all young lads from similar backgrounds where disagreements, whether major or minor, were always going to be sorted out with a scrap.'

None of these Merchant Navy candidates would have ever been reprimanded or thrown off the course for their unruly behaviour, the reality being that they were probably showing some of the qualities required in their future employment on board ship. They had to be tough to get through some of the exercises they were given. 'We had to climb into the back of an open truck for one of them,' Roy tells me, shaking his head, 'then we were driven into the countryside and when the truck had reached 30mph on a straight road, we were ordered to jump off the back one by one. If you hurt yourself, it was hard shit, you still had to find your own way back to the training centre.'

Roy completed the course successfully, passing all of his tests with flying colours, complete with his newfound memory skills which would become of huge benefit to him in his later life. It would have been one of the very few times in his life so far where Roy had achieved a pass mark in any form of test. For his efforts, Roy was given his very own Federation Pass Book which was effectively his passport to becoming a Merchant Seaman and the chance of a new life away from the troublesome existence he had become used to. It would also be giving the Grangetown Constabulary a bit of a welcome break too.

9

Roy went back to the local Federation Office in Middlesbrough, where he'd originally applied, clutching his Pass Book with pride. There were jobs coming in all of the time with ships arriving at different ports all over the country… the Mersey, the Humber, as well as our own River Tees among others. He was told told there was a boat in the Tees, the McCauley, it was going on a six week trip to Florida and did he want to go on it?

'That was my first trip to sea on the good ship McCauley… to Florida, my big adventure, never been out of the country before and now I'm off to America. I imagined myself as Seaman Staines from Captain Pugwash off the telly,' Roy laughs. 'What I hadn't anticipated though was the heavy storm we came across in the Atlantic. I was really bad, throwing up over the side. I was bad for a week. Not only me, most of the crew were ill, some so bad they were even bringing up blood. My throat was so sore, I couldn't keep any food down but we still had to work, there was no one else to do it. The only time I felt any better was when I was laid flat out on my bunk on a night, but then I had to get up again at 5.30am for work. The McCauley was an ore carrier, we were carrying what was called black salt. It was white powder actually, something that was used in paint. It took us eight to nine days to get to Florida and, being my first trip, I really didn't know what to expect but everyone on the boat was friendly, told me how to go on and I thought this is the life for me. On arriving in Florida, we berthed at Jacksonville alongside a paper mill. Now, I'd already heard people say that everything's bigger in America and when we said that we'd like to go into town, we were told there was a bus stop at the other side of the mill. Well, we had to walk through the paper mill to get to the bus stop and, fuck me, if it wasn't two and a half miles long. When we got to the other side, sure enough there was a bus stop, and there was four or five of us waiting for the bus. This was 1961 and when the bus came along we didn't know that in America – in this state anyway – black people sat at the back of the bus and white people sat at the front. We'd never experienced segregation back at home and nobody had even told us about it happening where we were. Not knowing about the rules, I got on the bus, walked straight to the back and sat down with the people who were already there. Before the bus moved away, the driver came to the back and in a broad American accent, which I could hardly understand, quite forcibly ordered me to sit at the front. I did as I was told but I just couldn't believe that that sort of thing went on. When we got off the bus I saw a sign saying 'drug store'. I said, 'Fucking hell, they're selling drugs.' Turned out it was a supermarket. It was massive, ten times bigger than our own Tesco and Morrison's are even today. I'd never seen anything like it for size before. The nearest things we had at home were our local Heagney's or Hinton's which were the smaller equivalent of the El-Supermakado you'd get to on holiday in Spain for your groceries and booze. Being Florida, the shelves were full of Disney related products… Mickey Mouse juice, Donald Duck ice cream, even a box of cornflakes with Disney characters covering it. There was a cafeteria inside the store where lads who were serving you wore uniforms similar to those we'd see on Thunderbirds off the telly, including the pointy hats. A lot of these were ex-army with shaven heads, whereas I had a full head of hair cascading off my shoulders, as was the trend back in the UK. One of the lads who'd been serving us actually thought I was a girl. He kept calling me 'Miss'. I said, 'Who're you fucking missing?' We got talking to a couple of the lads – this was after I'd explained to them that I was actually a male of the species – and they invited us to their home to meet their parents. What really struck me was that when we got to their home, they introduced us by calling their father 'sir' and asking 'Can they sit down, sir?' We were told to sit down and make ourselves comfortable, but it showed what respect they had for their own parents, again another eye opener for all of us rough sods. We struck up a friendship with these boys during our short time in Jacksonville, even keeping in touch by letter for a while when I got back home. We were walking along boulevards lined with palm trees. This was the first time I'd been out of my own country. I'd only seen stuff like that on Hollywood movies. There were long ornate Cadillacs with no roofs parading along the main road. The only cars I'd see on the road at home would be Ford Populars, and they'd have a roof to keep the rain off. Nobody here seemed to walk anywhere, this place was a whole new world to us.'

On returning to Middlesbrough, after receiving a cheque for his work on the trip, Roy registered back with the Federation Office and went on the list for any available jobs. He was asked if he wanted to go on the King Malcolm, which was a huge ship having been built in 1952 after the original King Malcolm was sunk by a German U-boat during World War Two in 1941. The ship was to leave Tilbury docks for a nine month voyage, taking in various ports on the way to South Africa and back. Roy immediately took up the offer and so, after waving girlfriend Sandra goodbye yet again, he jumped on a train to travel south.

On arriving at Tilbury, there was something of a surprise waiting for him.

'Bugger me,' Roy says, 'when I got on board there's a bunch of Boro lads already there… Billy Lodwick, Ray Blenkinsop, Arthur Mann and Joe Hammersley.'

Joe coincidently turned out to be the uncle of Roy's current driver, Keith, who he didn't meet until some years later. Joe was six foot two, as hard as nails and had been arrested by police after being accused of being behind local notorious riots in the tough Cannon Street area of Middlesbrough.

'I worked in the galley, peeling spuds and doing general kitchen duties, second cook and bottle washer.' Roy smiles as his thoughts go back to his spud peeling duties. 'As the boat swayed from side to side, the bucket I was dropping the peeled spuds into followed the motions of the boat, sliding from one side to the other. I'd chase after it, bring it back then peel as many spuds as I could before the bucket fucked off to the other side of the kitchen again. I'd feel the ship swaying then off it would go. I kept saying, 'Fucking hell here we go again.' I think I must have had an Albert Einstein moment 'cos I thought, fuck it, I'm just going to wait for the bastard bucket to come back to me. So I watched it slide across the kitchen floor, along the far wall as the ship swayed and lurched, then backwards and forwards in a zig-zag movement, finally coming back to its starting point where I was sitting, tatey knife in hand, then I'd peel like mad until it fucked off on its travels again. The motion of the ship was making me feel quite ill but I never told any of the crew that I'd spewed up in the bucket… didn't bother having any mashed spud that night.'

With the heavy swell of the ocean, it was obvious that the ship would sway quite heavily at times with Roy saying that he had to be strapped to whatever he was working with in the galley, whether it be a cooker or the kitchen sink… although I'm sure they're told not to use the word sink while they are on board ship.

Being in such a confined space with thirty or so other crew, there was bound to be the odd fall out or disagreement, but Roy says that Billy Lodwick took him under his wing and looked after him. Roy says, 'I could write a book about the fucking things he got up to, he had blond hair, looked a bit like Tommy Steele with the Teddy Boy look, and the pussy he brought back to the ship was unbelievable.'

The journey that the King Malcolm took to South Africa required a number of stop-overs on the way. Roy describes what happened after they left Tilbury docks.

'Firstly we had to go to Amsterdam to pick up cargo, sailing along to Portugal then on to West Africa where we stopped at Freetown in Sierra Leone and Monrovia in Liberia. That was the first time I'd ever seen any wild animals. We were sailing up river towards Freetown. It was a huge wide river with jungle on each side. Someone would shout the rest of the crew to come up on deck and we'd see maybe a herd of elephants come for a drink, but fucking hell we were getting bitten to death by mosquitoes. We had to take anti-malaria tablets. We'd even see the elephants jump back as a crocodile attacked. Natives would come alongside our ship in carved out canoes. There was one came up to us, and he was wearing a bowler hat. I haven't a fucking clue where he would have got a bowler hat from, but he just had a bit of cloth covering his arse and tackle with a bowler hat on his head. There were other ships the size of ours coming along the river as well. This chap would shout up, 'You gimme, gimme, you gimme, gimme,' and gesturing with his hands as though he was begging for money. The captain was with us and he said that what they want you to do is to throw some money into the river and they'll dive for it. The river was fast flowing filthy fucking water like the bucket when you've just finished washing your car, full of straw and bits of shit. We threw some coins into the river near his canoe and, sure enough, off came the bowler hat and he disappeared under the murky water. He seemed to have been gone ages before he reappeared looking straight up at us with what looked like a cheesy grin on his face. The cheesy grin though was our coins lined up in between his lips, staring back at us like the worst ill fitting dentures I'd ever seen. They'd tie hand-carved animals, elephants, crocodiles, giraffes to a piece of string and we'd pull them up to the deck of the ship where a bit of bartering would start. 'You pay two pounds!' 'No, I pay one fucking pound.' 'Okay you pay one fucking pound.' Then they'd go off to one of the other ships. Dangerous way of making a living, if you ask me but that's how they did it. I brought loads of those hand-carved animals home, gave 'em to me dad, but I don't know where they are now. They're probably being passed around car boot sales… 'You pay two pounds!' 'No, I pay one fucking pound.' 'Okay you pay one fucking pound."

After the ship had off loaded at Monrovia and Freetown it went to another dock, taking on cargo before heading off to South Africa then sailing up the east coast to Mozambique.

Roy says, 'At Lourenco Marques in Mozambique, we had a few days off while the ship was being loaded and the captain let us go ashore. He said, 'Be back at six for evening meal.' We went to the beach where there was a little hut. I thought it was where you went to have a slash but there was a man sat inside, taking money for the use of the beach and going into the water. It wouldn't have been much money but we could see that beyond this section there was nobody on the beach or swimming in the sea so we said fuck him and went over there. We were only in the water a few minutes when a black chap ran up to the water's edge, jibber-jabbering in a foreign language and shaking his arms around like fuck. We all thought he was just after some money off us and ignored him until one of the lads screamed, 'Shark, fucking shark!' He'd seen a shark's fin coming towards where we were swimming… which was what this chap had been waving at us for. It turned out that the section of beach and sea water that you had to pay for had been cordoned off with a sharks net that they couldn't get through. Fuck me, don't think I've ever been so scared in my life. Mombasa in Kenya was our next stop where we loaded animals – lions, tigers and the like – to take to Whipsnade Zoo. They were all on the deck in cages and wooden boxes and it was our job to feed them. There was a section in each box like a serving hatch that had to be opened to throw the meat in, or whatever they were fed on. I was asked to feed the ostrich and was given a metal bucket with corn in. There was a qualified vet on board with the animals who gave us instructions of what to do. He told me to stand well back holding the bucket towards the ostrich. I didn't know why. I held the bucket like I was told and opened the hatch, and fuck me, quick as a flash, the ostrich shoved his head through and loafed it with its beak. The bucket just folded in half while I still had hold of it just like it was sheet of newspaper. If he'd have hit me in the head, I'd have had no fucking chance, I'd have been dead. The vet just said, 'I told yer!' I'll never forget that. There were monkeys that would come and sit on your knee and play. They would shit all over the place and we'd have to clean it up, but it was still fun having the animals on board. We'd been allowed ashore while we were in Mombasa but, after leaving the port to continue our journey, a few of the crew – including me – started feeling not too well. I was itching all of the time and had a sore throat. Every ship has a medical officer, but I think they just read it out of a book if I'm being honest with you. I had to see him and, after testing me, he said that he thought I had a touch of malaria. Two days later as we were going through the Suez Canal, I was getting really bad so they wrapped me up like a turkey in fucking tin foil. I couldn't work, and they were giving me Lucozade, stuff like that to try and keep my energy up. Once we were through the canal and into the Mediterranean, a radio call was made to a nearby Royal Navy Ship and while both ships were sailing alongside each other, two Royal Navy Medics came on board, swung over in a basket. After having taken a look at me, they said that I was in such a bad state they would have to take me back with them and I was flown by helicopter to a hospital in Valletta, the capital of Malta. At the hospital, I was injected with what was probably an antidote to combat the malaria and when they were satisfied it was working, I was flown back to the ship which had continued its journey through the Med. I must have been away a couple of days. The captain said he thought I must be a fucking jinx 'cos after I'd got back one of the engines set on fire and we had to be towed into Barcelona. We were there for ten days but it was like having a holiday really, as we could go where we liked and do what we wanted. The captain said, 'You can all go ashore, we'll be here for a while, just make sure you don't run out of money.' Once ashore, we walked about two miles to the beach, stopping at an open-air swimming pool where bronzed young lads were throwing themselves off a diving board that was about sixty feet up. We all thought, fucking show offs. The girls, all beautiful girls, were going crazy at the sight of seeing these young daredevils putting a performance on just for them. I said, 'I'm gonna have a go at that.' 'Don't be daft, you must be crackers.' Anyway I did and, fucking hell, it was like doing a parachute jump without the fucking parachute.

When I hit the water, my trunks came up nearly to my fucking neck. At seventeen you don't really have any nerves and when I got out of the water, the lads I was with were crying laughing. One of them said, 'When you jumped off, it was like a meteor coming out of the sky and when you landed there was no water left in the pool.' I said, 'Fuck orrrrfff!' but it was funny, though I didn't seem to be attracting any attention from the girls. We had a great time in Barcelona. I bought a few things and we all got tans. After a week, I was almost as black as the ace of spades.'

The King Malcolm returned to Tilbury after its nine month voyage where Roy and the rest of the Boro lads made their way back to Teesside. They all registered back at the Federation Building for their next trip and ended up all together again on a ship that was part of the Red Line Shipping Company.

'We kept on getting into trouble while we were away,' remembers Roy, 'sneaking offshore when we were told not to, and when the local police came on board at one port and we were all nearly arrested, the captain said he'd had enough. We all had our Merchant Navy passports stamped with a double DR, I never knew what it stood for but it showed that you had disobeyed orders or something like that. What it meant was that when you went to the Federation Building for your next ship, they would look at your navy passport and seeing that you'd received a double DR would say, 'Oh, trouble, hey?' which meant you went to the back of the queue for jobs. Could be a couple or three months before someone might take you on again.'

Whilst happy to be back on terra firma again and reunited with girlfriend Sandra, it now looked like Roy could be without work for a while if he persisted with his navy life. It was never sure how long you'd be waiting for work once you had a DR on your Merchant Navy licence, never mind a double one, but Roy wanted to avoid slipping back into his old ways of going from one job to another, yet still needing to earn a living. While Roy was away, Sandra had started working as a chambermaid in a Scarborough hotel and now Roy was effectively out of work, she had an idea that maybe he could join her there. Sandra put it to him that there could be some vacancies at the hotel where she worked, did he want go and have a look? Willing to give anything a go, especially if it meant spending more time with his girlfriend as well as keeping himself out of trouble, Roy joined Sandra on her journey back to Scarborough, totally unaware that his time in the seaside resort would result in some of the lowest points he would ever experience in his beleaguered young life.

10

Scarborough was a place Roy loved, having often been on holiday with his mam and dad as a kid, so he was looking forward to spending some time there. Still only seventeen Roy had probably already had more jobs, seen more of the world and been into more trouble than most of us would ever experience in a whole lifetime but, as fond as Roy was of Scarborough, it was unfortunately destined to be the place where he would meet his Waterloo.

It all started out so well, the hotel where Sandra worked was called The Southlands and as luck would have it, there was a vacancy for someone to wait on tables with the prospect of training up to silver service. Roy wondered what his mates Nanda Basset, Swet Parfitt and Gandi Jarret back in Grangetown would think of him poncing around dishing posh food out to a load of well to does, but then thought it's got fuck all to do with them, a job's a job. As well as his table duties at meal times, Roy was also required to do odd jobs around the hotel, acting as a general dogsbody.

Life didn't turn out to be as blissful as he imagined and it wasn't too long before Sandra and Roy fell out, with Sandra moving to another hotel. 'We were always arguing,' admits Roy, 'but this one was a fucking humdinger, a massive, massive argument and Sandra fucked off. Then I heard she was seeing another bloke, so yeah, I thought, two can play at that fucking game… you know what you're like at that age. Not long after Sandra had left, one of the women who worked in the kitchen asked me what I was doing that afternoon. We finished at 1.00pm and had the afternoons to ourselves until teatime. I told her that I wasn't doing anything, just going for a walk, so she said, 'Will you take our Christine with you?' Christine was her daughter, who worked at the hotel, waiting on tables like I did, lovely looking girl in all the right places but she was deaf and dumb. I said, 'I'd love to but I don't do sign language, how will we communicate?' She said, 'Oh that's okay, Christine is good at lip-reading.' So we went out for the afternoon, and we walked down to the Valley bridge. Just underneath the bridge, there's a gent's toilet. Well, as we were about to walk past it, she just dragged me in, got my willy out and gave me a wank. I couldn't believe it. That led to me and Christine going out for quite a while, shagging each other's brains out. Her mam seemed well happy, though I'm sure she must have known what we were getting up to with us unable to wipe the big broad smiles off our faces after every time we'd had one of our 'walks'.'

Having got Sandra out of his head, Roy was back to enjoying his time at the Southlands but as usual a curveball was just around the corner. 'There were two other lads working at the hotel,' says Roy, 'one was a kitchen cleaner and the other was a porter. One of the lads had been knocking around with a girl called Rita who was Sandra's mate from school. They had both started at the hotel together. He got a job at the hotel to be with Rita the same as I had to be with Sandra. He was little bit older than me, and said, 'We're going to break into a shop and we need someone to keep a look out for us, are you up for it?' I said, 'Aye, I'll keep a look out.' He said, 'We just want you to stand on the corner while we break into the shop. Whatever we get, we'll split.' I said, 'Okay then,' thinking I was bit of a fucking gangster. I didn't find out 'til we got there they were only breaking into a fucking gift shop selling buckets, spades and flags to stick in the sand. I'd had visions of us being the youngest Lavender Hill Mob, busting one of the high street jewellers. They said, 'We'll split whatever we get.' I thought I was going to get a Rolex watch and some diamond rings, thought we were all gonna be rich… not fucking buckets and spades with maybe a bag of marbles thrown in for good luck. The shop was just a short walk from the hotel and I was standing on the corner about thirty or forty yards from the shop door while the lads were using a jemmy to force it open. I was just leaning up against the wall, waiting for them to come back out when a man walked up to me and asked me what I was doing,' Roy confesses. 'Daft as arseholes, I whispered out of the side of my mouth, James Cagney style like, 'Sssshhh… I'm waiting for my mates… they've just broken into that shop over there.' He was only a plainclothes fucking policeman. No sooner had I said it than police cars pulled up outside the shop with coppers jumping out and running in through the front door. It appeared that when the lads had jemmied open the front door, it had set a burglar alarm off in the police station so we were all fucking nicked, weren't we? The three of us got thrown into the back of a police van and taken off to Scarborough Police Station. We got to the station and while we were waiting at the desk to be processed, a policeman came up to me. It turned out that during the arrest, one of the other lads had nutted a copper and this PC had decided it had been me. After accusing me of headbutting one of his mates, I denied it, saying it hadn't been me. 'I'll fucking teach you, you little twat,' was his response then he took his helmet off, swung his head back slightly before aiming his forehead towards my face. I saw it coming and quickly bent my head forward so he hit the top of my crown, probably the hardest place he could have it and busted his nose. There was blood everywhere. The Desk Sergeant who'd been watching all this gave him a right bollocking, telling him it was his own fault. After being 'signed in', I was kept in a cell for a few days before making an appearance at Scarborough Magistrate's Court.'

On sentencing, Roy's petty criminal history was taken into account, so whereas his two accomplices got six months suspended, he ended up going to borstal for two years after being initially sent to Armley Prison in Leeds for assessments.

Roy remembers, 'Immediately after being sentenced and the paperwork being completed, I was placed into a police van to be whisked off to start my sentence in Leeds. To get away from the magistrate's court and out of Scarborough, we partly had to drive through the town. It took us past the Wimpey Bar I used to go in and fuck me, who's sat in the window with big broad smiles all over their faces? Only them two lucky twats, tucking into plates full of burger and chips … and it was all their fucking idea.'

It was probably inevitable that Roy's wayward lifestyle would culminate in a custodial sentence somewhere along the way. Roy had become quite used to the Scarborough holiday atmosphere's fairground rides and the bright lights of the amusement arcades with their penny slot machines and one-armed bandits, but even the street-hardened young Roy Vasey wouldn't have been expecting the shock and awe that was to greet him as he arrived at his destination in Leeds, where he was to swap the Scarborough one-armed bandits for rubbing shoulders with the two-armed variety behind the grim walls of Armley Prison.

11

On arriving at their destination, if it hadn't been for the fact that the driver had the radio on playing Beatles songs, Roy might have thought he'd been transported back in a time machine and dropped in the middle of a previous century. Armley Prison epitomised one of those workhouses off a Dickensian film, a building that had been up since the eighteen hundreds with the highest perimeter walls Roy had ever seen in his life.

So magnificent was its structure that as they reached the main gate it wouldn't have surprised Roy if Henry VIII had stepped out of the ornate double facade to greet them in person. When reality finally snapped back into Roy's head, the one thing that he was certain about was that once you were through those gates, there was no way you were gonna get back out under your own steam… Roy was most definitely not a latchkey kid anymore!

'As we approached the prison, I remember thinking, God, this is frightening. If you can imagine what the Addam's Family house looked like on the telly, you wouldn't be far off,' says Roy. 'Once inside, I had to join a queue, there were probably about fifteen or sixteen of us, we were all given a blanket each, a set of overalls to wear, then our identification number, after which we were marched off to our cells. From then on I wasn't Roy Vasey anymore, I was just a number. It was three to a cell, which meant, embarrassingly, when it came to having a dump, you had to do it in front of your mates, so one of us would hold a blanket round the other while he did a shit. This would have to be performed at a specific time in the morning because after that there'd be a bell rung and the cell doors would be opened to allow you to go and empty your shit pot. There was loads of piss taking going on but then that's what you would expect if you were emptying the toilet bucket so often. You'd regularly hear some lag shout out, 'We all piss in the same pot, don't we?' Funny the first time you hear it.'

Roy had been detained in police cells before, usually overnight at the main police station in his own area at South Bank, but this was a very different experience altogether. Even the cell doors sounded different with each one echoing down the halls as they were slammed shut last thing at night. Roy knew that he was only to be at Armley temporarily while they decided the next move for him so when the lights went out on his first night, he could only curl up in his itchy blanket and ponder what was to come in the forthcoming days.

'Two or three times a day, the cell door would open and you'd hear 'Out!" recalls Roy. 'This meant it was exercise time in the yard with all of the other prisoners where, I must say, I saw a few things that were a little bit frightening for a young lad like me. On one morning, a guy got attacked. All the prisoners ran over to him and started kicking him, and they would have kicked him to death if the whistles and sirens hadn't gone off. Suddenly, it seemed out of nowhere, between fifteen and twenty prison wardens dashed out into the courtyard and we were all rushed back inside to our cells. I said to one of the lads, 'I wonder what happened there.' He said, 'That bloke had strangled two kiddies, he'll have been due a fucking good hiding, it's a good job it got stopped, they'd have fucking killed him.' I said, 'Well I wonder how they knew.' 'Oh,' he said, 'one of the screws would have told them, they fucking hate 'em. They know the lags'll dish out their own punishment to anyone who messes with kids and they just casually let it slip out which ones they are, then stand back waiting for the inevitable mayhem. Did you notice it didn't take the screws long to stop it when the siren went off? The fucking lot of them will have been tucked away in little hidey-holes waiting for it to kick off, then stop it just in time like they're doing their job.'

At Roy's assessment, he had to stand in front of a board of governors while they decided where he would be sent to next. Roy says, 'At that meeting, they looked at my offence then talked about my home life during which I was told that they'd contacted my father and mother separately and neither of them wanted me back. Mam was in Pontefract with Norman, and me dad had moved another woman, Betty who had five kids, into Essex Avenue, leaving no room for me. 'You'll just have to do your sentence, son,' came the authoritative tone from the main man as he ticked and crossed a few boxes on my form that he was filling in. It was normal to try and get young offenders back to their home environment as soon as they thought it was fit to do so, but if no one was willing to have you back then you were fucked. I was told I was being allocated to Wormwood Scrubs.'

Just the name Wormwood Scrubs was enough on its own to send shivers down your spine. The Scrubs was, and still is, a Category B prison infamous for housing the Kray twins over a month in the 1950s before they were transferred to another high security prison, so you can imagine that it would have been hosting some pretty tough characters at that time.

Roy had to stay another month at Armley before three other prisoners and himself were taken in a van to Wormwood Scrubs, where he would be fully assessed by a medical and psychiatric team before being sent on to the most suitable borstal.

There was a lot of form filling to be done before Roy went in front of the board. 'After reading the form that I'd filled in, or Billy's Weekly Liar, call it what you like,' Roy smiles, 'the suits behind the desk at my assessment said, 'You seem like a nice quiet lad, it says here your aunty is a Methodist Minister, you've probably just gone down the wrong road and fell off the rails slightly.' If it was the first time you'd been inside, and you seemed like a decent enough lad, you'd get sent to an open borstal that didn't have the same restraints as some of the others. That's what happened to me. I got sent to Guys Marsh near Shaftesbury, not far off the south coast. The transfer didn't happen immediately so while I was at Wormwood Scrubs, I was given a variety of jobs to do just like any of the other young lads who were waiting to move on. I was given the scary job of cleaning one of the lifer's cells out each day.'

It wasn't too long before Roy was off to Guys Marsh with a few of the other lads. 'Guys Marsh was so much different to Armley and The Scrubs,' says Roy. 'It had been an old prisoner of war camp and the billet huts were still there being used as dormitories for the borstal. We were all allocated a billet, about twenty four in each, lads from all over the country. We got to know everyone and made friends. The billets were given names and there would be competitions against each other… tug 'o' war, football, stuff like that. At the end of each month you would go in front of a committee who looked at your record and decided if you were going home or not. Most kids did about eight months, eleven months, really bad bastards would have to endure a full twelve months. I did my full two years 'cos I fucking hated everyone at the time. I was wayward, totally off the wall. If anybody said anything to me, I'd just punch them in the fucking face, I wasn't bothered. I consider myself to have been very lucky. I must have been in two hundred fights and still kept my teeth… they're in a jar at the side of my bed. No really, I had loads of black eyes, broken bones and bruises but always managed to keep my teeth intact. My motto is, 'Never smile when you're being punched'. When you're in borstal with something like another seven hundred lads who are very much there for the same reason as you are, there's always going to be trouble. You can't be on your own, it's no good thinking that you can just get your head down and do your time. Everyone gets labelled, the other lads give you a label more or less as soon as you get there, it's like they want to work out what you're all about. Could be they think you're a mammy's boy, or gay, or a trouble causer they want to give a wide berth. Once they've decided who you are, the vulnerable ones, the loners, get picked on and bullied. There was a ruthless atmosphere in the air and lots of the lads lived their sentences out in constant fear. I was as fit as a lop then, not an ounce of fat on me and I could handle myself, so I got picked on because lads wanted to prove they were harder than me. Problem was, it was usually a handful of three, four or five, sometimes more from one of the other billets who would set on me. There was no way you could just keep yourself to yourself so I became part of a gang, but there were always lads from other gangs looking out to catch rival gang members on their own, just to give 'em a fucking good hiding. There was all sorts of stuff going on especially between billets. The competitions we had created a real heavy rivalry which would regularly end up with someone getting a good going over. One Saturday morning, we had a football match between our billet and one of the other billets. The team we were playing against were well known as being some of the hardest lads in the borstal proper, gangster types, everybody avoided them. I was playing at right full back, it was a real windy day and I hoofed the ball forward, it caught on the wind, bounced once, hit their goalie on the head and ended up in the back of the net. Everyone on our team started cheering, 'Nice one, Roy' and jumping all over me 'cos I'd scored. The lads on the other team just stood looking at each other, grimacing with grinding teeth and pointing to me. The other team weren't used to anyone scoring against them, everyone was too scared to, and I must admit that my 'worldy' had been a bit of a fluke. I got set on by a bunch of them after the game and was left in a right state, needing medical treatment. I just told the screws I'd fell down some stairs. I don't think they believed me but they put me in the gardening party keeping the lawns and flowerbeds tidy while I healed 'cos it wasn't such heavy work. The lads still kept having a go at me, thought I'd be too scared to do anything about it. One of them, an Irish lad, picked a fight with me in a corridor, and during the scuffle he bit me so I battered him. I must have hit him forty fucking times, I was getting real pissed off with them by then. It continued for another four weeks, and by then I'd had enough. Being in the gardening party, I had the key to the shed which housed five lawnmowers, as well as all of the gardening tools and I knew there were some cans of petrol in there for the mowers. Their billet was the one on the end, so one night I sneaked out, went to the shed and took one of the cans, poured petrol around their billet then set fire to the fucker. It was like fucking bonfire night. This was two o'clock in the morning when the fire had to be put out. Afterwards, still early hours of the morning, we were all told to stand in line on the parade ground and to stretch our arms out in front of us with our hands turned upward. The Governor walked past us all, sniffing each lad's hands as he passed, until he got to me that was. Of course my hands still stank of petrol. He said, 'Vasey, come with me.' I admitted it, I said, 'They beat me up so I tried to burn the cunts to death.'

Roy's reluctance to toe the line and just see his sentence out had been his downfall again, but at the same time he was showing that he was nobody's fool and if anyone thought they were going to get one over on him, they should think again. Because of this, his cushy existence at the open borstal of Guys Marsh was about to come to an abrupt end. It was decided that the much stricter regime of Portland Bill borstal, probably the most brutal establishment in the country for young offenders, would be more able to handle Roy's erratic temperament. Just how wrong could they be?

Portland Bill, sounds quite romantic, trips off the tongue like Craggy Island, Postman Pat or Fireman Sam. There, unfortunately, the similarity ends, Portland Bill Prison was known as the toughest borstal in the land. Situated on the Isle of Portland off the South Coast of England near Weymouth, it couldn't have been any further away from Roy's home territory in the North East without being in another country. Although the prison itself was only a small part of the Isle of Portland, as they approached it, Roy's mind couldn't help but wander back to having recently seen Burt Lancaster in the film,

The Birdman of Alcatraz, being the only prison he'd ever known situated on an island. As Roy got closer to the gates, he could see that it had been built to be as escape proof as its San Franciscan counterpart.

On the lower level, in the basement, there was Verne Prison which housed lifers and some of the hardest criminals in the UK, then on the next level were their apprentices, if you like, the young crowd who were all in danger of following in their footsteps.

Mostly, any young lad sent to these institutions wouldn't complete their full sentence, being released early for good behaviour or something, but, seeing as good behaviour was not really one of Roy's main assets at that time, Portland Bill Detention Centre, to give it its full title, was destined to be his new home for the remainder of his two year sentence.

Quite dejectedly, Roy's thoughts go back to the time when he missed out on the emergence of the Beatles and all that was going on in the early sixties. It was all on the TV in the recreation room but that only rubbed it in even more. They say that you will always remember where you were when you heard that President Kennedy had been shot, and Roy certainly does, 'I was swilling out buckets of shit at Portland Bill borstal.'

There's a saying, 'If you can remember the sixties, you can't have really been there', and you'll see as we read on that, in Roy's situation, for a good part of the sixties he actually wasn't there. Well, not where it was all happening, that is.

At Portland everyone had their own cell, no en-suite in those days though. Roy's next door neighbour was in for poisoning his grandparents just to get their money. Yes, it was a violent place with the most violent of cohabitants.

There was a lad called Barney Mulraney who must have recognised Roy's accent.

He asked Roy, 'Are you from the Boro?' Roy said, 'Yes I am.' He said, 'I'm Barney, come from Brambles Farm.' Brambles Farm is an estate on the outskirts of Middlesbrough. Roy says, 'God, he was a big bloke, told me he was in borstal for snatching the money bag off the rent man then throwing him through a window. Said he'd pleaded not guilty but the police had him bang to rights being as it was Barney's own window that he'd thrown him through… from the inside. Barney was a year or two older than me and he went on to say, 'If you have any trouble, just give me the nod.' Then he said that one of his mates had just been released and I was the spitting image of him. Barney had nicknamed him Spud so he said, 'From now on you're gonna be Spud, I'm going to call you Spud.' Having my own cell meant we were allowed to put family pictures up on the walls to remind us of home, even if you didn't have one. The only pictures I had were of people who didn't fucking want me back. I had one picture that I tried to put up on the wall but the screws didn't believe me when I said Brigitte Bardot was me sister. I still had a couple of photos of my ex, Sandra, so I put them up to keep me company and have a cheeky wank over now and then.'

Now feeling on his own in life, having been disowned by all and sundry, it would have been understandable for Roy to start feeling sorry for himself, but a surprise visitor from home should have lifted his spirits somewhat.

Even though his mother's home situation had forced her to say she didn't want him back earlier in his sentence, Roy was still the apple of her eye. She made the arduous train journey from her home in Pontefract to Portland under a visiting order during his second year. This meeting of Roy and his mam was somewhat subdued after she collapsed on seeing where Roy was being detained. After recovering, they sat together, much in silence than anything else, because neither really had that much to say to each other. Still, it meant a lot to Roy that his mam had taken it upon herself to make the long journey to see him.

'I was coming up to my second year in borstal and I had such a vicious temper then that I thought that this was my life now. All I could really see in front of me was going from one incarceration to another. I'd been in four separate prisons already and it felt like this was going to go on for the rest of my life. I was out of control. Thought I'd be in and out of jail all my life, even thought with my temper I might actually kill someone, that's how my mind was working at the time.'

'Inmates at Portland were given different coloured overalls, the colour of your overall indicated whether you had been behaving yourself or not. I'd been in that much bother since arriving at Portland that I was given the second highest coloured overall that was available, yellow, with the highest a patchwork suit being reserved for the crackpots that had actually tried to escape, but I was to be kept an eye on.'

Roy was still unable to control his temper and found it extremely difficult to take orders from anyone so, after an encounter between himself and one of the most unpleasant wardens, and a metal bucket full of water, he found himself in deep trouble again, receiving a term in solitary confinement.

After the twenty one days in solitary, Roy was hauled in front of the Governor and told that from then on he was going to be his monitor. Roy says, 'The Governor told me he had to keep a close eye on me and my job in future was to clean his office every day, sweeping, polishing, getting him cups of tea, anything he needed me to do under his watch all of the time.'

Under the close scrutiny of the Prison Governor, Roy completed his twenty four months detention being informed that there were very few lads who completed their full sentences without being granted earlier release. Roy's uncontrollable temper and behaviour had been so bad that it hadn't warranted cutting his term down at all, but the day finally came when they couldn't keep him locked up any longer.

Well, not this time anyway.

12

On leaving Portland, Roy was given his train fare home, together with a contact address back in Redcar on Westbourne Grove where Alf and Mary took in wayward boys and gave them a home.

It was hoped that a relatively settled lifestyle in a caring environment with Alf and Mary at Westbourne Grove would help to bring these troublesome boys back on to the straight and narrow, though some would prove to be more of a challenge than others. Roy was now coming up to be twenty one and the Redcar lifestyle suited him. There was always plenty to do and he fitted in and made friends quite easily, but trouble would always be just around the corner.

'Arthur Sturt, who I'd covered in cement at Dorman Long a few years earlier, had a brother called Billy Sheakey, obviously they had two different fathers. They were both tough Grangetown lads, working on the doors in Redcar and Billy got me a job on the door at The Red Lion which had dance nights every Friday and Saturday. We all knew each from years ago, growing up together in the same backyard, and another proper hard case from Grangetown, who was also working at The Red Lion, got sent down for six months so he asked me to look after his girlfriend, Barbara, while he was in jail. I said, 'Don't worry, no one will go near her.' Barbara still came to the weekend discos at The Red Lion, so I made sure she got home all right, putting her in a taxi home to Dormanstown at the end of the night. That was until one week when on the way for a taxi Barbara said, 'I don't have to go home, you know.' I loved a bit of pussy and I did fancy her, so didn't need any encouragement and took her back to my flat in Westbourne Grove. Barbara stayed over regularly after that, then suddenly disappeared when her lad came out of prison. I figured they'd just got back together again and thought no more about it. What had really happened and wasn't to find out 'til later in my life was that Barbara had been pregnant and was having my baby. I knew nothing about it. She'd left the area, had the baby and got it adopted. She'd said nothing to anyone, just went off, probably frightened what her lad would say or do when he found out.'

Roy continues, 'I thought Barbara had taken back up with him so never pursued it. There'd been rumours about what had happened to Barbara but I knew she lived in Dormanstown not far from me mam so, after a few beers, I went and knocked on their door. I'd previously been told by someone that Barbara's dad was the sort you wouldn't want to tangle with and if you went to his house he'd be liable to stab you. I still went round, knocked on the door and this little old lady opened it. I said, 'I've come to see Barbara.' She thundered back to me, 'She doesn't fucking live here anymore!' and shut the door on me. That was the last I heard of Barbara, the end of the matter so I thought, still not knowing anything about her baby being mine While I was working the door at The Red Lion, I was always getting into fights, throwing lads out for one reason or another. The fifties and the sixties was an era where it was thought you hadn't had a good night out if it didn't finish with the resemblence of a wild western brawl before you went home.'

Roy continues, 'I'd got a job at ICI during the day and had to catch the bus, getting off at the ICI gates then walking in from there. This one day when I got on the bus, the conductor, who gave you your ticket and collected your money, came up to me to take my fare, then pushed his face right up to my face and said, 'Now then, you fucking bastard, remember me?' I'd thrown him out of The Red Lion the Saturday before, and at this point everyone in the bus turned round to look. He was really showing me up. I had a very short fuse in those days and this lad was starting to wind me up so I said, 'If I were you, I'd just shift your fucking face away from mine.' He said, 'There you go, not so tough without all of your fucking mates around you, are you?' Playing the big boy. So I lost it. I just jumped up grabbed hold of his leather bag that held his money and smacked him across the fucking head with it. The money flew everywhere, all over the bus. The passengers forgot about us, they were all on their hands and knees, picking the cash up and stuffing it in their pockets. I smacked him again, then the bus stopped and the driver rushed round. I said to him, 'Come on then! You as well!' and he just ran off, ran into somebody's house. I just scarpered out of the way through a nearby field, but someone must have recognised me 'cos the police came round, saying that I'd attacked the clippy on the bus. I told them he'd attacked me first and I was only acting in self defence but they didn't believe me, so I was up in front of the Magistrates where I was fined two hundred quid.'

Roy served another two separate six month prison terms, the first for punching a police officer outside The Berkeley Bar, one of Redcar's night spots. Roy was sent to do his time in Lincoln Prison, being ironic as that's where the Vasey family now live.

'As we arrived, I thought they must have taken a wrong turning and brought us to Butlin's Holiday Camp at Skegness by mistake. There was a fountain in the middle of the forecourt and I remember thinking that this looks a bit of all right. I certainly didn't have the horrible feelings I'd had as I'd arrived at my previous residencies.'

The second jail term was for stealing a car with a mate of his. He was locked up at Durham Prison, no fountain in the forecourt there, top security with some of the hardest criminals in the country doing their time. Hard to believe at that time but Roy must have been on his best behaviour as they let him out after three months… or maybe they'd just had enough of him. After each of these prison terms, Roy would return to Redcar which had now become his home and pick back up with his door duties at The Red Lion.

On evenings through the week, Roy would socialise in nearby pubs The Zetland or The Clarendon, known as the The Clarry, and would get talking to the regular characters. It was during one of those nights that Roy was to be introduced to someone who would become one of those lifelong friends you could always rely on. Marty Miller was a local greengrocer and, after being in Roy's company a few times where they got to know each other, Marty asked Roy if he was working. Roy being yet again between jobs, apart from his Red Lion work, told Marty he wasn't.

As well as his greengrocer's shop, Marty had a stall on Redcar High Street. It's still there today being run by Marty's family. He was well liked in Redcar and just about everyone knew him from seeing him in the High Street, shouting out how good his apples and pears were. Marty asked Roy if he fancied helping sell his fruit and veg on his stall.

Roy said, 'I've never done anything like that before.' Marty replied, 'Oh, you'll soon pick it up, you're a natural.' It was Christmas time when he'd asked and Marty was selling wrapping paper to boost his earnings. He told Roy the tricks of the trade shouting, 'Three for a bob, three for a bob,' then only putting two in. He said, 'They aren't going to stand in the middle of the High Street while it's snowing and count how many sheets of Christmas wrapping paper I've given them. They'll just call me all the cunts under the sun when they find out at home, but that's how you make your money.' Roy says, 'Then he asked me if I could drive. Well, I only had a provisional licence but I said, 'Yeah, course I can.' Marty asked, 'Do you want to take the wagon home?' So I did, never driven nowt like it before, it had a great big floppy gear stick with a knob on the end, trying find the right gear was like stirring a huge witches cauldron.'

To get the best fruit and veg, Marty had to be at the market in Hill Street in Middlesbrough no later than five thirty on a morning. After giving Roy the keys to the wagon, Marty then added that part of the deal was to pick him up from home at five o'clock the next day so they could get there on time.

Roy remembers those days with great fondness. 'I picked Marty up every day after that, arriving at his house in Dormanstown at five in the morning. Problem was Marty loved his bed and he was never up. Most mornings when I pulled up outside and sounded the horn 'beep-beep!' then 'beep-beep!' I knew he'd be taken no fucking notice whatsoever so I'd throw a few stones up at the bedroom window. Don't forget this is mid-winter so at five in the morning we were still in complete darkness. Marty would often stick his head out of the window and whisper down to me to be quiet or the neighbours would complain to the council. Sometimes if he wasn't taking any notice, I'd start singing at the top of my voice, The Four Seasons, 'Sherry, sherry baby, sher-ry sherry baby' or 'Big girls don't cry'! Marty would shout down in his loudest whisper, 'Shut up, you fat cunt!'

Roy continues, 'The market was a typical auction where you had to bid for whatever you wanted with the auctioneer shouting out at the speed of light, fingers going up in the air together with the odd wink as different people made their bids. Marty would pick out crates of bananas, oranges or whatever and make his bid to buy them. He said to me, 'For fuck's sake, don't poke your nose or we'll end up with a barrow load of shite we don't really want.' There was one morning when two of Marty's brothers, Billy and Malcolm, were there. They would normally drink together in a local pub called 'The Palmerston' but the previous night they'd had a big fall out with Billy hitting Malcolm across the head with a chair. Malcolm had only come to the market with a fucking gun looking for Billy. I was standing by the lorry, and didn't know about the gun. Malcolm said, 'Hiya Roy, Billy there?' I said, 'Yeah.' He said, 'Go and get him, will you?' I looked at him and saw the gun. I said, 'Have you got a gun?' I thought it was a toy. Malcolm said, 'Yeah, I'm gonna shoot the cunt.' I ran inside and told Marty. I said, 'Marty, Malcolm's outside. He's got a gun, says he's going to shoot Billy.' Marty said, 'Aw, the daft cunt,' and we went outside and me and Marty talked him into getting into his car and going home. The next day back in The Palmerston, they're both pissed together again. Marty said, 'I ought to explain something about my family, Roy, they are proper fucking barrow boys. What you saw at the market that day is just their way of handling things. Nowt would have happened.'

Under the watchful guidance of Marty, Roy soon picked up the necessary skills of the barrow boy, revelling in describing 'today's bargains' with his own flamboyant style at the top of his voice. 'Fanny crackers 25p each, come and get your fanny crackers!' For the record 'fanny cracker' was Roy's description of a cucumber. Roy's banter with the customers always drew a large crowd with Marty asking, 'How come you always manage to sell more than I do, Roy?' Joining Marty as a barrow boy had been a huge success for Roy, being able to use his natural comedy talent to attract customers.

Roy would be working all day on the market stall after picking Marty up at 5.00am then off out on the night drinking with his mates and climbing into bed around 2.00am, then up again at five. He was never going to make a lifelong career as a barrow boy, it was all casual work, off the record, being paid in used notes with no numbers running concurrently and Roy inevitably found himself a job back contracting at ICI, so he had to tell Marty that he couldn't pick him up anymore because he was starting a new job, so no one knew after that how Marty managed to get himself out of bed on a morning. At Marty's request, Roy continued to work the market stall on weekends.

Roy and Marty had become a great team during their days working Redcar High Street, forming a close bond that lasted a lifetime, with Roy standing as Marty's best man at his wedding to Sue. Sadly, Marty passed away in 2020.

Marty Miller left a huge footprint in Roy's life, being probably the first person to show him any kind of trust. He gave Roy responsibilities and showed him what hard work and dedication could achieve… lessons we all need at sometime in our lives. Many more people would leave footprints in Roy's life, and are still doing so. Some as treasured as Marty's, some not, but each one helping to eventually shape a life for Roy that he could previously have only dreamed about.

13

Roy's aptitude for drumming, or not being able to sit still… call it what you like, was now about to raise its head, although it was not always appreciated. Working on the ICI site, he'd begun staying over at his dad's house in Grangetown on odd nights, there being more room after Betty's kids had moved out because his dad had been too strict with them. He'd keep telling them, 'Take your elbows off the table!' and stuff like that, so it was no surprise that when Roy continuously rat-a-tat tapped on the dining room table, his dad would pipe up telling him to pack it in.

Encouragement though would come from an unlikely source. Roy's new job at ICI was with a contracted welding company and anytime he could he'd pick up a couple of welding rods and start tapping along on a bench or a table. One of the lads asked, 'Do you play the drums?' Roy answered, 'No I don't.' With the other lad coming back saying, 'Well you should, you're dead good with those rods.' I'm sure this chap was no Simon Cowell but his words have always stayed in Roy's head as giving him the drive to becoming a drummer in the first place.

Somehow Roy managed to convince his dad to buy him a drum kit, told him it would stop him tapping on the table at meal times. With dad having contacts at the Unity Club and still a regular member of the Methodist Church, he found out that the local Salvation Army had a set of drums they no longer needed. He went off and had a look, not really knowing anything about drums but ended up putting a few bob in their collection tin and bringing them home. It was a very basic set with a snare drum, one cymbal and a massive bass drum which had 'GOD' printed on the outer skin for all to see, but Roy thought it was great, spending every spare minute he had practising and practising until he thought he was ready to go public.

Roy would often go into the Station Hotel in Redcar where they had a resident pianist called Nancy Pinkney. Nancy liked a drop of Guinness… well, more than a drop really and, even if it hadn't been spotted beforehand, by the end of the night she sounded like she was playing her piano while wearing handcuffs. Not that any of the pissed up regulars would have noticed anyway.

The Station Hotel was typical of the day, air thick with fag smoke and the stench of stale beer and body odour, but it was popular with the locals… most of whom stank of fag smoke, stale beer and body odour, and still thought you hadn't had a really good night out unless there'd been a scrap at the end of it.

Roy was now quite a well-known character around Redcar so it didn't take too long before he wangled his way in to become Nancy's assistant on the drums. He did look slightly out of place though, with his Salvation Army drum kit and its bass drum inscription of 'GOD' staring disdainfully out at the ungodly goings on around him. Roy was in his element, getting paid – albeit in pints of beer – for doing something he really enjoyed for a change and he looked forward to his nights supporting Nancy on the piano. In Roy's world though, the tranquillity, if you could call it that, would turn out to be too good to last.

One night, a disagreement at the bar got out of control and quickly escalated into a cowboy saloon style brawl with somebody flinging a stool, which was evaded by a ducking punter, only for it to finish embedded in 'GOD'. Fucking heathen. Roy wasn't at all happy that his 'GOD' was no more and picked up the stool, taking God into his own hands, and wrapped it round the neck of the thrower. Not only was it the end of Roy's Station Hotel residency but his treasured Salvation Army drum kit had been demolished and gone to drum heaven in the sky with its forwarding address still on the front bass skin. Good thing Roy hadn't left the day job!

Roy's mam had now moved back to the area with Norman, living in Dormanstown on Staintondale Avenue and had made contact with Roy, asking to see him. Roy thinks that she'd heard about him staying over at his dad's and got a bit jealous so she asked him if he wanted to stay with her on the odd occasion. Not wishing to rock the boat, he agreed even though he had a disliking to Norman, who'd once told his mam that he knew Roy would end up in jail at some time, though he hadn't needed to be too clever to have worked that one out.

The stay overs got more regular so Roy, now contracting with Kellogg's at ICI, offered to give his mam some cash every week towards his food and the household bills. He said, 'I was working for Kellogg's. Everyone thinks they just do cornflakes but they are a huge American company into just about everything, and I was on great money, ten pounds a day. I'd give me dad money for a drink and also me mam a few quid. I'd been giving me mam about twenty quid a week and getting my tea done each night. Everything was fine, I was getting fed each night and keeping out of Norman's way, until after a few weeks on a Friday teatime, pay day, me mam brought my plate to the table and asked for her money. I said, 'I've lost it all at the bookies.' I was always in the bookies then, got the gambling bug. She just flung my tea at the wall, smashed the plate, leaving a mural of egg and chips staring back at us as it slid towards the floor, then told me to get the fuck out. That's probably where I get my short fuse, though there is a distinct difference between me and me mam… I would never waste a fucking plate full of egg and chips'.

Roy was well aware of how quickly his mam could turn so he very likely knew he was pushing his luck when he told her he'd lost all of his money and had none to give her. It would always have been only a matter of time before they had another massive fall out. Roy still carried on with his visits to his dad's but by then, it was becoming a matter of Roy carving out his own life in Redcar. Even as dramatic as his mam could be when they had their disagreements, since coming back to the area, reconciliations were never that far away, both knew each other for who they really were. After all, they were mother and son.

Standing on his own two feet had been what Roy was forced to do from an early age when his mam left home, so looking after himself was never going to be a problem anyway. The visits to his mam's or his dad's homes were as much to keep them happy as simply just getting a decent meal. Roy was never going to go hungry, especially after being the main reason that the pork pie was invented. By now, Roy's everyday life consisted of his ICI contracting job, helping Marty with his stall on a weekend and doing the odd shift at The Red Lion.

Roy's existence was now very much the same as many of the mates he socialised with on an evening, but I think as we've come to realise already with Roy, there's always a 'nobody knows what's around the corner' moment waiting to jump out.

One such occasion happened on an evening when Roy was enjoying a drink in The Clarry. 'I heard a bit of commotion,' says

Roy, 'When I looked over to see what was happening, there was a lad kicking bits out of a young girl. I went over, grabbed him and said, 'Hey, hey, what yer fucking doing?' He said, 'Get your fucking hands off me.' So I just hit him, sent him flying back through the front door. A bit later on, I was sat in the corner with my mates, when one of the bar staff came over with a pint saying, 'That girl over there asked me to bring this over for you,' and when I looked over she waved at me. It was the same girl whose boyfriend I'd kicked out earlier. Not long after, one of her mates came over and said that her name was Judy, which was coincidental I suppose seeing how I'd just given her boyfriend a punch, 'cos at seaside towns like Redcar, you'd rarely see a Judy without a Punch. She said that Judy wanted to know if I'd be going into The Red Lion later on, so I told her I would. There was always a gang of us who would walk the High Street pubs on a Saturday night if I wasn't working on a door. We'd start at The Clarry, onto The Park, The Zetland, then The Red Lion before we all went off to The Starlight, which was one of the few night clubs in the area.'

Roy and Judy met up in The Red Lion and spent the rest of the evening together. They would meet up regularly over the next few days with Roy saying that they consummated their friendship after about three nights – well, 'shagged' is what he actually called it – and from then, the relationship blossomed. Roy had enjoyed other female company with the odd date between jail terms and girls who had been attracted to his 'fanny crackers' on the fruit and veg stand, but Judy was about to become his first serious girlfriend since breaking up with his childhood sweetheart, Sandra.

Judy wasn't a local girl; she originated from Bellingham, which was in the heart of Northumberland. Judy's mam and dad had split up, her mam coming to live in Cleveland Street, opposite the post office with Harry who she'd ran away with. Judy had still been living in Bellingham with her dad but was a frequent visitor, staying with her mam and Harry. It had been during these visits that she'd taken up with her previous boyfriend who'd had the habit of knocking her about a bit.

She had now moved to her mam's permanently while still keeping in touch with her dad and visiting him back in Bellingham occasionally. Roy was sharing a flat in Saltburn with two other lads, Tommy Keegan and Johnny Horrocks, who he'd met in the wayward boys home on Westbourne Grove in Redcar. 'I had some great times with Tommy and Johnny, fun times. It was all just a laugh, good mates. We'd draw straws to see who was going to do different chores, make the tea, wash up, stuff like that and I was always able to take Judy to the flat when they were both out. Then I managed to get a flat above the hairdressers on Coatham Road, back in Redcar, not far from Judy's mam's house. It made life a bit easier and we were able to see each other more often. Judy was able to stay with me on the odd night even though it was a bit tight on space being a simple bedsit, but at that age I'd have shagged on a washing line if it would have taken my weight. We'd been going together about six months when I suggested that we got a decent size flat together, which prompted Judy to drop the bombshell she'd been keeping to herself for a couple of weeks. 'I'm pregnant.' I said, 'You what?' She said, 'I'm pregnant.' I said, 'Are you sure it's yours?' I still couldn't resist cracking a joke even then, it's always been my way of handling tense situations. Trying to get me to take it more seriously, she said, 'Roy, I'm fucking pregnant. Do you think we should get married?' I said, 'Do you want to get married?' Back in the sixties, it was generally accepted that if you got your girlfriend pregnant then you did the 'decent thing' and married her, but we'd been planning to move in together anyway so it seemed quite the natural thing to do. Judy said that she did want to get married and I hadn't thought about it before, but agreed that we should. After all, most of my drinking pals were settling down and getting wed, so to start with we managed to get a flat on Newcommen Terrace, opposite the Regent cinema. Judy was attractive and knew I had a jealous streak in me, so she would occasionally wind me up by saying things like, 'A bloke outside the pub told me how lovely I was and would I like to go for a drink sometime.' One day she came in and said that two lads in a van outside Birkbeck's electrical shop had told her she was the best looking girl they'd ever seen. Birkbeck's shop was just around the corner from our flat on Station Road so I ran around there as quick as I could. I was fucking raging, but there was no one there, no van, fuck all, but if I'd seen anyone I'd have given them a fucking good hiding. I went back to the flat still raging, but by then it was because I'd let Judy wind me up yet again. Before I ran out after some blokes who weren't there, I'd filled the bath up so I just picked Judy up and threw her in, it had cooled down by then and was fucking freezing. She shouted, 'Yer fucking bastard!' Soaked through to the skin she was.'

Having new-found responsibilities of providing a roof over his and Judy's head together with the prospect of a forthcoming child, Roy resigned himself to getting back to doing the bit jobs that came his way. Every penny counted now. The flat itself wasn't altogether suitable. It was on the top floor of three and, being directly opposite the cinema, could be quite noisy on a night.

'We got married at Guisborough Registry Office,' he says, 'had our reception in The Clarry with a few drinks and a bite to eat, concluding the festivities by spending the rest of the afternoon in Garvey's betting shop, picking out 'winners' and 'losers'. Some wedding day that turned out to be.'

After getting married, Roy and Judy qualified to go on the housing list, finally getting a council house at number 36 Cedar Grove and settling down to being just another married couple with Richard, their first baby, having been born to make the unit complete.

Roy had now relaxed himself into the typical married man with, hopefully, his feral days behind him. Those wild nights drumming along with Nancy in the Station Hotel were now just a distant dream and thoughts of ever picking a pair of drumsticks up again never entered his head. A second child, Robert, was born but, just as Roy was about to slip into being suburban Mr Vasey, his life was about to take yet another detour when opportunity came knocking at a time he least expected it, the impact of which would be instrumental in the birth of a whole new career, but also in the inevitable breakdown of his marriage.

14

There are certain times we can all look back to in our lives which we regard as turning points. One was just about to happen for the wayward Roy Vasey and, although not realising it at the time, would turn out to be the catalyst that would change his life forever. It was 1969 BC (Before Chubby), the year Neil Armstrong set foot on the moon, whilst back on Earth another small step was about to make its first teetering, yet galactic imprint.

Roy's cousins, Dek and Lee, both a bit younger than Roy – in fact Lee would only be in his early teens – were already talented musicians, being self taught on bass guitar and lead guitar respectively. Dek was part of a local band made up of Grangetown and Boro lads working the pubs and clubs of the surrounding area. Unfortunately Lee is the only other surviving member of that time. He's now a highly regarded musician living in Norwich, and looks back to those days with great fondness.

The group was called Pipeline and had been formed by the lead guitarist whose name escapes Lee after all these years. Other members were Tony Morris on rhythm guitar and lead vocal, with Geoff Briggs on drums, affectionately known as 'stiff arm' because of his drumming technique. The lead guitarist, who we'll call Eric to make life easier, was the only one in the band with any equipment, so even when Tony recommended bringing Dek Vasey into the band on bass guitar, they all had to plug their instruments, including the only microphone they had, into Eric's Vox AC30.

Just to give you the Stephen Fry bit here, for those who aren't aware, a Vox AC30 was an amplifier, the most common in the 50s and 60s, but was generally used for one electrical instrument only, not designed for everyone to be plugged in at the same time, although I'm sure a lot of bands had to start out in very much the same way. To see a Vox AC30, you only need to look at any of the early Beatles stage photos.

Fourteen year old Lee, who was already quite useful on the guitar himself, used to tag along with his brother when Pipeline were playing at local gigs. Dek was a top bass player, playing a Hofner violin bass, the same one Paul McCartney played, and Tony had a great lead voice, but both of them didn't think Eric's lead guitar playing was up to the job and that Lee would fit in better, so during one of the band's practice sessions, they kicked Eric out of his own group and installed Lee. In a typical 'I'm taking my ball home' moment, Eric, who wasn't at all happy, unplugged his AC30 from the wall and stormed out of Tony's house, carrying both guitar and amp under each arm, then jumped on to the next trolley bus home. It appears that nobody ever saw him again, but that also left the band with nothing into which they could plug their instruments.

There was always someone on the periphery of joining a band who had an unemployed amp who would be only too willing to lend it out in the hope that they might get to join in, so it wasn't too long before Pipeline were back on the road again, even if they did have to travel to each gig by tram. Not long after Lee joining the band and even with the shortage of proper amplification, Pipeline were doing very well, securing themselves a regular weekly slot at The Magnet pub in Grangetown, where Lee and Dek lived.

The Magnet was just one of the many drinking holes for the hard workers of Grangetown to get away from it all for a few bevvies, some often calling in on their way home from shift still covered in coal dust so nobody would recognise them and 'sprag them to their lass'.

What made The Magnet stand out though was that through the week, in the lounge area, there would be a band playing, a different band for each night. There was a small stage to appear on and it was as if The Magnet was Grangetown's very own miniature version of The Cavern in Liverpool, because we all thought if you got a gig at The Magnet, you'd made it big. Many of the workers who drank in there didn't take much notice of what was going on in the lounge, but The Magnet actually was a magnet for young musos, members of other bands, who would come along to see who was doing what.

Pipeline became regular performers at The Magnet, but one week, drummer Geoff 'stiff arm' Briggs, the only one with a proper job working for the council, informed the rest of the lads that he would be going on holiday in a few weeks time, so wouldn't be available to play. Tony, Dek and Lee didn't want to lose their Magnet night in the weekly rota of groups, as well as the pittance of cash that went along with it, so it was decided they would still go ahead with the gig.

Dek had been spending more time in Redcar, having moved into a flat on Newcommen Terrace, overlooking the boating lake, along from where Roy and Judy had been living. Dek and Roy were now in regular contact but Lee hadn't had much to do with any of the other members of the Vasey family, so he didn't really know much about Roy. That's probably because, while Lee was growing up, Roy had been spending most of his time at Her Majesty's Pleasure for one reason or another. The lads knew of Roy's drumming escapades in the Station Hotel and Tony said to Dek, 'Why don't you ask your Roy to fill in for Geoff?'

Dek went to see Roy and asked him if he fancied playing drums for them while Geoff was away on holiday. Roy said, 'When is it?' Dek said, 'Tomorrow night at The Magnet.' Roy's Salvation Army drum kit had been destroyed in the pub brawl a bit back, so he said to Dek, 'I haven't got any drums.' Dek said, 'Geoff's left his kit at Tony's, you can use that.' 'I've never played with a band before, you know that, don't you?' 'You'll be all right,' said Dek, 'it's all four-four time rock 'n' roll, straight forward stuff. You'll be fine. We can have a bit of a practice tomorrow afternoon.'

This would be Roy's first venture into the world of show groups. How could any of them know it was also the start of a hugely successful showbiz career that is still in as much demand today as it has ever been, fifty plus years later.

By this time, each member of the band had managed to obtain a small amplifier, with Tony getting hold of a PA system to sing through, although he still had to plug his guitar into Lee's amp. Most equipment was bought from Hamilton's Musical Store in Middlesbrough, usually on the never-never where a customer would pay their deposit and never be seen again. Not sure where Pipeline's gear came from but the increasing amount of it was now causing a problem of its own with none of the band, apart from Geoff, who was on holiday, having any transport of their own, so getting the whole band plus guitars, amps and drums to The Magnet caused a bit of a conundrum.

Tony worked on the trolley buses, or trams as they were also known. He was a clippy, a conductor taking fares and handing out tickets, not the one Roy bashed over the head with his money bag. He knew most of the drivers and was quite sure that if everyone got on at different bus stops, they could all get to Grangetown together by tram without causing too much of a commotion. Roy's – well, Geoff's – drums as well as the band's PA system were at Tony's house in North Ormesby, just outside Middlesbrough, where they had been practising. Dek was staying at his girlfriend's house in South Bank which was on the way, and Lee lived in Grangetown anyway, though it was still decided that he would also jump on the bus so they all arrived together.

Roy had met up with Tony at his house as arranged to help him get Geoff's drum kit to The Magnet where they'd asked the manager if they could go in on the afternoon to do a bit of rehearsing.

The tram terminus was North Ormesby and the bus stops weren't too far apart, so it was decided that because Tony would probably know the driver and conductor, he'd be first to get on with his equipment, with Roy waiting at the next stop with the drums. Tony had plenty of time to get on and get sorted because the bus would wait at the terminus for a good five minutes before setting off again, so on he got on, putting his equipment in the storage section under the stairs and sitting just inside the tram being able to keep a close eye on his gear. It had just started raining but most of the bus stops had shelters so it was thought that everyone on the way would be able to keep dry until the bus arrived.

 Coincidentally, also getting on the tram at the terminal was a man carrying a snooker cue in its case and, being the length that it was, he was unable to get right into the bus nor put his snooker cue in the luggage section under the stairs. Consequentially, he had to stand on the open platform where passengers got on and off, holding his snooker cue in an upright position.

Just as the tram was pulling away very slowly, a manly figure in a gabardine mac and flat cap came into view, running after the tram. He managed to catch up and jumped onto the platform, grabbing hold of what he thought was the attached pole that everyone used to steady themselves as they were getting on or off. What he'd actually got hold of was this chap's snooker cue which he wasn't letting go of, and there began quite a tussle between the two of them, culminating with both unceremoniously falling off the bus together. The rain had suddenly turned into a deluge as they both hit the floor, still refusing to let go of the snooker cue, landing in a puddle of water with a great splash just as the tram slowed down at Roy's bus stop.

The trolley buses didn't like to stay at one bus stop for very long because they came along every five minutes, so Tony got up to help Roy on with his drums, with Tony standing on the bus's platform while Roy passed them one at a time over the top of the prostrate pair who were still arguing whose fault it had been. Roy and Tony were past themselves laughing uncontrollably as the bus pulled away ever so slowly, leaving the drenched pair stranded. I must say, Tony lived off that story for a very long time.

So with the drum kit taking up two sets of seats either side of the aisle, it was off to South Bank, only a few miles away, where Dek was to be waiting at St Peter's Church bus stop, with bass guitar and amplifier, keeping dry under the bus shelter. Dek attempted to climb on to the bus with guitar in one hand and amp in the other, but Dek was a slip of a lad and struggled to get the amp on. Roy got off to give him a hand and the three of them managed to get it far enough onto the bus so it could be pushed behind a seat out of the way. By now passengers were straining their necks to see what was going on and the poor conductor, who Tony knew well enough and hadn't charged for the journey, was sweating in case one of the inspectors (remember Blakey from On The Buses) got on and caught him at it… letting anyone off paying for their fare would usually end up with instant dismissal.

There was now just Lee to pick up a couple of stops before The Magnet Hotel, so when the bus arrived at his stop, it seemed crackers that the only place he could put his guitar and amp after getting on at the back of the bus, was right to the front where there were empty spaces. By the time, Lee had dragged his gear all the way to the front, with people trying to squeeze past him to get off at the next stop. The bus had gone past the first stop and was slowing down as they got nearer to The Magnet. The lads couldn't stop laughing. Tony was still telling everyone about the snooker cue incident, but the antics on the bus had even the passengers giggling, with Roy telling everyone that the fares had gone up 'cos there was a band on.

The bus stopped just around the corner from The Magnet so, after getting off the bus, and managing to get their equipment bit by bit to the front door, they all walked in together with Tony flinging his house keys up in the air and catching them again as if they'd just got out of a van.

Roy remembers, 'Geoff's drums were a magnificent Premier kit. I'd never set one up before. It had everything, snare drum, tom toms, hi-hat, the sort of things I'd only seen in Hamilton's Music Store or on the telly. I didn't really know how to set it up, it was nothing like my old Salvation Army kit that got destroyed at The Station, but I got it sorted with a bit of help from the lads.'

The rehearsal went well and the evening went even better, so after The Magnet, and with the next few gigs they played while Geoff was away going so well, the boys came to a decision that they wanted Roy to be their permanent drummer. Tony said to Dek, 'Will you ask Roy if he'll stay on fulltime? He's keeping the beat better and he's more powerful.'

Geoff didn't take the news too well on his return from holiday and left the band under somewhat of a cloud.

The very first Pipeline photo – circa 1969
Dek, Roy on drums, Tony and Lee

Roy was still working on the door at The Red Lion when Dek asked him to stay on in the band and, with the weekends being their main gig nights, this left Roy with the decision as to which was more important to him. Thankfully he chose 'showbiz'.

Another problem was that Roy didn't have a kit of his own, so he went to see his dad, who took him to Hamilton's where they went straight upstairs to the drum department before anyone recognised Roy from his LP nicking antics a few years earlier. Roy picked out the kit that he wanted and his dad signed the credit forms to make payments on a monthly basis.

Pipeline were now starting to get noticed and getting plenty of bookings through local agents, as well as securing a few of their own gigs, namely The Magnet, The Normanby Hotel and a regular Thursday group night set at the local night-spot of South Bank Sporting Club.

The lads had been begging and borrowing transport in the form of anything from anyone who would be daft enough to lend them and had got a local lad they knew, Norman Pinchbeck – one of the few around in those days who actually had a full licence – to drive them around. Norman became the band's first roadie, even though they were still without a proper van of their own. They were getting most of their club bookings through a Normanby agent called Frank Feeney whose agency was predominately country and western, so to have a pop band at his disposal was a bonus. Frank must have seen some potential in the band because, knowing the transport problem they were having, he offered to buy them a van at a local car auction.

The lads couldn't believe their luck and on the day of the auction they went off all together, including Norman, to The Yarm Saleroom, where second hand vehicles were auctioned off 'sold as seen'. On the way there, they were overtaken by an Austin J4 van, which was unusual for Frank because if anyone did any overtaking in those days it was Frank. When they got to the auction while looking around at what was going to be up for sale, they saw the very same J4 van on display and having already seen it perform on the way there, it was decided that Frank would bid for it.

He was successful in securing the van, giving the keys directly to Norman, telling him and the rest of the lads that it was to be driven by Norman only. I'm betting you could already see the glint in Roy's eyes as he said to Frank, 'Aye, okay then'. The Austin J4 van was the type being used by the police at the time so on further inspection and having been thrown into the back of one a few times, Roy felt right at home. To give the van its own identity, Dek covered it with his own painted handprints from front to back.

Three months later, Pipeline were working on the M and D Social Club in Stockton when a couple of blokes came along and stood at the side of the stage. After the first set, Roy went over to them and asked who they were. One of them said, 'We're from Hamilton's.' Roy said, 'What do you want?' The other one said, 'Your drum kit.' It turned out that Roy's dad hadn't been keeping up the monthly payments and these lads had been sent to repossess Roy's set of drums. Roy asked them, 'Can you wait until the end, we've got another set to do?' They said, 'No problem, we're enjoying the show.' Then at the end of the night, they just picked up Roy's drum kit and left.

'Dad never had anything on 'tick' before. He always paid cash and wouldn't dream of getting into debt, so when I went and told him what had happened, he was mortified. He'd just completely forgot about the payments. He said, 'I'll go to Hamilton's and sort it out, son,' which he did and I got the kit back, eventually using it as part exchange for a Carlton set. This chap Carlton had worked for the Premier drum company but had split away to form his own business. I bought a red kit and painted flowers all over it.'

Dek, Roy and Lee sat aloft the early Pipeline van with roadie, Norman

Pipeline had now become a fully functioning, bona fide show group on the road in the great North East of England. They had their own gear, a van and a roadie with a real driving licence. There would be no stopping them now. With so much going on keeping Roy away from his home, it was getting more and more likely that this would have an effect on his family life.

15

Cedar Grove was on a housing estate in East Redcar, minutes from the sandy beach. On a still evening whilst lying in bed, you could hear the tide's gentle roar washing back and forth. The comforting hum of trains passing through on a nearby track took Roy back to his childhood in industrial Grangetown. On a warm summer's day, even with the cool breeze swinging in off the North Sea, Roy thought there was no better place to be on Earth. It was idyllic.

Yet there was still something missing and Roy just couldn't put his finger on it, until one of his mates at the pub said to him, 'Yer not properly married and settled down 'til yer've got yerself a shed, pal.'

Roy looked at his friend, twisted his head slightly frowning as he did, taking in what had just been said, then excitedly blurted out, 'That's it! A fucking shed, you've got it! I've got to have a shed,' but coming back down to earth with his shoulders dropping more by each second, dejectedly following it up with, 'But I can't afford one, we're only just making ends meet as it fucking is.'

His mate carried on, 'You don't have to buy a new one, Roy, a pal of mine got the back end off a Welford's Bakery van and made a shed out of it. Looks great, he got it from the scrapyard at Warrenby. I'd get down there straightaway if you want one, those Welford's Bakery vans go like hot cakes.' Funny bugger.

Warrenby was just on the other side of Redcar to where Roy lived, so he went the next day and, as luck would have it, staring him in the face as he walked into the scrapyard was an old Welford's van. It could have even been one that Roy himself had worked on when he was a van boy back in the day. After close inspection, the back end which would have carried loaves, cakes and other baked goods looked in decent nick so Roy bought it for next to nothing.

Roy says, 'They delivered it for me, but it was so fucking big we just to say managed to squeeze it down the passage between the two houses. We lived in an end terrace of four with a small gap before the next row. After huffing and puffing for what seemed like fucking ages, I thought it was never going to fit through, but we eventually got it where I wanted it. It looked great but it was enormous by shed standards when I looked around to compare it with what everyone else had. That caused a problem in itself, as my next door neighbour came straight out, complaining that it was blocking the sun out of his garden. 'My plants aren't getting any sunshine, my tomatoes won't grow.' After he threatened to tell the council about it, my 'shed' had to go back to the scrapyard. They didn't give me back what I'd paid for it either, fucking robbers. The house itself looked like it hadn't had a lick of paint on the outside since the day it was built. I fancied myself as a bit of a handy man, especially with a paint brush, so I sanded the front door and window frames down then gave them a nice bright new coat of paint. When I'd finished, it looked great, I was chuffed to bits. That was until I got a visit from a council chap carrying a clipboard under his arm. He said, 'Who's painted your house?' I said, 'I did.' He came back with, 'Well, you'll have do it again, put it back the way it was.' I said, 'You're fucking joking, aren't you?' He said, 'No I'm not joking, it has to look the same as the other three houses it's joined on to.' I liked my newly painted house and was determined some fucking stuffed shirt from the council wasn't going to make me undo it, so I knocked on the other three doors and asked them if I could paint their houses too. They were only too happy to have their flaky drab doors and windows brightened up so I did one house a week over the next three weeks until we all looked the same. Council were happy enough too. Dave, a big mate of mine, had a huge fall out with his wife and split up. I said to Dave, 'Where are you going to live now?' Dave said, 'Don't know, Roy. I've got nowhere to go.' I said, 'Come and stay with us, we've got a spare bedroom.' So Dave came and stayed in our spare bedroom at the back of the house.'

Pipeline were getting plenty of bookings, so with Roy working through the day and playing on an evening he was spending less time at home. With Judy being left at home so much while Roy was out with the band on an evening, Davie – Roy's mate – and her had been getting close. Roy says, 'I returned home after a gig one night, about half past eleven to find a note on the kitchen table. It said, 'Roy, I know you'll go mad, but I want you to understand that Dave and I fell in love and we can't live without each other.''

'Robert was only a baby,' continues Roy, 'only about five or six months old, and the letter finished off with, 'Once you've settled down, because I know what you're like, I'll be in contact with you. Don't bother looking for us, we've gone off to Newcastle.' I was torn but not that bothered really. I wasn't sure how I felt, daft things go through your mind like, did I love her enough to commit murder for her? I let it go but after about three months I contacted the Police and the Salvation Army, hoping they weren't going to ask for their drums back, to see if either of them could find Judy and make sure she was alright. They both came back to tell me that they knew where she was but couldn't tell me but she was okay. I figured it out for myself that she'd very likely have gone back to her dad's place in Bellingham.'

It must have been a bit like being back in solitary confinement, only with his own key, though Roy has never had a problem with being alone in his own company, so he just got on with it. Yes, Roy was a latchkey kid again. He says, 'I still had female company, bringing the odd girl back to the house, some more odd than others. I brought this huge girl home one night, she was like a fucking house end, I couldn't find my way round her. I made a joke up that I would use on stage at the time, I said, 'Come on then, fart and give us a clue'.'

Although home alone, as Roy was, he always found plenty to keep him busy. The previous tenants had left an old upright piano in the living room and Roy thought it would be a good idea to wallpaper it with some of the group's advertising posters that he'd taken from club walls at the end of their shows. Roy hadn't taken up playing the piano by then. Adorned as it was, this piano had now become the main focal point in the whole of the room but, sadly, was to come to a watery end during some publicity photographs later on.

After Roy had been on his own about six months, Judy got in touch with him. 'She rang me out of the blue, told me she was at her dad's house in Bellingham. I said I'd guessed that was where she would be. Dave and her had split up, but Judy had a couple of brothers who would be looking out for her. She knew I'd be missing the kids and said that I could visit them if I wanted to. I drove to Bellingham in the group's van. When I got there, I stopped at the end of the road trying to look all inconspicuous in our bright yellow van that I'd painted flowers all over. I could see Judy's dad's front garden from where I was and there were two very young lads playing, one had blond hair and, from a distance, I wondered if they must be Richard and Robert. Anyway, that first time I bottled it, I just turned the van round and headed back home. I hadn't told Judy I was driving up to see them so she wouldn't have been expecting me. I talked to Judy on the phone a few weeks later without letting on I'd been, and arranged to go visiting the kids, spending the day at her dad's house. I only stayed for one day and didn't sleep over, but it gave me the chance to get to know the boys all over again. Robert had been just a baby when Judy left so I must have seemed like a bit a stranger to him, but Richard responded to me immediately as he had been a bit older.'

More visits were to follow where Roy was able to regain the trust of the boys and consolidate their relationship all over again, though another Judy bombshell was waiting to be dropped not too far down the line.

16

In contrast to Roy's married life, Pipeline continued to thrive, with Roy discovering yet another enterprising string to his bow. Roadie Norman remembers that the very first time Roy told a joke on stage was when they were playing Sunderland Catholic club. The lads were part way through their first set when the group's PA system started playing up, with sparks flying from the amplifier. Roy shouted to Norman to try and sort it out, but the result was that the show had to be stopped and Roy, realising that the audience were getting a bit restless, came to the front of the stage and shouted out a few gags which calmed the situation and was going down really well until he made a crack relating to a crucifix that was hanging on one of the walls.

Initially nothing was said, the electrical problem was soon fixed and the band carried on to finish their set, at which point the concert chairman blazed into the dressing room to tear a strip of Roy for his 'blasphemous' remarks during his joke telling stint. Roy had never intended to be blasphemous, he'd just spotted a comedy opportunity and took it with both hands… a rare gift that was to cause him many problems in his early career but stand him in greater stead throughout his rise to the top. Quite a lot of people in the room had even found it funny, though this may have been an early indication of the no holds barred Roy Chubby Brown that we've come to know and love over the last half century.

Roy had a twinkle in his eye though at having got laughs for the first time, and his second chance to show off his joke telling also came as the result of another electrical problem… a regular occurrence in the old, under-maintained social clubs. It was during a booking at Haverton Hill Workmen's Club that this happened. The electricity cut out in the middle of the first set, plunging the club into complete darkness. This left Roy banging away on his drums by himself and it was a few seconds before everyone realised what had happened with Roy still, head down, tapping away, oblivious as to what was going on. He finally lifted his head up to see that the rest of the lads in the group had turned around and were looking straight at him, not playing their instruments.

Tony shouted over to Roy, 'The leccy's gone off, Roy!'

Roy immediately shouted at the top of his voice, 'Don't panic! Don't panic!' A phrase he'd heard Corporal Jones saying on Dad's Army. The audience responded with loud cheering and laughter.

Up until then, at Dek's request, Roy had been introducing some of the band's numbers from behind his drums. Even then he couldn't resist putting his own spin on some of the introductions. He'd often say things like, 'The next song is I've got you… by The Dooleys' or 'I'll never get over you… so get out of bed and make the tea yourself.'

These venues had made it their business to be ready for any blackouts and Haverton Hill Workmen's Club certainly was. There were storm lanterns (probably 'borrowed' from the local shipyards… ahem!) positioned around the room, so quite quickly they were lit and distributed to various tables. Roy, who had always been one for clowning around, having being the school joker, was still behind his drum kit when he just stood up with a broad grin on his face and shouted out to the audience, 'Did you all like the drum solo? The leccy's gone off. Tell one of them tight committee men to put two bob in the meter'. At which point, the few people that were in the concert room gave another cheer and a muted round of applause. These crowds loved it if ever anyone had a dig at the committee.

The room was now quite dimly lit from the lanterns as Roy got off his drums and made his way toward the front of the stage.

'We're all still here even if you can't see us,' Roy shouted to the audience, 'takes more than a blackout to get rid of us.' Then he added, 'I thought it was unusual to see a committee man smiling, then I realised it was the piano with its lid up.' The crowd loved it, which gave Roy the impetus to deliver more gags.

It was regular material but, even in those days, Roy had an eye for a crack that he knew club people wouldn't have heard before. Every now and then he'd slip in one of his own gags to see how it would go. Thankfully it wasn't too big a room so, with the PA system having been cut off the same as everything else had, Roy's booming voice was able to be heard around the room. The small crowd roared with laughter as Roy delivered joke after joke, which were flowing easier and easier with the adrenaline that was being created by the audience's feedback. Tony, Dek and Lee had left the dressing room and sat at the front of the concert room to enjoy Roy's performance.

Roy had kept the audience entertained for about twenty minutes, when the lights flickered back on. Tony, Dek and Lee jumped up on to the stage and picked up their instruments as Roy finished yet another joke. The people in the audience gave Roy a big round of applause, with a number of them standing up as he gave them a wave and turned round to sit back at his drums.

The band struck up straight into Creedence Clearwater Revival's Bad Moon Rising, at the end of which the Club Secretary beckoned the lads off, asking over the microphone, 'Please put your hands together for the Pipeline,' finishing off with a typical Club Secretary comment, 'not that you've seen much of them,' without once showing his appreciation for Roy filling in the middle of the show.

Once in the dressing room, the secretary came in and, again with no mention of any thanks for keeping the show going, while looking quite flustered, said, 'That was a close thing, lads. If the electricity had been off any longer, we'd have had to cancel the bingo. There'd have been a riot.'

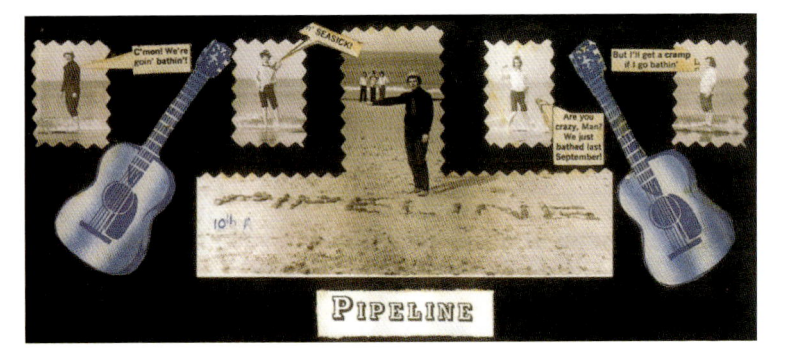

Roy was now showing the confidence to do more comedy as well as the realisation that including comedy got the band an extra tenner on their fee, so whenever the occasion arose, usually clubs rather than pubs, he would get up in the middle of the first set and tell some jokes. These episodes usually went down a storm with audiences, but Roy would always insist that the rest of the lads didn't leave the stage. Not yet knowing how long he could hold an audience, Roy needed the safety net of the lads standing behind him, strumming quietly in the background, C, Am, F and G and so on. Then, however long his joke telling went on, the band would be ready to go straight back into the next number without any gaps.

The group was doing quite well, but historically our local groups hadn't generally stayed together for very long and, after a short time, it was Tony who got itchy feet and took the opportunity of joining a local close harmony band, the excellent Music Book, after their lead singer/guitarist had decided to leave. This left the rest of the lads on the hunt for a new lead singer, but it also heralded a new chapter for the band which would see them change direction into more of a comedy unit over the following six months.

The search for a new singer didn't take too long as waiting in the wings was Ernie Goult which, at the time, was a bit like finding gold dust under a pebble on Redcar beach. Ernie had established himself as a prominent frontman for a number of bands since the beginning of the sixties. He was a good looking bloke, with a great voice who had effectively been there and bought the t-shirt. So, after half a dozen practice sessions, the first of which was at Grangetown Boys Club on 21st April 1971, they were ready for their first gig.

Ernie's background had, as said, seen him front a number of bands with him taking centre stage in his adopted stage name of Shane North. One of the bands he had formed himself decided after buying a treasured echo unit, a small electronic repeating tape machine that gave vocalists the same rock 'n' roll echo sound that you would hear on early Elvis and Buddy Holly records, that they would call themselves 'Shane North and the Echoes'. They played some of the bigger venues in the area, having already performed at The Empire Theatre in Middlesbrough when they were called 'The Rhythm Riders'.

Shane North And The Echoes

When Ernie wasn't working with his band, The Echoes, he would regularly make appearances with the dance band at The Pier Ballroom in Redcar. The Pier Ballroom was a popular place for its Thursday dance nights and a regular visitor had been Roy Vasey with his then girlfriend, Sandra. Ernie would regularly wander through the audience with microphone in hand whilst crooning a ballad and, when passing tables, would often sing directly to the girls who were sat there.

A tale that has circulated locally for a number of years is that one night he went up to Roy's table and started to sing A White Sport coat and a Pink Carnation, a popular tune of the time, in the direction of Roy's girlfriend. Now what happened after that escapes Ernie's memory, but folklore has it that after Ernie had sang 'a white sport coat' and before he could continue with 'and a pink carnation', Roy thumped him. Ernie's pretty certain that it never happened but, after Ernie admitted that he had been seeing Sandra on the quiet for a while, I'm not so sure.

Back to the Pipeline, after rehearsing the show for a few weeks, it was time for the new outfit to perform their first booking. This took place at The Westminster Hotel in Middlesbrough on 21st May 1971. The Westminster Hotel was a bit like Grangetown's Magnet Hotel where most local acts would appear from time to time. Their next gig was in Middlesbrough again only a few nights later at The Clarence Club, where they amazingly lasted all night doing two spots, the second for dancing. I say lasted all night because The Clarence Club was notorious for paying bands off at half time, thus having to pay them only half of their fee, then filling the rest of the evening in with bingo, so to get to play the full night means you had to be of a reasonably high standard.

They played a number of other nights together but it was decided that for whatever reason, things weren't quite working out as hoped. It was probably because with Roy becoming more involved within the programme, the band was now starting to lead towards becoming a comedy show group and Ernie was more of a stylish musical band frontman. The last booking with Ernie played out at the Skelton Green Workmen's Club on the 30th May 1971, after which he and the band split on amicable terms and, even if the incident in The Pier Ballroom actually happened, Roy and Ernie have stayed firm friends ever since.

Ernie resumed his original passion for singing as a frontman when he reformed his own band with new musicians calling themselves 'Shane', which included ex-Pipeline roadie Norman, playing the pubs and clubs of the North East for quite a number of years before he finally hung up his microphone and called it a day. People often say that Ernie 'retired' far too prematurely, but he can rest on his laurels with the full knowledge that he was one of the early pioneers of the Redcar area's local band scene right back from the early sixties, without whose influence none of us, who followed in his steps, might even have picked up a musical instrument in the first place.

I'm guessing that with the show becoming more comedy orientated, it was probably decided that Ernie was too good looking to be in a comedy show group. Though it could have been that he was a bit of a ladies' man and none of the other lads were getting a look in. Whatever the real reason for the break up, this happened to be where I joined in as Ernie's 'no fucking oil painting' replacement and where the band became more comedy orientated.

Roy Vasey as he was then, not Brown and only chubby by nature, was becoming better known for his comedy than he was for his drumming. Although it wasn't apparent at the time, Roy was now at the very start of his long journey to becoming the UK's King of Comedy. If you thought Roy's life so far had been a bumpy ride, please hold on to your helmets for the rollercoaster that's to follow as we discover how Vasey became Brown first, then 'Chubby' later, amassing a worldwide army of loyal fans on the way.

17

I played in a group around about the same time as Pipeline. Our group was made up of various members of the youth club that we attended. I played rhythm guitar and took on a bit of the vocals. Our drummer had been plucked straight out of the Boy's Brigade, so people would usually march to our music rather than dance. The bass player was the drummer's mate and had never held a guitar before in his life. The singer was a pal of mine who played centre forward for our football team, and thought he had a good voice… apparently the only one who did.

At that time the two loves in my life were playing the guitar and footy. I really wanted to be a professional footballer, but the Boro weren't looking for a short-sighted goalie at the time. I think they already had one. I digress though… to finish our group off, thankfully we had someone who could actually play an instrument, Ritchie, our lead guitarist, so some of the tunes we played were almost recognisable.

Our first ever booking was at one of our own youth club 'disco' nights where we performed our set during a break in the playing of records on the club's Dansette record player. After our first number, a young girl came up to the stage, which was a few wooden boxes we'd dragged together, tugged at my trousers and asked rather unpolitely, 'Can we put the record player back on yet?'

I tell you all this to draw a comparison with Pipeline, now a consolidated outfit that was getting a name for itself as one of the top groups in the area. South Bank Sporting Club was a nightclub situated just around the corner from myself and I was a regular visitor. Shows that appeared there included the likes of The Nolan Sisters, Sid and Eddie who later changed their name to Little and Large, as well as Shane Fenton aka Alvin Stardust, all later to become big names in the entertainment world. Pipeline had secured a regular spot on Thursdays as one of the groups for dancing, so there would be no comedy included on any of those nights, but this was a testament to their musical sound that they had been chosen to take part.

During the day, Norman, the group's roadie, worked on a local building site in Grangetown, driving a dumper truck, where I too was working, sweeping up houses, having left my previous job in the laboratories at ICI because it had turned into shift work, which didn't fit in with a sixties social lifestyle at all.

Norm would regularly come to work bleary-eyed the day after having roadied the lads to a gig, sometimes as far away as the Lake District. I remember him once saying to me, 'It was rough at Brough', having had a tough night at a venue in Brough. 'It was rough at Brough,' became a regular comment within the band whenever there was a comparison to be made of a tough night, of which there can be quite a lot in the 'Workies' clubs of the North East.

There would usually be a story to tell of the goings on from the night before, one such tale being of Roy performing his party piece of spinning around on the dance floor to music during the band's break in performances, not unusual in itself you might think, but Roy would be spinning around on his bare belly. It appears that one night, while performing his party piece, a drunk stood on Roy's hand, so Roy jumped up and immediately flattened him, causing a bit of an uproar in the club with the band having to make a hasty retreat from the venue. No doubt the Club Secretary would have seized that opportunity as a solid reason for not having to pay the band their fee, non payment of fees for whatever reason being a regular occurrence in those heady clubland days, a few more free beers for the commitee lads.

As I said before, Norm would often come to the building site the day after a long trip which meant a late night dropping all the members of the band off at their various homes. He appeared to be coping quite well with this, telling us all stories, until one day he got the sack after falling asleep while driving his dumper truck and ending up in a ditch.

Norman had taken ill, spending a period in hospital, which meant he had to give up his position as the group's roadie. Norm played the guitar, as I did, so having built up a friendship at the building site, we decided to try our luck forming a duo after he came out of hospital. We practised and we practised, and we practised and we practised, never did any gigs, but, unbeknown to me at the time, the link between Norm and the Pipeline group, who now had Jim Rudd doing the roadie work, would eventually be my introduction to Roy, and a working relationship and friendship that has so far stretched to fifty years.

Having been in a band before, I was eager to get out and perform the songs we'd rehearsed. Norm hadn't, but after practising for so long, the courage was eventually built up for us to enter a talent competition at Redcar Workmen's Club. I think we sang Leaving on a Jet Plane or something. The contest was won by the Entertainments Secretary's eight year old niece who sang a rendition of The Good Ship Lollipop, which sank like the Titanic before she had screeched out two lines. The result was quite normal for these talent nights, the winner usually being a relative of someone on the committee, whereas we didn't get on the rostrum at all. We walked off to the sound of our own footsteps.

In the audience that night were Dek and Lee Vasey, supporting Norm as their ex-roadie, but after watching me and Norm perform, they noticed something that I had that was missing from their act now Ernie had left, namely a PA system. Joke (I hope), but it did appear that in those days if you had a van or a PA system you could get into most groups in the area.

What really happened after that night was that Pipeline, now re-christened as The New Pipeline were looking for a replacement for Ernie. Through Norm, I was approached about becoming the band's lead singer, also playing rhythm guitar, a decision that didn't take me too long to make. I met up with Dek and Lee, who apparently hadn't told Roy about their plans, but was assured that he would be happy to go along with any decisions they would make. I had never met Roy Vasey up until then but I was well aware of his larger than life characteristics. Norman, incidentally, went on to work with Ernie in his new band, Shane. It was all a bit of a merry-go-round with band members then.

Dek had a new vision for the band. He wanted to revolve it around Roy's comedy talent which was becoming more evident with every club booking they had performed. The musical content had improved too with the introduction of new equipment, and Dek wanted to make a show which included a mixture of both music and comedy. Thankfully, on meeting Roy at his home in east Redcar, we hit it off immediately, having very much the same sense of humour.

Roy and I come from similar backgrounds, Roy having been

brought up in Grangetown on the outskirts of Midddlesbrough, whereas I had been brought up in South Bank, affectionately known as 'Slaggy Island' – after the slag tips, not the women – which was just a couple of miles away. Probably the only real difference would have been with Roy being slightly older than me was that while I was being an alter boy at St John's Church in South Bank, Roy was serving time in a jail at Portland Bay, to name but just one of the many of Her Majesty's establishments he had frequented over those early years. Having been around the block a few times since then, we were both very much on the same wavelength, although my naivety did raise its comical head every now and then.

One such occasion was during the time Roy was helping out behind the counter at Alleycat's second hand shop in Redcar where quite a few of us who had time on our hands would meet up for a bit of banter. One day, there was a few of us in the shop with Roy sat in his usual chair to one side of the counter when a quite officious-looking suit walked in carrying a briefcase, approached Roy and said, 'Are you Royston Vasey?' Roy, who had always avoided officialdom like it was the plague, replied, 'No, I'm George Proudman'… my name. I immediately jumped in without thinking, squeaking out, 'Eh no, you aren't, Roy,' a bit Kenneth Williams like, 'tell him who you really are,' similar to the way Roy had told that plainclothes policeman in Scarborough that his mates were in the gift shop robbing buckets and spades. I dropped him right in the shit, but we still don't know where the bloke was from to this day.

From our first meeting at Roy's house, it was pretty apparent that this big bloke with the reputation of 'asking questions later' if there was any trouble, was not only warm and friendly, but had the knack of making people feel right at home in his company. I'm pretty sure that anyone who had been on the end of one of his 'ask questions later' moments even felt the love just before receiving the first punch. Nowadays Roy is much more likely to do the question asking immediately in order to diffuse any situation, but still be aware that he's nobody's fool, and like the rest of us does not like to be taken for a ride, having put his trust in too many people who have let him down over the years.

Dek came to my house and, in our front living room with copious amounts of tea from my mother, we concocted a first half forty five minute routine that included hits of the time, standard songs and a couple of comedy songs Roy had recommended, a bit of Bonzo

Dog, stuff like that. This was all to accompany the extra comedy routines that Roy had created which we would blend in at rehearsals. The show included a ten or fifteen minutes stand-up session with Roy telling jokes, most of which he'd made up himself, many that we didn't get to hear until he told them on stage.

We rehearsed the new act in a few clubs around the Redcar area, anywhere that would have us really, paying for their generosity by doing a free gig. Free gigs didn't bother us at the time because we were having such a ball we just wanted to perform, whether we got paid for it or not. I think it was the same for most bands when they first started off, a different era where the money wasn't the be-all and end-all. Whatever we got from performing would usually be spent on a porterhouse steak at the Europa restaurant in Middlesbrough before we went home from bookings anyway.

It was decided, for the first half at least, that we should wear something a bit different for the comedy set and thought we might find some suitably ridiculous outfits in second hand shops. Most groups were dressing themselves up in the smartest kit they could get, whistle and flutes like the sixties Mersey bands used to wear, but we had chosen to clothe ourselves like some beggars that had just spent the night kipping in a council skip. We looked funny though, and I'm sure we gave audiences the immediate impression that this wasn't going to be just another one of those musical evenings… or that a bunch of tramps had just walked in.

Unfortunately, that didn't go down so well at every venue we were sent to, especially Friday heavy nights. Friday heavy night was the one night of the week certain pit village clubs would cater for the younger crowd who would be expecting a band to play heavy rock music. If we were ever sent to one of these nights by some deaf, blind or drunken agent, you can imagine the reaction when we opened up with The Beatles' Octopus's Garden.

On the whole, the new show group, which got called The Dek Vasey Four Man Band, was going down a storm at most venues. We were all just having a great time and to mark the occasion we launched Roy's wallpapered piano into the North Sea from Redcar beach, having our photos taken for posterity into the bargain. I say 'launching', it was more of a sinking because as the tide came in and washed over us all, the piano slowly sank further and further into the wet sand. It's probably still there now.

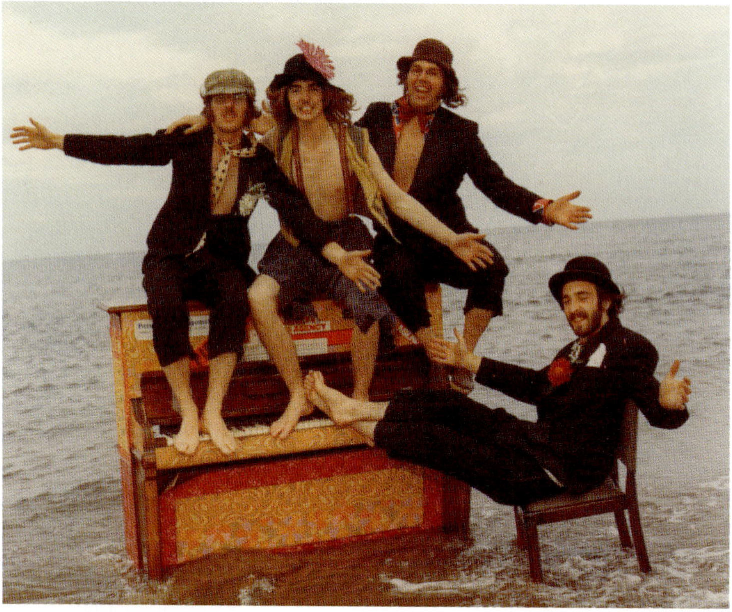

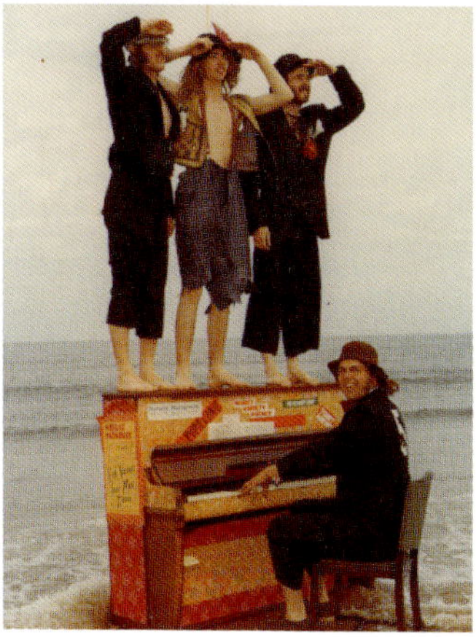

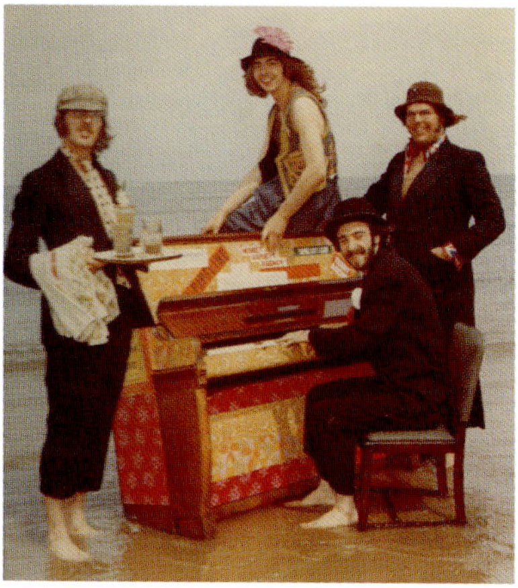

18

Having become prolific with his drumming and joke telling, Roy was about to be spotted for a totally different talent. He had become a prominent figure on the high street as part of Marty's emporium on the fruit and veg stall where a couple of local entrepreneurs had noticed that this lad could probably sell snow to Eskimos. Roy had also been working on the door at The Starlight nightclub, keeping troublemakers out.

Gerry Hartley was the owner and, together with two members of the resident band, Back Door, Ronnie Asprey and Colin Hodgkinson, had opened up a small music shop on Lord Street. It wasn't the size of Hamilton's in Middlesbrough where most would buy their first guitar, but through creating a more intimate atmosphere, it attracted the more established musicians, selling brass instruments, acoustic guitars and sheet music, along with other associated musical products.

Ronnie and Gerry told Roy they were looking for someone to look after the shop and did he fancy doing it. Being between day jobs, the only income Roy had coming in was from the band, practically all of his 'bouncing' money from The Starlight club bounced straight over the counter at the nearest Ladbrokes. A job in a shop looked like the perfect fit, especially a music shop, and the hours wouldn't interfere with his night time group commitments so Roy took up their offer. He hadn't been there very long when Gerry told him that he had what can only be called a mucky bookshop on West Dyke Road and was going to clean it out and take everything from the Lord Street shop there because it was in a better position for passing customers.

He asked Roy if he would like to move to West Dyke Road with him. It sounded like a good idea so he went along with it and Gerry opened up Alleycats where, as well as the musical items previously on sale, people would bring their unwanted bric-a-brac and Roy or Gerry would offer them a price, hopefully selling them on for a decent profit.

Once Roy was behind the counter at Alleycats, it became a bit of a magnet meeting place for anyone in a band who had fuck all else to do during the day. I still had a proper day job then but had played the 'bad back' card so I could get some rehearsing in with the group. I was one of those who spent many an amusing hour in the shop. The banter was great, but if you didn't like having the piss taken out of you it was best that you stayed away. I'll wager a lot of Roy's early material was probably thought up from encounters with his customers, or one of us.

Ex-Pipeline roadie Norman remembers being in Alleycats when two policemen came in and said to Roy, 'Where have you stashed the stuff, Roy?' Roy simply replied, 'No comment.' When continually asked the same question over and over again, Roy's answer was the same, 'No comment.' The two policemen had no alternative but to end their interrogation and leave. Norman says that he never found out what it had been all about.

'I was working Alleycats by day and the group by night,' says Roy, 'so I didn't open the shop too early, about ten. From home I would generally walk through the town, often stopping off at a different café on the way for a bit of breakfast. There was one café in particular that I would visit on the sea front called The Tower Café where there was an attractive girl I used to talk to called Beryl Hawthorn, serving customers, and I eventually asked her if she fancied going for a drink one night. I asked her if she was married, she said she was separated and that she'd been living in Middlesbrough but now had a flat with her young son just around the corner from the café. We went out for a drink on a few nights though she didn't invite me back to her flat.'

Roy seemed to be gaining a rare state of normality… a regular job, working with the band, plenty of female companionship, and was still keeping in touch with Judy and visiting the boys regularly. All was to change though when, during one of his trips to Bellingham, Judy, right out of the blue, said she wanted to come back to Redcar. Roy says, 'It took me completely by surprise. Dave was well out of her life and, with her mam still living in Redcar, she thought it would be good for the boys, so she asked me if I could find her somewhere to live. I left Bellingham with a lot to think about, but by the time I got home, I realised the only solution was for Judy, Richard and Robert to live in Cedar Grove while I found myself a flat. It would be great to have the boys around again. I told Judy over the phone what I thought, telling her everything was as she left it including all of the furniture. I didn't tell her the piano had sailed off into the sunset though, not that she'd have been that bothered. Judy was delighted and soon moved back after I had found myself a flat at the far end of Coatham Road.'

The flat was only a short walk from Alleycats and after acquiring a few bits of furniture to make the place feel like home, Roy continued on with his life almost as it was before. 'I'd been seeing a girl called Maureen on and off after meeting her while I was doing some shopping. She worked in Iceland and would come round to the flat during her lunch breaks for a 'bit', though when she told me she was on the till, I thought she said she was on the pill, and I think you can guess what happened next.'

'Once again I didn't find out until much later on in life, but Maureen had become pregnant with my child. I found out later that she'd moved to Thornaby and was back at home living with her family. I still didn't know she was carrying my baby.'

After a few months, Roy got the chance to move further up Coatham Road nearer to Alleycats and the town centre when he found a flat at a house called The Ponderosa, opposite the library. It had three floors where the rooms had all been turned into self-contained flats, but Roy says it attracted all of the dropouts in the area so it was hoped his stay would only be short-lived.

'Everything else was just like it had been. I'd had a few more dates with Beryl, still having not been invited back to her flat and continued working at Alleycats during the day. One day, it would have been mid-summer, there was nobody in the shop so I was standing at the front door taking in the lovely sunshine when Beryl walked along, took out a front door key and opened up the door which was right next to the shop. She hadn't spotted me so I called her and she turned towards me. I said, 'What are you doing here?' She said, 'I live here, I live above the shop.' All that time over the last few weeks I'd been taking her out for a drink, we'd been going our separate ways afterwards and she'd been living in the flat above the shop where I was working… if I ever joined the army they would never have had me in the fucking Observer Corps. After that, we started seeing each other on a more permanent basis with her coming in the van to the odd gig. One of the bookings she came on was Lingdale Workmen's club and as we walked into the concert room, the committee man on the door demanded twenty pence cover charge for Beryl before he would let her in.' Twenty pence doesn't sound much now but in those days if any club had charged more than that to get into a concert room, there would be outrage and a total boycott of the club. I said, 'You're going to charge twenty pence to come in? You must be fucking joking!' He said, 'Either she pays twenty pence or she's not coming in.' I said, 'If I have to pay for my wife to come in and watch me, I'm fucking leaving,' and we got back in the van and went home. I hadn't been in very long when the phone rang. It was the agent asking, 'What the fuck's going on?' So I told him and he went crackers saying, 'I've had trouble with him before, he can be a right awkward cunt!'

Roy was still living at The Ponderosa, though constantly on the look out for somewhere else when a small flat upstairs on the other side of the landing to Beryl's was about to become available. Roy says, 'Mick Boothby, a bass player with one of the other local bands, The Jason Jones Trio, was living there with his girlfriend, Julie. They'd found themselves a house to rent and Mick said I should move in and get away from The Ponderosa. I moved into the flat with the result that Beryl and I became even closer.'

Alleycats and Roy's new flat

Roy was now as near to Redcar town centre as he probably could be, with the Royal Standard pub directly opposite. Because of its situation, especially on weekends, Roy would be able to hear quite rowdy behaviour, with people milling in the streets as the pubs and clubs kicked everyone out. 'It would be about one in the morning when I heard a commotion across the road outside The Standard so I opened the window and shouted down, 'Don't you ever go to fucking bed, you noisy bastards, there's people up here trying to get some sleep.' One shouted back, 'Shut your mouth, you nosey cunt! So I thought, right. I stormed downstairs and opened the front door, there were about six empty milk bottles on the step which had been left out for the milk man the next day. I just picked them up one by one and flung them in their direction. They were ducking and diving to avoid them when one of them went straight over their heads and through The Standard window. The police station was only just around the corner so within no time a handful of coppers appeared and I was carted off to spend the rest of the night in Redcar nick.'

After a short while, Beryl managed to get herself a council house, so her and Gary, her young son, moved out, with Roy taking the opportunity of moving into her now vacated larger flat. It was huge as far as flats went, covering the whole of the street corner. It had a three piece suite with separate sleeping and washroom. I can remember attending a few parties there with members of local groups, and great nights they were.

Initially Beryl got a council property in Norfolk Close with Roy dividing his time between his own flat and Beryl's new home. The Closes, as they were known, were pretty run down and attracted a lot of antisocial behaviour so Beryl soon put a request in to the council for a move or a swap.

Roy says, 'After waiting a while, the opportunity came up for her to move into a house on Lime Road. I said, 'That's the next road to where Judy and the lads are living, there in my old house on Cedar Grove.' I never officially moved in with Beryl, still keeping my own flat on above Alleycats, but spent quite a lot of time with her in Lime Road. It was great because my kids, Richard and Robert, could walk round the corner to visit us whenever they wanted.'

So much had happened in such a short space of time since Judy and the kids left, some of it good, some of it bad, but most of it out of Roy's control. His group work had been one of the few consistencies Roy had been able to rely on, but as his and Beryl's relationship became stronger, maybe, just maybe, this might turn out to be the chance for things to start settling down again.

19

Jim Rudd was the group's roadie when I joined the band, having followed on from Norman after he had taken ill and left. He'd met Roy from being a regular at the Berkley Bar, as well as being a frequent visitor to The Station Hotel when Roy was drumming with Nancy. Jim had been working in London, returning home for weekends, but had recently got himself a job on the British Steel site. He was one of those rare breeds of the time with a full driving licence so was the perfect fit for the now unavailable Norman.

Roadie Jim joined in with the piano launch

With Jim established as the band's roadie, he started sharing a flat with Dek on the seafront. Money was tight so there would usually be a number of people sharing these flats, even though they were only meant for single residency as there was generally only one bed, albeit a double. You can cram a lot into a double bed… well, you could in those days. We would all stay over on occasion, just crashing out on the floor.

As brilliant a musician as Dek was, Jim remembers one day walking into the flat and catching him balancing an egg on the end of a spoon whilst holding it under the hot tap.

Jim said, 'Dek, what are you doing?'

To which Dek replied, 'I'm boiling an egg.'

Jim can't recall how he actually started to drive the group to bookings, but it was probably through his Redcar associations with Roy and Dek, and being asked in a drunken stupor at The Berkeley Bar one Saturday night.

Jim warmly remembers his days spent with the band and has stayed in contact over the years with most of the people who were around at the time. His memory of events is really clear, although after hearing a few of his tales, you'll wonder how anyone could ever forget them anyway.

There were no sat-navs to help find venues then so when reaching a town or a pit village where the gig was, finding the actual social club was only ever achievable with local guidance. One night, they were playing at a club in Rowlands Gill near Newcastle and were running a bit late, nothing unusual, so Jim was looking out for someone to ask directions to the club. Having spotted someone, he pulled up alongside and Roy, who was sitting in the front passenger seat, wound the window down and asked for directions.

The man told Roy in a thick Geordie accent, 'Well, you go along here and turn right where the old police station used to be, follow that road until you get to where the cinema was then turn left. The club is just along there next to the church that was demolished by a bomb in the war.' 'Thanks, mate,' said Roy, then wound the window up and turned to everyone else in the van, who were creased up laughing, and said, 'How the fucking hell are we supposed to know where the old police station, cinema and church used to be?' Jim pulled away looking for someone else to ask with the gent still waving to them as though he'd just done his good deed for the day.

Eventually, having found the club, there was quite a rush to get the equipment in because it had turned eight o'clock and these clubs were on a tight schedule to work around the bingo. The concert room was upstairs, so getting the gear in wasn't a cakewalk, through the front door, up the stairs and right through the concert room to the stage. The lads were on stage setting up their amps with Roy doing the same with his drum kit when the Club Secretary walked up to the front of the stage with his left arm in the air, pointing at his watch.

He said, 'I want you on in ten minutes so you'd better get a move on,' to which nobody took any notice. Then a few minutes later, he did the same thing again, only just raising his left arm and pointing to his watch.

The lads were still getting their equipment ready so Roy went to the front of the stage and beckoned the secretary over then asking him for a look at his watch. Mr Secretary obliged by lifting his left arm towards Roy, pulling his sleeve back and pointing at the time again. By now Roy had lost it with him and promptly whacked his watch with the heavy end of one of his drumsticks. There was glass, springs and little cog wheels everywhere, leaving only the leather strap remaining of a timepiece that was probably presented to him for doing a hundred years down a coal mine.

The secretary was left screaming that the band were now not going on and demanding they left the club immediately, long way to go for no remuneration. Still, Mr Secretary wouldn't have had any idea if the next night's acts were turning up late or early, would he?

On another occasion, which Jim recollects with not so mixed feelings, Dek wanted to take his girlfriend, Elaine, to one of the bookings. She had a friend that Roy had been keen on so they both, Elaine and her friend, came along to make up a foursome. It would have been a tight squeeze in the van they were using at the time, so Roy asked Jim if they could go to the club in Jim's prized Mini, which he had bought only recently. Jim, I'm sure reluctantly, agreed to allow the four of them to travel in his car while Jim and the rest of the band plus equipment travelled in the van. Roy, who only had a provisional license at the time, would drive the Mini himself, leading the way with the van following them, as Jim didn't know the way to the club which was in Sunderland.

They arrived at the club okay and had a good night, but as they came out of the club to go home they were met with dense fog, a pea-souper where you couldn't see much beyond the end of the car. Jim asked Roy to drive in front very slowly so that he could still see him as he didn't know the way back home. They set off and managed to find their way out of the built up urban area which was pretty well lit up, but once they were out of town, the street lighting disappeared and Jim was hanging on to the tail lights of his treasured Mini that Roy was driving in front. Even so, the fog was so thick that Jim was driving close enough to notice that Roy was leaning out of the car having opened the driver's side door in order to get a better view of where they were going, but also probably just having a bit of a laugh with Dek and the girls.

Still in the van with Jim were Tony and Lee who, together with Jim, were having a bit of a giggle at Roy's antics, when WHACK…! Roy, in front, had noticed that he had strayed over the central dotted line in the road and was now approaching a roundabout on the wrong side of the road, slamming his anchors on in blind panic, so I'll say it again WHACK…! Jim following on so close behind had ploughed into the back of his own prize Mini, almost writing it off.

Jim, who was now crushed up against the windscreen, the group's speakers and amplifiers having slid forwards with the impact, managed to twist his head around towards Tony, who was in a similar position, only in the front passenger seat, and said, 'I don't think I'm gonna be able to drive home like this, Tony!'

Everyone got out of their respective vehicles in somewhat of a daze, Dek and his girlfriend who had been sitting in the back of Jim's Mini were still pulling shards of glass from each other's hair and Dek's beard. With closer inspection, and after pulling bits of car and van back into place, thankfully both were still drivable, so they amazingly got back to Redcar without any more mishaps. As they approached Redcar, there was just Jim still driving the van, having dropped the lads off at home on the way, with Roy in the now even minnier Mini. They both pulled into a lay-by to decide what they were going to do.

Jim said to Roy, 'I'm going to leave my car in The Lobster car park 'til in the morning,' the Lobster being a local pub near to Jim's flat.

To which Roy replied, 'Don't leave it there, mate, there'll be nothing left of it in the morning. Follow me and we'll put in on Fisherman's Square car park.' Fisherman's Square was where the local fishermen parked their fishing cobbles and tractors.

Jim agreed with Roy's advice, so followed him to Fisherman's Square, parked the car up and Roy dropped him back at his flat before going home himself. All were glad to get home and to bed after such an eventful night.

The next day having not slept that well, Jim was up early and off to pick up his car. On arriving at the car park, Jim was greeted with the spectacle of his car propped up on house bricks having had the wheels removed, not only that but the Redcar piranhas had stripped the entire vehicle of everything that was worth removing, leaving only the skeletal bones of what used to be Jim's pride and joy Mini. Jim dejectedly walked the short distance to Roy's house to tell him what had happened.

Roy simply said, 'Fuck me, you can't trust anyone round here, can you? Good night though, wasn't it?'

As I said before, Jim was roadie when I joined the band and there was one night after arriving at a club in the Tyneside area we needed to back the van up to some double doors which would allow us to take the equipment straight up the fire escape stairs and into the concert room which was on the first floor. I was sat in the front passenger seat, next to the door, so I was able to stick my head out of the open window, as Jim did out of the driver's door window, to give directions that the way was clear.

'Okay my side,' I said to Jim.

'Same here,' said Jim as he slammed the van into gear then, as if he was auditioning to be Reginald Molehusband's stunt double, that's just for those who can remember who Reginald Molehusband was, he reversed it straight into a reinforced concrete pillar.

CRUNCH!!!!!! The van came to a sudden halt. We jumped out, myself with Jim and Roy, who had been sat in the front between me and Jim, to see what had happened only to find that we'd backed into a concrete post which was holding the first floor of the club up. As I had been looking out of one side of the van and Jim out of the other, the post had been out of our line of vision so neither of us could see it. The van was crammed to the roof with amps, speakers and drums so the rear view mirror never came into the equation either. All of this taken into account still didn't stop Roy calling us both a pair of blind twats though, but thankfully the damage was minimal and it didn't take too long before we all saw the funny side of it.

Although Jim was the regular roadie, another lad who also drove from time to time was Chris Barnes, a giant of a bloke with an appetite to go with it. As well as The Europa, a regular stop off would be at a Chinese take-away in Gateshead, if we'd been working in Newcastle. The take-away was situated on a main road in the district of Low Fell and had a sign across the full width of the shop just above the door saying 'Low Fell Chinese Take-away'. One night while we were all in the shop, Roy went up to the counter and asked the Chinese lad serving, 'Is Low in?' as if Low Fell was the Chinese name of the owner… we all just fell about laughing.

On visits to the Chinese, we would always get a meal each, apart from Chris, who would probably just get himself a portion of chips. This was always expected because the meals were quite large and more than any of us could manage, so Chris would then polish off what everyone else had left.

I was always the one to get dropped off first and we'd all pile into my house for a nightcap. If it was a Sunday and we'd been out all day doing a lunchtime gig as well as an evening one, my mother would always plate up a Sunday dinner for me. As we would usually have had a Sunday night visit to the Chinese, I was always too full to tuck in, but never fear, Chris would be at hand to rescue the situation by polishing it off on top of his own take-away leftovers to the amusement of the rest of us.

There was a lad who used to come along on gigs, I didn't know too much about him or where he came from, but remember he was called Derek. We nicknamed him Spotty Muldoon, after a sixties comedy character created by Peter Cook. We would all bring the odd mate or girlfriend on a gig at times but to this day I still don't know if he knew anyone in the band. It was as if he was just masquerading as a non-driving, not helping with the gear roadie, though, try as he might, he didn't quite blend into the background owing to what he insisted on wearing.

It was always a long shoulder to ankle length coat made with the type of heavy, rough tweed material you'd only ever see as part of your art teacher's jacket… without the leather elbow patches, that is. It was well worn and very drab, looking like it had come from a church jumble sale. We all thought it was Derek's attempt at looking a bit trendy as he'd wear it throughout the year, not taking it off even in the middle of summer. Derek and his coat almost appeared to act as two separate entities because, with it being so thick and long (the coat, not Derek… although I'm not so sure now), almost touching the floor, if ever Derek turned quickly to the left or right, the coat would refuse to co-operate, staying straight in the 'looking forward' position. We were never 100% sure whether Derek brought the coat with him on gigs or the coat brought Derek, or if he actually had a real pair of legs underneath it at all.

One night during our break while the bingo was on, Roy and the rest of us lads including Derek had gone into the lounge area for a drink, sitting around a table just inside the door. After a few minutes Derek and his coat went off to the toilet but as he left, a couple of good looking young girls walked in and stopped to see if there were any seats left. Roy started having a bit of a crack with them and, as there where no other seats available, asked them to join us, one of them sitting in the seat that Derek had vacated.

These two girls were really stunning and dressed to kill, leaving very little to the imagination. The lads couldn't take their eyes off them. Suddenly Derek and his coat appeared at the door that was adjacent to the table, he looked straight at this gorgeous girl and blurted out dozily, 'Hey, dat's my seat!' Then stood behind with his hand on the back of the chair, waiting for her to stand up, which she did. Then, together with her friend, she promptly marched straight out of the door and out of our lives for good. We all looked at each other in astonishment then glared straight at Derek, who was now established back in his seat. Roy shook his head, saying in slow amazement at Derek, 'What the fuck?'

Jim says, 'Derek once told Roy that he was going to be a drummer. Roy asked why he hadn't kept it up then, with Derek answering that it hurt his neck. It was probably 'cos he'd have to take his fucking coat off.'

Jim Rudd took Roy on a number of gigs later on, after he had gone solo, one of which was at the Quoit Club in Guisborough. 'Roy wasn't having such a great night,' says Jim, 'then part way through his act, stopped and just said, 'Well, you're all a pack of bastards,' threw his microphone down on the stage and walked off. The Club Secretary stormed into the dressing room and said to Roy, 'You can't say that to our members, get back out there and apologise.' Surprisingly, Roy stood up, marched back out on to the stage, picked up the microphone and said, 'I've been asked to apologise for calling you all a pack of bastards, so to those of you who aren't bastards, I'm sorry… the rest of you are still a pack of bastards!"

Jim Rudd is the absolute representative of the group's roadies which, as well as himself, included Brian de Bear, also a club DJ in his own right, Norman, who was the first roadie, Chris Barnes and Barry Watson. Without these people, the 'well-oiled machine' that was seen on stage in those early days would have been much more difficult to achieve, so a big thank you goes out to them all, even if the wheels did come off on the odd occasion.

20

Dek Vasey's Four Man Band went from strength to strength in the workmen's clubs of the North East. We would do two sets in each club either side of the main event of the evening, namely the bingo, usually finishing off with what they called their flyer card which could have a jackpot prize of anything between fifty and a hundred pounds, big money in those days. Then followed a stampede akin to an early Californian gold rush as the room half emptied after the flyer, as if someone had just announced that the club up the road were serving free beer.

That was the way it was. Most club audiences considered the act on stage as just a bit of an annoyance to be tolerated once or twice a week, particularly certain committee men who would never put a foot in the concert room if it wasn't to collect their free pint tokens for turning up to check a winning bingo card. It's probably not a wonder why so many of those establishments eventually bit the dust, but hey, this was club-land's heyday, and we too were riding on the crest of their wave.

As I said earlier, we would generally perform two sets at each venue, the first being predominately comedy routines revolving around Roy which we all joined in with, padded out with pop songs of the day. Roy would often surprise us out of the blue by presenting us with a new version of one of the chart hits he'd been working on, to which we would hastily add the music in order to perform it that night.

Even in those early days of his career, Roy would spend hours alone creating his own comedy identity, the like of which our workmen's club circuit in the North East had never seen before. The end product would usually have us all rolling about the floor in fits of giggles well before it had been performed on stage. It was a regular occurrence that when performing a new routine for the very first time, we would often not get through it for laughing hysterically, usually with the audience staring at us stony-faced, wondering what on earth was going on, or words to that effect.

Our first half comedy show would start with just three of us on stage, Dek, Lee and myself, opening up with The Beatles' Octopus's Garden. As the audience resigned themselves to the fact that we were going to be yet another pop group that had just come along to spoil their evening, even though we were dressed in the most ridiculous clobber, Roy had infiltrated the crowd quite inconspicuously, as if he could, wearing a vicar's cassock and hat.

Please allow me to diversify at this point because having used the word 'crowd', which was a regular way of describing our audiences, I decided for the first time to look it up in The Oxford English Dictionary. Its official meaning is: 'a large number of people gathered together in a disorganised or unruly way.' So I'm afraid I will have to take that back because there was never a large number of them, just usually an unruly mob.

Back to Roy. Having manoeuvred himself among the throng, somehow without getting noticed, he would make himself known to us part way through our opening number by causing quite a bit of a stir. It was intended that the audience would think that this was for real with Roy dressed as a vicar shouting abuse up at us from the concert room floor. People would be turning round to see what was going on as Roy advanced toward the stage, eventually climbing up with us by whatever means were available.

Once on the stage, Roy would strip off his vicar's cassock to reveal similar attire to ours, with his shirt undone to reveal his belly with the word 'Empty' written on it in black felt pen. He'd then sit behind the drums, give us a loud heavy drum start to bring us into our second tune of the evening. Hopefully, by then, we would have got the attention of the people in the room and, with a bit of luck, the crowd had turned into a receptive audience.

The beginning to our show was not always executed in the way it was intended though. On one particular summer's evening, we were performing at The Chicken Ranch in Stokesley, North Yorkshire. Our dressing room was also used as the changing room for the club football team, so as well as there being an opening leading to the back of the stage, it also had a back door leading out to the football pitch.

Roy thought it would be good and raise more laughs if, after the three of us had opened up the show, he would sneak out of the back door, walk around the side of the building and back in through the front door. It sounded like a great idea, so Dek, Lee and myself went on stage and, as we were announced by the Concert Chairman, broke into Octopus's Garden.

As we completed the first verse, the three of us were distracted by Roy walking past the window of the concert room dressed in his vicars' outfit trying to be all nonchalant, as if it was a normal thing to do. He looked hilarious and we all started laughing uncontrollably. But that wasn't the end to the hilarity, as, when Roy reached the entrance, the doorman wouldn't let him in because he wasn't a member so, without Roy's intervention, we had to play the last verse of the song over and over again, still giggling from the sight of Roy walking past the window.

It looked like Roy was having a hard time trying to convince the jobsworth doorman that he was a member of the band, and the vicar's outfit wasn't helping him one bit. It was as though this confrontation had become part of the act, and it was a pity we couldn't have used it every night. Roy eventually got into the concert room and onto the stage in his usual way, but it wasn't until the break that we all found out what had happened and fell about laughing. The story is one of many that always comes up whenever we all get together… still laugh at it every night.

Roy did many parodies of chart songs for the show. Among the favourites was his rendition of Benny Hill's Ernie (The Fastest Milkman in the West), which was always a great hit with audiences. Roy would come on stage dressed as a milkman in a white shirt and pinny, carrying a milkman's crate that he probably acquired illegally. The words 'Sterilised', 'Pasteurised' and 'Circumcised' were written in strategic places on the pinny. It usually had the crowd in stitches and would get one of the biggest ovations of the night. One of my own favourite routines was when Roy would put a dress and lady's wig on to impersonate

Mary Hopkin, who had recently been a winner on Hughie Green's Opportunity Knocks. She'd had a hit with her first single, Those Were The Days, to which Roy had changed the words with hilarious results. The chorus sticks in my memory to this day. Anyone who can't remember the song or maybe wasn't even born then should google it and sing along to the chorus with Roy's words. They went like this:

> *Those were the days with Bill, when she was on the pill,*
> *Out every night and dancing with the crew.*
> *She goes out with the lads, likes playing mams and dads,*
> *Then sneaking home while Bill's on six till two.*

The audience would already be in hysterics long before he started to sing, at the sight of Roy coming back on stage dressed as a woman, who, admittedly, looked rougher than a badger's arse, and did not appear to have just come off the catwalk. In fact she/he looked a bit like the type of groupies we used to attract. We would regularly have to wait until the furore died down before getting into the actual routine, or nobody would have heard a word Roy was singing.

After Roy had finished and taken his bow, still with applause and laughter ringing in our ears, he would turn his back to the audience as he left the stage only to reveal that there was no back to the dress and that he was not wearing any underwear. There would always be screams of derision and that was only the blokes in the room… in fact, generally audiences would fall about, creased up at the sight of Roy's bare arse, you never normally saw a bare arse on a workmen's club stage, unless it was that of Big Boobs Babs, the stripper on a Sunday lunchtime.

1972 saw Chuck Berry top the charts with the novelty song My

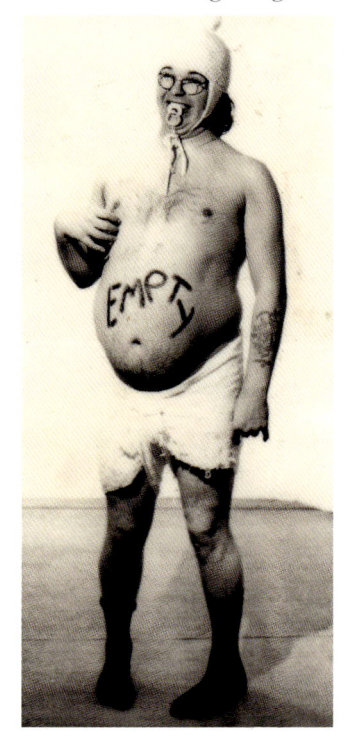

Ding-a-Ling, and it was crying out for Roy's special treatment. The words were not tampered with at all, but Roy visually attacked it by appearing on stage wearing a baby's nappy (terry towelling, not disposable), a white knitted baby's bonnet and sucking a large dummy. Roy's exposed belly still had the word 'Empty' written on it, which always raised another titter, even though it had already been seen at the beginning of the show as it obviously was not 'Empty', quite the opposite from the look of it. It was during this routine that Roy perfected his trademark of occasionally scratching his balls, an action you can still see him performing on stage to this day… always gets a laugh. Roy's comedy dancing was something else that came to fruition over this period and still gets a laugh before he's even opened his mouth.

As fast and furious as our first set was, it homed in towards the climax of a solo stint where Roy would stand alone at the front of the stage telling jokes. Roy liked the three of us, Dek, Lee and myself, to stay on stage while he did his 'stand-up' because in the tough workie clubs of the North East, his ten to fifteen minute's worth of joke telling could sometimes be only two to three minutes then back on the drums to finish the set off. Generally though, Roy's bit in the middle would be the highlight of the show with even ourselves falling about laughing having not already heard half of the jokes.

Jokes at the time might be… Christmas was coming and I said to my dad, 'I've got my eye on a bike.' Dad said, 'You can keep your eye on it 'cos you won't get your bloody arse on it.'

Another was… I took a girl home the other night and afterwards I said, 'In nine months time you might have a baby, you can call it Roy, if you like.' Then the girl said back, 'In nine days time you might have a rash, you can call it measles if you like.'

Roy would often attract hecklers but would always have a few well-rehearsed put downs to shut them up. 'They named a town after you, mate… Leatherhead!'

Other comedy influences which Roy shared with Dek Vasey's Four Man Band was through the choice of certain songs included in the first half of the show, one of which was Jollity Farm by Bonzo Dog Doo-Dah Band… nobody else in the North East club circuit was doing such material.

When the band performed Jollity Farm, it had been decided that it would be comical to throw bananas into the audience, to which they were always gratefully received with the recipients usually tucking in immediately. The routine would see Roy leave his drums and pick up the bananas, which had been placed on top of one of the amplifiers in front of him ready to be used, then toss them into the audience so people could catch them.

On one particular night, Dek, who didn't have any other income streams other than his earnings from the group, hadn't eaten for about two days, and had already tucked into the bananas while no one was looking, leaving only the skins. Roy left his drums and came forward, leant down for what should have been the usual bag of bananas, but because of the stage lighting didn't notice that all that was left were four empty banana carcasses.

Having wrapped his hand around what was left of the bananas, it became apparent what he was holding before he launched his first missile, but still decided to let the audience have them. The people in the audience that caught them weren't best pleased, but their friends who were sat with them thought it was hilarious. Roy had a real go at Dek when he found out what had happened, but with everyone seeing the funny side of it, we laughed all the way home. Needless to say that Roy kept a keen eye on the bananas from that night on, although they wouldn't be the last banana skins Roy would encounter during his rise to fame.

The tough northern workmen's club circuit was the perfect training ground for someone like Roy and it was as if he had taken on an imaginary apprenticeship to learn the skills of his trade. Roy's always said, 'It takes lots of hard work over many years to become an overnight success.'

21

Dek was seeing Elaine Richards in the late 60s, early 70s, and Elaine's brother, Davy, who everyone knew as Davy Rich, owing to his dad having been a well-known local boxer called Kid Rich, started coming along on gigs with us in the van. Davy had only recently returned to the area in 1970 after living in London, but more recently had been singing with a band in Grangetown, and had only known of Roy Vasey through reputation of being a Teddy Boy, but had come across him briefly before they met through the Four Man Band.

Roy had become a well-known character in the Grangetown area and a proper Ted. Yes, most people in Grangetown knew Roy for a variety of reasons and he came with a bit of reputation as something of a tough nut.

One night, when Davy and his mates had been practising in the front room of the drummer's house, there was a loud tapping on the front window. Davy went to investigate, only to find Roy Vasey standing at the front door. Davy had known of Roy, as said before, but had never met him.

Before Davy could say anything, Roy jumped in with, 'I can play the drums better than him. Can I join your group?'

Given that Roy came with such a reputation, and being only half his size, Davy gulped and said, 'Well, it's not my group, but I'll go and ask my mates,' not wishing to give Roy an abrupt answer of no.

The lad who ran the band went to the front door and was there for a few minutes. After he came back in to the room, Davy asked him, 'What did you say to him? He told me he wanted to join the group.'

The reply was, 'He said that to me too, but there's no chance, he's too rough for us lot. Didn't dare tell him that though, just told him that once we'd got rid of our drummer, the job's his.' The band carried on with their practising and never heard from Roy again.

Davy, like most of us at the time used to like going out to see local bands, and Dek had started going out with his sister, Elaine. Davy would go and watch Pipeline whenever he could at The Normanby Hotel or if they were on at South Bank Sporting Club, with Dek and himself becoming good friends.

Even though having very little, Dek was a kind-hearted bloke and would always try and help people out if they needed it. Davy tells of one day when Dek was looking out of his flat window in Redcar, which was a number of floors up, and noticed a tramp sitting on the pavement outside The Regent Cinema which was slightly further up the promenade, so Dek went down and invited the tramp in to stay the night. Davy says, 'Dek slept on the floor after giving up his bed for him to get a good night's sleep, but the tramp had been scratching all night. The following night, after the tramp had left, Dek slept in his own bed and awoke the next morning scratching like fury having caught what must have been a dose of crabs that the tramp had left the night before'.

Dek then said to Davy, 'Just goes to show you… one good turn deserves a dose of the crabs.'

Davy started coming on gigs with us, by which time the show was developing into a pretty well packed first half comedy act and we were introducing various props to add to the comedy element. One was a table with Queen Anne legs, standing about a metre from the floor, something you might have had in a hallway with flowers on. There was a hole drilled through the top of the table just big enough to fit a clenched fist with a small flip top rubbish bin with no bottom placed over the hole in the table.

Now this might be one of those occasions when you just had to be there, but we'll give it a go anyway.

The idea was that at sometime through the act, one of us would say, 'Alright?' then in a deep gruff voice someone else would say, 'Alright!' at the same time as the flip top of the bin opened and a toilet brush was pushed through for everyone to see, the illusion being that the toilet brush was saying, 'Alright'. Okay, I know I'm milking it but it was 1971 and it got some great laughs. Anyway, in order to perform this we needed someone to crouch underneath the table for the full length of the first half, usually about forty five minutes. Davy, who thankfully was somewhat shorter than the rest of us and fit perfectly, got the job. We disguised him by draping some old curtains over the side of the table, right to the floor, so nobody knew he was there. He did this for a full six months and the poor lad still walks with a humpty back.

The flip top of the bin was operated by Davy pulling on a piece of string from underneath the table which occasionally snapped at the vital point in the programme, to which after 'Alright?' and 'Alright', everybody would then hear 'Shit, the fucking string's broke again!' from underneath the table, which usually got a bigger laugh from the audience, even though they didn't know what was going on, and an even bigger laugh from all of us.

I remember Roy saying to Davy once, 'It must be tough on your back, crouching underneath that table every night. If you ever want to stop, just let us know.' Davy's reply was, 'What, and give up show business? No chance.' Davy would eventually escape the confines of the curtained table to join us all at the front of the stage.

In between gigs, mainly through the mid-week, Dek had started playing bass at a Middlesbrough nightspot called The Contessa. With him were local jazz musicians… Joe Boston on keyboards and Paul Barker on drums. This was definitely Dek's musical preference so it came as no surprise that when Joe was offered a job in far away Rhodesia and asked Dek and Paul to accompany him on the trip, Dek had no hesitation in accepting and informed the band that he was leaving.

By now we had become a tightly knit group and, although everyone gave Dek their blessing, we knew he was going to be a hard act to follow and replacing him would be difficult. Dek had other ideas though and was determined that little Davy, although never having picked up a bass guitar in his life, would be his ideal successor.

Davy knew the act back to front, probably more back than front seeing as he'd viewed it from under his table every night for the previous six months. Dek told Davy he wanted him to join the band and so did the rest of us, so Dek gave him an intense crash course, practising every night for two weeks, culminating with his first performance around Christmas 1972.

Davy, in his own admittance, would never be the bass player that Dek had been, but he had a fabulous rough tuneful voice that had become more fashionable with the emergence of the likes of Rod Stewart, and brought a new dimension to the musical aspect of the band. He also brought a few reggae tunes in as well too, so Davy and I started to share the duties of lead vocals between us. It also helped that after dressing up he looked as daft as the rest of us did.

Without Dek we could not keep calling ourselves Dek Vasey's Four Man Band so we needed a new name. After throwing one or two names around, it was decided to go with a name that expressed the comedy style of the group and came up with The Nuts. We all liked it and dressed appropriately to suit the name. When looking at Nuts photos we pulled out to go in the book, Roy said, 'Put that one in George 'cos I like the face you were pulling.' I said, 'I wasn't pulling a face.'

If anything, The Nuts were even more madcap than Dek Vasey's Four Man Band. I worked with the band for a short while, before leaving to work as a solo act doing the rounds of the North East pubs and clubs, although Davy and I did do some work as a duo called Fingers and Thumbs, probably named as a tribute to my guitar playing.

The Nuts: Roy, Davy, George and Lee

A great routine The Nuts had was, with Davy being so minute, in comparison to Roy that is, he fit perfectly into a large suitcase. At the beginning of the act, Roy would walk on stage with the suitcase, place it in the middle of the stage, open it up and Davy would roll out, always got a laugh. One night after the first half of the show, when it had been obvious Roy struggled bringing the suitcase on, he said to Davy, 'Davy, you're gonna have to go on a fucking diet, I can't hardly lift you anymore.'

The Nuts carried on as a trio, Roy, Lee and Davy and, as none of them had any ties to hold them down, they decided to travel further afield to get bookings.

Davy tells of a trip to South Wales where he'd been given the job of finding accommodation for the week, but on arriving in Cardiff realised that he'd left the details of the digs at home. After plucking up the courage to tell Roy and Lee what he'd done, the three of them found themselves high and dry in what they thought was a foreign country with nowhere to stay. Davy then had a bright idea and said,

'Pull over at that telephone box,' and then said he'd remembered that the lady who owned the digs was called Mrs Jones.

Roy went into the telephone box, which was obviously used as a night time toilet, then came back out and blasted Davy with, 'Just because you can do a handstand in a shoebox, Davy, doesn't mean you can also pull a random name out of a fucking telephone book.' Roy showed him the two phone books he'd brought out from the telephone box and said, 'This book is the one with everybody else's names in and the other is the one with everyone who's called Jones,' then said, 'they must like sandwiches round here, they're all interbred.' Roy, having finally finished his ranting, smacked Davy over the head with the book full of Jones's. Roy rang the agent they were working for, who was able to put them in contact with the right Mrs Jones in Rumney, just outside Cardiff, and they enjoyed her wonderful hospitality for the duration of their stay.

Lee, Davy and Roy

When working away, the days can be quite boring, so they would regularly go into Cardiff centre for a walk round and see what was going on. Davy says that they were walking past a theatre where comedian Harry Worth was appearing and there was a life-size cardboard figure of him standing outside advertising the show. Harry Worth was a huge name at the time, having his own comedy series on the BBC. Harry would always start off by saying, 'My name's Harry Worth, I don't know why, but there it is…' It was the way he said it.

Roy, still with the same instincts he'd grown up with, said, 'Let's nick it,' and before anybody could reply Harry was under Roy's arm as he legged it up the road with Davy and Lee chasing after him. Managing to reach the van without being stopped, they bundle poor Harry into the back among the equipment and set off back to the digs. On arriving at Mrs Jones's house, it was getting near to mealtime, which was always provided in professional theatrical digs in plenty of time for the acts to eat up and get on their way to their evening's booking. Roy thought it would be a great ruse to take Harry down and sit him at the table with us.

Mrs Jones had poor eyesight and wore beer bottle bottom glasses which she would take off whilst cooking because they used to steam up. Roy placed the Harry Worth effigy at the head of the table, which was the furthest seat away from the door that Mrs Jones would be bringing our food through. He then shouted through to the kitchen that they'd bumped into an old friend while in Cardiff and had brought him back for some tea. Mrs Jones came to the door without her specs, then looking over the long table, squinted to see Harry Worth sat at the opposite end, put a thumb up in the air and said, 'Yes, no bother, Roy.'

She then brought everyone's meal out, putting one in front of Harry and telling him to tuck in, while the rest of us including some other acts that had come in for their meal were sticking serviettes into their mouths to stop laughing. After sharing Harry's meal out between themselves, the boys took him out to the van and never mentioned him again. And neither did Mrs Jones.

On a Nuts trip to Sheffield, the boys were booked into digs at the same time as Bobby Thompson (The Little Waster from Geordie Land) and Johnny Hammond, one of Roy's comedy heroes. Davy remembers getting back to the digs late one night after their booking, Bobby was still up so they all sat talking and laughing at each other's stories. That was until the lounge door swung open and standing in the doorway was Johnny Hammond, stark naked apart from a bowler hat. He said, 'Can't anyone get some fucking sleep round here?' then turned around and disappeared back upstairs, while Bobby and the lads' jaws just dropped open as they stared at one another.

The Nuts returned to performing North East clubs but their sense of humour still wasn't 'got' by certain venues. Davy remembers a club somewhere in Sunderland where the secretary threatened not to pay the lads for the night's entertainment. Roy had noticed earlier in the evening, standing next to the regular organ – always a permanent fixture on most of the club stages – there was a brand new Techniques keyboard. Roy had recently become more interested in playing the piano and electric keyboards were still very much in their infancy, with Techniques being one of the top makes.

Roy just said to the lads, 'If we aren't getting paid, that fucking keyboard's coming home with us.'

Davy says, 'Thankfully our second set had everyone up dancing and by the end of the evening, all was forgotten and we got our money.' Davy finishes off with, 'As we were leaving, I still think Roy had his eye on that keyboard though.'

An occasion that brings a smile to Davy's face was when the van broke down on Stockton High Street. There was a problem under the van, then a scissor jack appeared from nowhere, and Davy was volunteered to slip under the van to have a look, which he did with a great deal of uncertainty, going in on his back, head first. Davy could still see as far as the kerb of the pavement and it was obvious to him that a crowd had gathered to see what was going on. A broken down van wouldn't have normally attracted such an audience only Roy had grabbed hold of Davy's left leg by the ankle and was lifting it up and down as though he was pumping up the scissor jack with everyone having a good laugh at it.

Whilst back in the North East, The Nuts continued to work as a comedy trio, then, as happened with lots of groups, it ran its course and disbanded amicably with each member going off to do their own thing.

22

A school mate of mine, Alan Earl, had been working the North East clubs for a couple of years and knew a lot of the local agents. He also had a telephone which was a rarity in itself in those days, so said he would look after our bookings for us. Alan had only recently got married and bought a house in Pym Street at South Bank for which he had taken out a mortgage of £500. We all said he was mad and that he'd have it hanging around his neck for the rest of his life.

Because of the fact that Alan was my friend, as well as looking after our bookings, if ever there was a problem while we were on a gig, it was always me who would be delegated to make contact with him to try and sort it out.

This included whenever the van broke down, which was an all too regular occurrence, and one time that springs to mind is when it happened on the way back from a booking further up north when the van came to a halt right outside Middlesbrough General Hospital, refusing to go any further.

We went through the same old routine of lifting the bonnet up and making mumbling noises as if we knew what we were looking for until, inevitably, Roy said, 'You'll have to phone Alan to come and get us, George.' We're talking somewhere around midnight here and I didn't really like to be bothering someone who I knew would have been tucked up in bed, apart from having had to ring him so many times recently for the same reason. Alan was a rare phenomenon in the entertainment business of the early 70s. He was teatotal – a non-drinker – so there was no problem of him having had too much alcohol to drive.

With no other option available, I said, 'Okay, Roy, we'll have to go and find a phone box.' No mobile phones in those days.

Roy said, 'There's one just along the way at the traffic lights on Linthorpe Road. I'll come with you.'

So off we trudged with no real drama, we were all getting used to this and considered it just part of being on the road. We reached the telephone box and scratched around for some coins to make the call. The country had only recently gone decimal in February 1971, and we were all still getting used to it.

The price for using a telephone from a public phone box had gone from four old pennies (4d) to two new pence (2p). The new two pence piece though was the same size as an old halfpenny piece, usually called a ha'penny (pronounced ape-nee), and would fit into the slot perfectly for making phone calls. The ha'penny would have been approximately an eighth of the value of a new two pence piece so people held them back for such a reason, and we kept a few for that purpose. Now, you didn't think you were going to get a history lesson as well, did ya?

So, after rummaging around in his pocket, Roy passed me a ha'penny and I went into the telephone box. I'd been an avid reader of Superman comics when I was a kid, so whenever I went into a telephone box I always felt a bit Clark Kentish… never came out as Superman though.

Once in the telephone box, I got on with the job of phoning International Rescue to come and pick us up once again. Alan answered the phone and we were in deep conversation when suddenly I felt a warm sensation around my kneecaps. I looked out through the telephone box window to see Roy very close to me but with his head looking skyward and whistling, then I looked down to see what was happening, all the time still in conversation on the phone. Roy had been caught short and must have decided he couldn't hold on any longer and was having a slash up against the side of the telephone box, of which neither of us had been aware until now that from waist height downward there was no glass, so the warm sensation I could feel was Roy pissing all over my jeans.

In an attempt to make Roy aware of what he was doing, but still not wishing to alert anyone else on the other end of the telephone, I gently tapped on the window. Alas to no avail, Roy, oblivious as to what was happening and continuing to stare away, probably looking out to make sure no one was watching, still gushed. I knocked harder and harder on the window, until Roy eventually turned round, having just about finished emptying his bladder. He looked toward me with in inquisitive look on his face and mouthed, 'What?'

I looked him straight in the face and, whilst still talking to Alan, just pointed downward with the index finger of my left hand. Roy looked down to see what I was pointing at and realised that where he'd been pissing, there was no glass, then immediately burst into fits of laughter. Not at my wet jeans, he says, but at the look on my face when he finally looked back through the window.

When we got back to the van, Roy couldn't tell the lads what had happened for laughing, but when we finally got home, I had to explain why I had pissy-wet jeans on… still don't think anyone believed me, though it was a scene that was to become famous later on when Roy used it in his film, UFO.

Waterworks were to play a starring role yet again during another incident not much further down the line when, on the way to a gig one night, the van caught fire on the A19. The fire was underneath the van, not too far away from the petrol tank, so we all jumped out with the intention of extinguishing it somehow. It would never have entered our minds to carry a fire extinguisher and, with no source of water in sight, it was decided the only way to put it out was to piss on it.

Roy was first, didn't want a slash, so nothing came out, then little Davy Rich couldn't do it for laughing, so Roy said, 'You'll have to have a go, George.' I said, 'But I don't want one.' Roy said, 'You'll fucking have to, the van's going to go up with all of our gear inside.' I really didn't want a slash but got on with it anyway. I struggled to start with then after a second or two, woooshhh, I was away and couldn't stop. Roy shouted, 'The fire's out, you can stop now,' but I couldn't, I carried on for what seemed ages. All the lads were back in the van ready to go before I'd finished and sorted myself out. 'Fucking hell,' Roy said, 'didn't want one, hey? I'd hate to be stood next to you in the gents when you really do fucking want one.'

We continued on our way to the venue in Newcastle, thinking we'd just had a lucky escape but brushing it off as we had many other times already. We reached our destination without any more problems but on the way back we hadn't gone but a few miles when it started playing up again. Jim was driving and thought we ought to pull in somewhere so that he could have a look. He knew a bit about motors, the only one of us that did.

We turned in to Birtley service station, just south of Newcastle on the A1 where, after pulling into a parking space, the van seemed to give out one last gasp. Looking ever so tired and overworked, our trusty old van appeared to slump down on its own four baldy tyres, with shoulders sinking from sheer exhaustion.

After looking under the bonnet, Jim declared, 'This old thing ain't going anywhere tonight. It might have even had it for good.'

Roy looked over at me and, without saying a word, I knew straightaway I'd have to make the dreaded phone call once again. This was without doubt the furthest we'd asked Alan to come out to rescue us and I was sure he wouldn't have been too happy, though not that surprised, when I rang.

The only option left for us while we waited was to go into the service station café where we were able to get something to eat and drink. One of the lads had brought a couple of friends along that night and Roy had decided it was his job to keep everyone entertained. Well, you couldn't shut him up. It was one gag after another, then another one followed by yet another. I was the only one there with a proper job and, with this being a Sunday night, I had to be at work the following morning. I was shattered and, quite frankly, though I've never told him to this day, Roy's constant gag telling was getting on my fucking nerves.

It was almost morning by the time Alan picked us up, managing to get us all, plus our equipment, into the back of his van, so they dropped me, bleary-eyed, at work on the way back. The van was left where it had finally given up the ghost and we never saw it again. Although Roy did get a visit from the police, having been traced as the owner. Roy told them he didn't really want it back so one of the police officers offered him fifteen quid for it. Roy said, 'Twenty and it's yours,' so he got a few quid for a van that he never thought he'd ever see again anyway.

23

Roy left Alleycats after Gerry started moaning that he wasn't making enough cash from sales, probably because it was always full of us waifs and strays who weren't going to put our hands in our pocket, but it could also have been because it was full of shit nobody wanted to buy. While The Nuts had been doing well and travelling away occasionally, Roy thought it was best to move on. He had always thought that the flat above the shop was too big so at the same time as leaving Alleycats, he also moved into a new flat directly above a ladies hairdresser's shop on Coatham Road.

Roy began to turn his flat into a comfortable home by getting a few bits of furniture from the local saleroom. The flat already had a rickety old bed, and the ceiling had more cracks in it than Ken Dodd and Tim Vine's acts put together. Something that Roy hadn't noticed before though was the stink of perm solution which was so strong that you could actually taste it. Roy said if you made a sandwich the crusts would curl up all by themselves, and if he stayed in the flat too long, his lips would also start to curl as though he was doing an impression of Mick Jagger!

It was at that time that Roy bought his first piano – a bargain at £5 from the saleroom – although I don't think the man in the flat next door would have agreed, as he died soon afterwards with Roy's piano playing finally killing him off... as well as the fact that he smoked a hundred Woodies a day.

Davy Rich tells of the day the piano arrived at the flat... Roy had commandeered Davy's help along with a couple of mates, having already managed to get the piano into the back of the group van with the help of the saleroom's staff. Roy's flat was on the first floor above the shop, so getting a piano up there was always going to be a tough job, and it took them a whole half a day to achieve their task.

Davy recalls how hard Roy would practise on his new piano, and says, 'Not many people really know how dedicated Roy has been to perfecting his art. He was never one who would come out drinking with the rest of the lads.' Something I can endorse from my time working with Roy. Davy continues, 'He'd practise day and night until one day, he asked me over to his flat because he had something to show me. When I got there, he couldn't wait to play me a note perfect rendition of The Entertainer, a piano piece even Liberace would have found arduous.'

Roy would to tell a tale in our stage act. 'I used to go to piano lessons and the piano teacher said to me once, 'You know, Roy, I've never seen anyone play the piano quite like you,' then she slammed the lid down and broke two of me toes.'

He'd also say, 'I used to play the piano by ear, but I kept banging me head on the lid.'

Roy's pride and joy was a Dansette record player with a five watt speaker. You would have had to put your head under the lid to experience surround sound, but Roy thought it was marvellous, and in its time was regarded as 'straight out of the ark technology!' The rent for the flat was £10 per week, so it always left him with enough money to buy a few records. Luckily there was a second-hand shop just around the corner that had loads of old records that they sold dirt cheap. The only record collection that Roy had been able to amass up until then would have been police records.

Roy was now writing a lot of his own stuff and he would jot little lines down about things that he'd seen while he'd been out, and it was then he realised that when you go shopping, just look around, there's something funny happening all of the time, you just have to pick up on it.

The flat wasn't perfect. The floor was sticky around the piss pot… 'Can't imagine why,' says Roy. And so were the sheets, but that's a different story. Roy had never been much of a handyman, but when a knob came off the electric cooker, he thought it would be a good idea to stick a fork in the hole where the knob had been. Not one of his better ideas.

There was a flash and a bang, resulting in Roy flying backwards across the room doing about forty miles an hour, hitting the wall on the other side of the kitchen at such a force that his cap fell off, with the electric shock turning his hair into a crew-cut, and his eyebrows smoking away like they'd been blow torched. Embarrassingly, Roy says, 'What a silly fucker, but I suppose you'd expect that from somebody who burns salad.'

Roy says the flat was a good move for him, giving him the time and space to help perfect his dream of becoming the top performer that he is today. During his time at the flat, Roy accumulated a fair selection of books written by some of his comedy heroes… Charlie Chester, Chaplin, but Roy's all time comedy hero had to be the late Sir Ken Dodd. He also took up playing the ukulele, which he mastered after buying a tutor book.

Roy's work philosophy has always been, 'You only get out what you put in,' and Roy certainly puts a hell of a lot in. What you see on stage is only a fraction of the work Roy puts in to keep his live act having that fresh look.

After The Nuts ended, Roy had been asked to do the odd stag do by local agent Brian Findlay. Roy hadn't performed solo before, let alone stag shows, and wasn't sure whether he should. Brian, who was a larger than life character, said, 'Go on, you'll be alright. You don't do very long at stag shows… about twenty minutes. They're more interested in the stripper, just drop a few swear words in with your jokes and you'll be fine.'

Roy took up the challenge and, although there wasn't that many jobs coming in, he was doing okay when one night the pub manager that had booked him said he thought he needed to spice his act up, be a bit naughtier, bluer even, before he would have him back for another stag night.

Roy would often bump into Mick Boothby when he was about town. Mick was the one who'd had the small flat above the shop before Roy moved in. Mick was no longer working with the Jason Jones Trio and was now doing the clubs as a guitar vocalist going under the name of Oliver Lee. With having similar interests, they always had something to chat about, and Roy would ask Mick what kind of a weekend he'd had on the clubs. They became quite pally and, after one tough weekend, Mick, knowing that Roy was only doing the odd booking, said, 'Why don't you come with me on a gig? Bring your drums and back me, tell a few jokes.'

Roy really had nothing to lose, so agreed with Mick that it might not be a bad idea after all, and went along with him on his next booking. Roy took his drums and his comedy gear with him, did some comedy routines around Mick's songs and had a great night. After that they decided to go out permanently as a duo calling themselves Jason and Everard.

Mick got the Jason name from the seventies TV series called Jason King where the main character sported probably one of the most famous handlebar moustaches ever seen on telly, and Mick had a great one. I remember we all tried to grow a Jason King handlebar moustache but most of us couldn't get it to join at the side of our lips, leaving a little bald patch that some of the lads would fill in with their sister's mascara.

Again it was another venture for Roy but he remembers one night working not too far away from home when the act wasn't going down very well. Half way through the first half after he'd left the stage for a quick change, he sneaked out of a side door, got in the van and fucked off home, leaving Mick still playing on stage by himself. The routines were very much like we'd had in the band where Roy would regularly disappear off stage for a quick change and, on this occasion with the act going down like a lead balloon, he'd just had enough.

Roy says, 'We were having the shits of a night so when I came off stage during the act, I just slipped out, got in the van and drove off, forgot all about Mick. I'd only been home about ten minutes when the phone rang. It was Mick wondering where I was. I said I'll come straight back for you, mate. Mick had been playing the same song, repeating the same verse over and over again, waiting for me to come back on stage. After finally realising that just wasn't going to happen, he came off and saw the van had gone as well as me so he guessed where I would be.'

Mick and Roy worked the North East clubs as Jason and Everard for a period before, as everything else had done, it had its time and they went their separate ways, but Roy and Mick's paths would cross again at a later stage in Roy's career.

Jason and Everard

24

It was 1973 and so much seemed to have happened over such a short period from the back end of the sixties, bringing with it new musical genres. The Beatles had split up and gone their separate ways, Motown and soul music had slipped in through the back door after being so successful stateside during the sixties. We still had rock bands and Elvis and Cliff continued to have hit records, so there was a real mixture to keep everyone happy, including the mams and dads.

The speed of change and different experiences was also something that had been happening in the Teesside area, of which Roy was now becoming a prominent figure within the club circuit. Having worked in the bands and a stint with Mick Boothby as Jason and Everard, Roy approached me about forming a double act to work the clubs. Since leaving The Nuts, I had worked solo, as well as having done a short run with a local band, and at the time I was again working the clubs and pubs as a guitar vocalist, so when Roy suggested us forming a double act together, I was immediately up for it.

Workingmen's clubs would always expect any act to perform two spots, where you'd usually be ignored in the first half, then during the second half everyone would get up dancing until by the end of the night… they wouldn't let you off. Roy would still be playing drums, myself on guitar and vocals, with our first half being a mixture of standard songs wrapped around Roy's comedy routines. So effectively I was to be Roy's 'straight man' for our first half performances, but we now needed a new name.

Thinking of a new name might not seem so important or that difficult really, but you need something that is not too hard to remember and hopefully sticks in peoples' minds… for the right reasons, of course. To reach our decision, it was decided we might need a bit of alcohol-related help, so Roy and I went off to my local, The Oak Leaf, which was just at the bottom of the street where I lived. We went into the small lounge, which was usually occupied with CID from the nearby South Bank Police Station, got a couple of beers and sat down in a quiet corner.

We had a few sherbets and tossed around a variety of options to call ourselves with neither Roy nor myself being able to recollect any of the other names, but do remember both of our eyes lighting up, although that could have been the ale, when one of us blurted out, 'Alcock and Brown'.

Alcock and Brown were British aviators who made the very first non-stop transatlantic flight in 1919, setting off from Newfoundland in Canada and landing in County Galway Ireland.

Having had a few more drinks, we started to get a bit giggly while deciding which one of us was going to Mr Alcock and who would be Mr Brown. You all know the answer by now, I'm sure, but not only was this the birth of Roy Vasey becoming Roy Brown but, with the aviation connection, Roy's trademark flying

Allcock and Brown

Photo: John Herring Sunderland

helmet also got its introduction. Needing some advertising material, we booked ourselves into John Herring's Theatrical Photographers in Sunderland. John was well known within the industry and was usually employed to take the photos of most of the acts in the North East, so we knew we would be in good hands. We'd used Johnny before when we had our 'Nuts' photographed, if you know what I mean.

Because of the Alcock and Brown reference from way back in 1919, we asked John if he could give our photos a vintage feel with some sepia toning, which he did to great effect, then put two L's in Alcock, leaving me with the name of Allcock.

We decided that, being a new outfit, we'd rather perform our first gigs out of the area where we weren't known by anyone, just in case we fell flat on our arses, so we managed to get ten days work in South Wales for Cardiff agent Chris Banks, taking in two weekends. At the time I had a proper job in the labs at British Steel so I put a week's holiday in to cover our ten day run, rather than say I had a bad back which I'd used many times before.

In order for me to get to my solo gigs, I'd bought a second hand Red Morris 1000 van complete with starting handle, the same vehicle postal workers were using at the time. This was now Allcock and Brown's regular mode of transport, becoming quite the Chitty Chitty Bang Bang of clubland. We shared the driving, even though neither Roy nor myself had a full driving licence… please don't tell anyone. So, we set off with some trepidation on the long journey into the unknown.

We had digs with Mrs Jenkins in Neath and our first booking was a Friday night at Swansea Docker's club, which wasn't too far from Neath, so we were able to check in with her before we went to the club. Friday was one of the big nights at the Docker's club so the concert room was full. We were on with another comedy act called Johnny

Where do you put the petrol?

Goon Tweed. Johnny had been in the business a long time and had a terrific act taking off all the characters from the Goons, including Spike Milligan, Peter Sellers, Harry Secombe and Michael Bentine. We were asked to open and close the show with Johnny doing his spot in the middle. His was a highly polished act where, as we were performing ours for the very first time in front of an audience, we didn't really know how it would be received.

To put it bluntly, we died on our arses, not a titter in the first half at all, with most of the audience not even turning to look toward the stage and acknowledge we were there. Johnny went on after us and didn't fare any better. We had heard so much of Johnny without having actually seen him, so we watched his show and he was brilliant, but still didn't get any attention from the crowd. As he came off stage, we went back into the dressing room where Johnny was nonplussed by the reaction of the audience, and as we tried to console each other with the way things had gone, Johnny just said, 'This place is a graveyard for comedy. I didn't tell you before you went on because you told me it was the first time with your new show. You'll be okay with the rest of your bookings in the area, I'm sure.'

Kind words from Johnny, but Roy and I were so despondent at the response of the first half comedy show that we contemplated packing up and returning to Teesside. Second half, the crowd were pissed off their faces, dancing around like lunatics and wouldn't let us off, so we reluctantly did as few encores as we could get away with, just wanting to get the hell out of the place.

We were due to play Ringland's Social Club in Newport the following night, which was a Saturday, yet we still hadn't convinced ourselves that we shouldn't just get in the car and head off home. We got back to the digs where, after mulling over the events of the evening, it was decided that we would stay in all day Saturday and spruce up our first half comedy show, then see how it went the following night in Newport.

We did as we said, spent all day Saturday working on the act, taking out what we thought had struggled, which was most of it, and replacing it with other things we had up our sleeves, but it was effectively very much the same style of act that we'd performed on that fateful Friday night. Hadn't a clue how it was going to go, but we needn't have worried… we stormed it, had a brilliant night which gave us the impetus and a kick in our step to go on and have a great run in the rest of the South Wales clubs.

Pictured below… Allcock and Brown picking up their first pay packet at Ringland's Social Club in Newport. Chairman doesn't look like he wants to let go of it. Notice the eyes… I'm thinking, 'Bugger me, a whole twenty five quid, I can get a few beers tomorrow night.' Roy's thinking, 'I'm going to go to the bookies in the morning and blow the fucking lot.'

One for you, two for me!

Roy did and still does like a flutter on the horses, but I'm not sure if I'd ever been in a bookies before, didn't know the front of a horse from the back. While we were in Cardiff, with very little to do during the day, Roy decided that the betting shop would be a good way of filling some time in so, as we did everything together, I went along with him. While Roy busied himself studying form, using all the paraphernalia at his disposal, I simply went up to the board, spotted a name on it that I liked the look of, Precious Will, and put my hardearned 50 new pence, as they were called then, on the nose (I'd heard someone else say it while I was standing in the queue to pay).

'It's a fucking donkey!' was Roy's laughing reply when I told him what I'd done. 'It's got no fucking chance.' Then stood in complete silence, with his mouth wide open, as my horse romped home at 25 to 1, while his brought up the rear. From then on just the mention of Precious Will brings groans of disapproval from a disgruntled Roy… still scarred by the incident.

During the week we had occasion to visit Chris Banks, the agent, at his office in Cardiff, where we were greeted at the front door by Chris and his pet Labrador.

We followed Chris and his dog along the passageway and into his office/living room where we sat on a couple of chairs in front of his desk. The Labrador was giving both of us quite a lot of attention but mainly making a big fuss of Roy's bollocks. Roy tried to make a joke of it saying, 'Eeeh, get off me, will ya,' but after pushing him away a few times to no avail, he gave him a rather heavy tap on the end of his nose while Chris had his back turned. The dog gave out a bit of a yelp which made Chris turn around quickly to see what was going on, looking toward both me and Roy as we shrugged our shoulders and shook our heads… dog didn't bother either of us again.

We concluded the ten day run successfully with the first night at Swansea being the only bad night we had.

On returning to Teesside, we started to get regular work and it was decided that Allcock and Brown was worth having a crack at full time, so I handed my notice in and we both became 'full time pros' for the very first time, mainly working the North East club circuit, as well as travelling the country.

Up to then, the recent years had seemed mainly for the young 'uns, but the Workmen's and Social Clubs of the area were still being run by the old guard. Because of this, the sort of comedy that you could get away with in these venues was limited to say the least. You had to be very careful what was said. This became apparent on an evening working Queen's Club, Thornaby, for an all male audience when at half time we were told in no uncertain terms that we wouldn't be required to perform a second spot.

After asking why, it was explained that Roy had said 'bastard' during the act, only once might I add and let's not forget it was an all male audience, but it prompted a small meeting of committee men in the passageway who came to the decision of paying us off early because the act was too blue. Even in those early days that wouldn't be the only time the act would be considered too naughty for certain venues, yet today you will hear far worse in your own front room on the telly.

To perform our shows, we were reliant on the musicians, usually organist and drummer, supplied by the venues, so we had our musical accompaniment professionally transcribed by Gordon Scurr who was the musical director at The South Bank Sporting Club. The musical arrangements, or 'dots' as they were known, were often above the capabilities of your regular club backing because of our many stops and starts throughout, and they would often just busk along in the background.

Allcock and Brown became reasonably popular in North East clubs, then on a night working at The Beechwood and Easterside Club in Middlesbrough, one of Roy's first windows of opportunity opened when Peterlee agent Vince Richardson from Spotlight Promotions was watching in the audience. He approached us after the show and asked if we would like him to become our manager, telling us about all the contacts he had throughout the country and that he could get us work just about everywhere.

Up until then we had been finding our own bookings through different agencies, which in itself was a bit of a pain so, although having not given a decision on the spot and having heard promises of the 'big time' before which never materialised, we eventually decided to give Vince a crack of the whip. He invited us to his office in Peterlee where he had contracts waiting for us, all very official we thought. We signed on the dotted line, effectively allowing Vince to take 15% of anything we earned. What bothered me more was the fact that I was still playing weekend football at the time and Vince told me I had to pack it in because if I had a serious injury or broke anything other than me glasses, the show would be off the road, so I reluctantly agreed.

Vince was true to his word regarding his contacts in the business, as very quickly we were touring the country from Lands End to John o'Groats, doing the same circuit as up and coming acts like Sid and Eddie, who became Little and Large, and Cannon and Ball, while having a great time too.

Gigs were now flowing in with a mixture of club bookings, hen nights, stag nights, corporate shows, weeks here and weeks there… you name it, we were working it. Yes, Vince was definitely keeping us busy, and our little trusty (or was it rusty?) Post Office van was working very hard too.

25

Allcock and Brown were doing okay but, even after having our backing music written perfectly by a professional, the resident musicians at most workmen's clubs were usually employed on a price basis rather than expertise. Most drummers couldn't read music and many organists just couldn't be bothered. They were used to getting their instructions from acts of what to play scribbled on the back of a fag packet, 'If' in f, for example.

There was one night at a club in Doncaster where, part way through our comedy first half, the drummer reached down, picked up a trumpet and blew on it with all of his might, taking us both by surprise. The audience, who all seemed to be waiting for it to happen, cheered and laughed uncontrollably. Seemed he did it to all acts during their first half, just for a laugh, but this time he had done it right on one of Roy's crucial punchlines and he showed his displeasure to the drummer with a glare that would have melted his cymbals. It was probably the fact the drummer was an elderly statesman that saved him from getting his trumpet pushed so far down his throat he'd have to blow up his own arse to get anything like a squeak out of it.

Admittedly that was an extreme example, but it was a case that the resident backing provided at most venues could not keep up with the stops and starts we had in the act to accommodate Roy's quick changes. Having put up with it for so long, we were now getting a bit fed up, and both of us came to the same conclusion that we needed to become a self-contained unit that didn't have to rely on anyone else.

In order to do this, we would have to bring someone else into the act, and we both knew who would fit the bill perfectly… Mick Boothby, who Roy had previously worked with as Jason and Everard. Mick was still doing the clubs as guitar vocalist Oliver Lee and delivering school meals during the day but he was up for it immediately. Mick was initially a bass player and a natural harmony singer, which was what the act needed and, although I knew Mick, I hadn't worked alongside him before, but we hit it off straightaway and he fit into the show like a glove. Sadly, Mick is no longer with us but both Roy and I remember the times we spent together on the road with great affection and regularly have a good laugh at some of the antics that we all got up to.

With the new line up being a trio, we contemplated changing our name, but considering that Allcock and Brown had gained a reasonable reputation, we decided to hang on to it and became Hall, Cock and Brown, with myself and Mick having to toss to see who would be Mr Cock, with myself getting the honour and Mick becoming Mr Hall, Roy retaining his Mr Brown status.

Having watched comedy bands that we admired, such as The Nobodys, Cresters, Paddy Green set, as well as The Rockin' Berries and the Black Abbots, it was noticed that they all looked polished and smart, even if that was only at the beginning of their show. So to achieve this we decided to get ourselves togged up with some proper stage clobber, and the three of us walked into Burton's tailoring shop on Redcar High Street. We must have looked a right sight, both Mick and I had long early seventies hair, with both of us dressed in our scruffs, and Roy was never seen without his blue dungarees, cap and Jesus sandals, which he always found difficult to walk in, blaming me for introducing him to them.

Now, I'm sure these tailor shops would not normally have three grown up blokes coming in together but, nonetheless, the assistant came towards us, rubbing his hands and asking if he could help. Roy said, 'I need a new suit. I've had mine since it was a pair of gloves.' The assistant gave a very polite nervous laugh, obviously still with his mind on any business he could get out of us.

After much deliberation, we came across some striking tartan material that hit us straightaway, and thought it would make a great impact onstage. Mick and I ordered three-piece suits in black and white Shephard's tartan with Roy taking on a more recognisable red and black tartan suit. You could almost feel the assistant's elation at getting rid of some material that had probably been laid around for years gathering dust. Incidentally, the Shephard's tartan has become very popular recently with everything from jackets and trousers to hats and scarves being sported by a very trendy public, but let it not be forgotten who started it all off.

We delayed having publicity photos taken until our new stage clothes had arrived, but once they arrived we booked Johnny Herring to do the job again.

Vince Richardson was still our manager, and initially had been opposed to us becoming a trio, nothing to do with Mick, who he had never met, but I think more to do with the opportunities that were available for a comedy duo. Nonetheless, Vince soon realised that working as a self-contained unit meant we were able to perform venues that had been out of our reach as a duo, so we were soon off and running and back on the road again, still with the Post Office van to start with.

Vince was selling us out to other agents for £225 a week net, that would usually be to complete a set number of shows in seven days which would have included Sunday lunchtimes and 'doubles'… fitting in two clubs a night, normally a social club then going on to a night club.

£225 for a week's work doesn't sound too bad, does it, for the early seventies? That was for three of us, could be anywhere in the country and, as said, would often have us playing two gigs per night. It was classed as good money back in 1974, but we had to pay all our own expenses out of it, including petrol and maintenance for our transport, which by then had become a transit van.

We had persevered with the Post Office van, or Tardis, as we called it, as long as we could but, because we were cramming more gear into it, the only way we could close the back doors was if two of us pushed each side in while the other one quickly turned the door handle and locked it when the doors eventually met up. That was without accommodating three grown up blokes… one of whom was Roy. It was like playing a game of sardines every night.

Also from our pay packets we had to fork out for our own digs, as well as hand over 15% of our fees to Vince, our manager, for getting us the work. As we were now travelling up and down the country, we could be going all the way to the south coast or up to bonny Scotland for the same money. It was a good job none of us had big mortgages or bothered to pay bills because usually, after boozing and betting for the week, we'd come back with nowt.

Working for the princely sum of £225 between us for a week's work, less all expenses, you don't need to be any Carol Vorderman or Rachel Riley to work out that we were probably living on our arses, so when it came to needing new equipment for the show, a certain amount of juggling had to be performed. Having relied on Hamilton's Music Store in Boro for all of our earlier purchases, we'd discovered a company called Bell Accordions in Newton Aycliffe, Co. Durham that was giving credit to anyone who walked through the door that was still breathing, and anybody that played an instrument in the North East took full advantage. I'm guessing most would have ended up in County Court for non-payment.

Roy decided he would like an electric piano and headphones so he could continue practising his new passion while we were on the road. The piano he wanted was in Hamilton's, who were a bit stricter than Bells when it came to offering hire purchase. My mother had a good job and a decent credit rating so she offered to sign the hire purchase contract to get Roy his piano. I think it worked out at £5 a month.

It was planned that each month, Roy would give me his £5 and I would pass it on to my mother, but when the monthly request came along it felt a bit like I was the Provident Man knocking on someone's front door with Roy hiding behind the curtains, pretending not to be in. Roy would always say, 'I never knew what it was like being in fucking debt 'til I met you, George,' before he handed over his fiver.

Mick kept our 'new' tranny van in working order with his excellent knowledge of what went on under the bonnet, whereas Roy and I were only familiar of what might go on in the back of a van if we were ever given the chance. Not that we were. Mick was able to get behind the steering wheel wherever we were in the country, regardless of what time we finished, and bring us safely home even after a skinful, but don't tell anyone.

One night during a long drive home from the South West after being away for a few weeks, there was a problem with the van and Mick had to pull into the hard shoulder of the motorway. It had to be in the early hours of the morning, having not got out of our last venue until well after two am with Mick having enjoyed a few beers, to say the least.

He had his head under the bonnet when a police car pulled up to see what was going on. Roy and myself were watching developments from the comfort of the van, when we saw one of the policemen go back to his car and come back with a torch shining it onto the engine to help Mick see what he was doing. It wasn't long after that Mick got back into the van turned the key, with the van starting up first time. He jumped out, pulled the bonnet back down, shook hands with the policemen, and got back in the van and took us home. Thankfully the traffic cop probably couldn't smell the alcohol on Mick's breath because of the fumes from the engine.

Roy's always been one for getting his words mixed up. Examples are: when talking of the City Birmingham he says 'Berningham', and 'thief' always comes out as 'feeth'. So when, during the day whilst working in Rotherham, the three of us walked into a baker's shop. Roy was first in the queue and asked the lovely looking girl behind the counter if she had a strawberry flange, both myself and Mick knew that he was really asking for a strawberry flan. After seeing the shocked look on the girl's face, and as we couldn't keep a straight face anyway, we turned straight around and went out of the shop. Roy wasn't far behind us, telling us that the manageress, having heard what he had asked for, told him to get out or she'd call the police. Roy said, 'I wouldn't care, I was going to give her a lick of my cream horn,' so on that occasion I'm pretty sure Roy knew exactly what he was asking for.

An indication of how different audiences reacted to the material Roy was doing came as we were returning after a week's visit to workmen's clubs north of the border. Our manager had fixed us up with a Bank Holiday Monday engagement at Seaton Delaval Social Club, the other side of Newcastle, on the way home. Roy had heard a new gag while we'd been away and, although he would normally do his own material, decided to give it an airing during our first half. Make your own decision as to whether it was worth a paying off or not:

Roy says… Teacher says to the class, 'We are going to do some geography. Can anyone tell me where the Nigerian border is?'

Little Tommy jumps up and says, 'He's at home in bed with me mam.'

Can't believe it? Neither could we, but we were escorted out of the club before the bingo started with no pay for the night. To be honest, we weren't all that bothered because, after a week in the Scottish clubs, we were all really just looking forward to getting back home.

There was another occasion where we managed to get paid off from a whole week's work in South Wales. We'd been asked to do a week for an agent called Peter Groves, and he booked us on what turned out to be his own venue, The Candlelight Club in Llanelli. We were scheduled to perform one cabaret show each night from Sunday right through to the following Saturday. On the first night, we put on our usual show which had been going down very well all over the region. This being a dining club with entertainment, it was noted before we went on, that the diners were all holding their cutlery and drinks with their little pinky fingers sticking up into the air.

Being a Sunday night, there were not many people in the club, so the mild applause we got at the end of the show wasn't anything to write home about but we never thought any more about it, took our bows and left the stage. Almost immediately as we got backstage, the dressing room door burst open, and Peter Groves, agent and owner of the club, stepped in not looking very happy, and, before even introducing himself, he turned to Roy, blurting out in quite an effeminate and not too menacing a voice, 'You can't say 'shit' in my club.'

'I didn't say shit, I said shite,' was Roy's immediate stern reply.

Then, looking even more flustered, Mr Groves continued, 'You'll have to do something different or you can't come back tomorrow night,' then, pointing to Roy, he added, while gesticulating the motions, 'Can't you twizzle your drum sticks around your head or something?'

By now myself and Mick were looking at each other anxiously, both of us thinking that if he didn't shut his face, there was only one place that Roy's drumsticks were going and that wasn't around his own head.

We didn't give him an answer immediately, but left it until the next day to inform him that we wouldn't be changing anything in the show so subsequently would not be appearing at his club anymore that week.

It was essential that being such a close-knit unit, in each other's pocket 24/7, that we all got on. We didn't have arguments as such, differences of opinions maybe, though on a night in Gainsborough, Lincolnshire, on leaving the stage after our first set, Roy complained that my guitar playing was too loud and drowning his comedy vocals. I disagreed and a heated discussion followed. Mick could see that Roy was getting agitated and stepped in between us with Roy disappearing out of the dressing room door.

We hadn't a clue where he'd gone so Mick and I just got a drink and parked ourselves at an empty table to relax during our break. We must have been sat there about twenty minutes with no sign of Roy, when he suddenly appeared carrying two double whiskys for me and Mick, sat down and cracked on with nothing else said about the earlier incident. I've never ever mentioned to Roy about me standing directly in front of his drums with every thud ringing in my ears throughout the show, but then again you can't turn a set of drums down, can you?

Top and bottom of it is that we were all good mates and still are to this day, and even though Mick's not around anymore, Roy and I still talk about those times as if he'd never left us.

Hall, Cock and Brown all grown up – in the dressing room at Middlesbrough Town Hall in 2015

26

Hall, Cock and Brown were now regularly on the road and doing well, but of all of the different areas we would work, South Wales was probably our most prolific. It could have been that, coming from the North East and playing clubs in many of the pit villages, there was a similarity between the audiences we had at home and the folk in the valleys.

Generally we performed at social clubs, but one particular week in the middle of the summer of 1974 we were asked to do a Sunday night show at The Queen of Hearts Club in Nelson, South Wales, then go on to do one show at The Stoneleigh Night Club in Porthcawl on the Monday night, returning to finish our run Tuesday to Saturday at The Queen of Hearts Club. We hadn't booked any digs for that week because, up until the previous day, we thought we were going to Nelson in Lancashire and had booked accordingly… we never were any good at geography. We spent the Sunday night after the show sleeping in the van at the top of a Welsh mountain. We didn't have much trouble getting to sleep because we just had to look out of the window to count sheep.

On the Monday morning we set off for Porthcawl on the coast, arriving mid-afternoon and went straight to the club. There we were on the billboard in the club window advertising the forthcoming shows, right alongside big names of the day including Frankie Vaughan and Anita Harris… we thought we'd made the big time. We were the support act for Monday night and were able to get into the club on the afternoon because the top of bill act were rehearsing in the cabaret room.

We walked in and realised that topping the bill was a group called Fairfield Welles. We'd seen them at our own South Bank Sporting Club a few times, and they were brilliant with a fabulous girl lead vocalist. We watched them for a while, introduced ourselves, then set our equipment up in front of theirs, as we would be opening the show later that evening. While setting up, the club manager came in to talk to us about the evening's show during which he asked us where we were staying.

Roy said, 'With some sheep.' We'd still not arranged any digs.

'Some sheep?' asked the manager.

Roy said, 'Yes, some sheep. Looks like we'll be sleeping in the van again.' Then told him why we hadn't arranged accommodation.

The manager said, 'I've got a caravan on the local camp site. There's nobody in it this week… you can use that for tonight, if you like.'

If you like? Too well we'd like, we all agreed. There was four of us that week as my brother had put a week's holiday in and came along on a working holiday as non-driving roadie. At that time, Porthcawl had one of the largest caravan sites in Europe so, after setting our gear up, we got the keys and directions off the manager then went and made ourselves at home for a few hours.

Being in the middle of a hot summer, we were all feeling a bit uncomfortable after our night in the mountains, so Roy was the first to say he was going to take a shower and headed off to the shower block with his towel tucked under his arm. He hadn't been gone very long when he came bouncing back into the caravan shouting, 'I've been stung, I've been fucking stung.' We all turned towards him inquisitively. 'I went for a crap first and a wasp came in and stung me on me fucking arse,' an obviously pained Roy cried out. I don't remember any of us actually inspecting the affected area, but a short sighted wasp had probably been scanning the whole campsite looking for a target big enough that even he couldn't miss before finding it on Roy's derrière. (French wasp… well it had a stripey jumper on).

On the night at The Stoneleigh there was a good holiday crowd in and we were due on for one comedy cabaret spot at 9.30pm with Fairfield Welles topping the bill at 11.00pm. The audience were brilliant and we had a great night, getting brought back for a couple of encores at the end of our show.

The manager thought we'd had such a good night that the following day he informed us that there'd been a change of plan and we were to stay at The Stoneleigh for the rest of the week, sending Fairfield Welles, who'd also been well received by the previous night's audience, to complete their week at The Queen of Hearts in Nelson, leaving us to top the bill at Porthcawl's biggest night club… it was the only one but there you go.

Stoneleigh Club, Porthcawl 1974
Mick, Roy and George
(Not a great picture but it's the only one we've got)

The club manager said we could use the caravan for the rest of the week. It was four berth with a double bed and two singles, Roy and myself squashed into the double… it was what you did when you were on the road. One night after the show, Mick and my brother Colin brought a couple of girls back for the night, entertaining the girls in their front section of the caravan while me and Roy were in the double bed towards the rear. There was a pair of curtains pulled across the middle in a pathetic attempt to give the separate sections a bit of privacy. It didn't work as both myself and Roy crept out of bed in turn to look through the gap in the middle and giggling like little girls at what was going on in the front. It resembled a tag wrestling match I'd watched on World of Sport a few weeks before.

Even though there's only the two of us left to reminisce, we still look back on that week we spent in Porthcawl as one of the best times. It was a new experience for us to be doing a week's work in the same venue, allowing us time to relax through the day before performing on the night, lovely weather, bit of a paid holiday really. We all struck up relationships of a sort, my brother eventually marrying the girl he'd brought back to the caravan that night. Roy, himself, got real 'friendly' with a young local girl, although how friendly, no one ever asked. So, at the end of the week, packing our gear up at 2.00am early Sunday morning after the club had shut, we were all saddened to leave people behind us. None more than Roy.

Topping the music charts at the time, and never off the turntable at the club, were The Three Degrees with When Will I See You Again, which, whenever I hear it, always reminds me of that special week.

On another night in the West Country, Somerset or Cornwall, we'd been asked to do a double, working a social club then going onto a night club and, as it was the weekend during the summer holiday period. When we arrived at the night club, it was packed full of revellers already in party mood with the dance floor swamped. The DJ, who appeared to be in charge, told us that we were to perform on the stage in front of his equipment, but we couldn't see any stage, the whole place was just full of bodies bouncing up and down.

Roy asked sarcastically, 'What stage, mate? It looks like it's fucked off, got the last stage out of town.' None of us were really looking forward to this at all.

'No,' he said, 'the stage is tucked away underneath me, you have to pull it out and set your gear up on it.'

'You're joking, aren't you?' said Roy.

'No,' said the DJ, 'everybody does it. There's three rope handles at the front. It pulls out easily.'

Turning away, Roy muttered, 'For fuck's sake!'

Reluctantly, the three of us went on to the dance floor and pushed our way to the front, then with Mick to the left of me and Roy to the right, we bent down with each of us grasping a roped handle. 'After three,' Roy shouted, then thundered out above the music, 'FOUR!' It was always a little joke of his. We pulled it with all of our might. It was heavier and not as easy as we had been told but still this was showbiz, mate, so get on with it. It was only about a foot high and hardly worth standing on but we eventually got it fully out, and being so heavy it was dropped with quite a thump.

Being the summer, I had taken to wearing Jesus sandals – no socks, of course – and when the stage was dropped, it marginally missed my exposed toes but landed on the small bit of leather sandal that was protruding at the front. Job done, Roy and Mick buggered off back to the van to bring the gear in, but what they didn't know was that my sandals were now trapped under the stage and I couldn't move. There were people dancing about me and, as it was difficult to keep my balance, I just looked like one of them. Thankfully it wasn't too long before Roy appeared with part of his drum kit and spotted me. After showing him what had happened, he couldn't stop laughing, but still wouldn't help me out of my predicament until Mick came back in so he could show him too. After lifting the 'stage' so I could get my feet out, Roy said, 'We wondered where you were… thought you'd pissed off to the bar again.'

Pissed again!
Late pint at our digs, Station Hotel in Shotts,
during a small tour of Scottish workies in 1974

Roy looks back on his group days as some of the happiest of his career. There are many more stories from those days. Some have already been told, some will have to be kept for a later date though most, unfortunately, will never be told, having sadly lost so many original band members, together with their memories, over the years. So it is important that those of us who are left recollect whatever we can before we all lose our marbles, leaving the history of Roy Chubby Brown's rise to comedy stardom unfinished.

Hall, Cock and Brown came to a natural ending over the Christmas of 1974. Roy teamed up with a comedy impressionist called Terry

Harris, who had been front man for North East group, Sugar and Spice. Mick and I stayed together as a duo calling ourselves Tim Buck Two for the next ten years, before I realised I didn't have any talent and became an entertainment agent.

Drumming with Allcock and Brown – Station Hotel, Shotts, 1974

Immaculately ready for stage at Allcock and Brown's 2nd gig – Ringland's Social, Newport, 1973

If the cap fits, 1973

27

Roy frequented the Stockton Fiesta regularly during 1974, meeting up with other acts for a drink and wind down after gigs. It was there that he came across Terry Harris. Terry was a talented front man for a North East show group called Sugar and Spice, and he did impressions of popular TV characters of the time, such as Frank Spencer and Norman Wisdom.

Roy says, 'I was talking to Terry at the bar in the Fiesta one night and told him I was thinking of going on my own.' He said, 'So am I. Why don't we form a duo?' I said, 'I don't know, I'll have to think about it.' Terry said, 'I can play guitar for you while you do your routines. They always want two spots, then you play the drums and I'll do the singing for the second half.' I thought it would be so much easier than having to do it all on my own.'

It sounded like a good idea… two comedians on stage together should get laughs from start to finish. The act had to be funny, there would have been no doubt about that. The problem was a clash of personalities, and, alas, it turned out to be a mismatch not quite made in heaven. I have known Roy for fifty years plus now and am very aware that apart from professional expertise and willingness to do the job, any co-worker connected with Roy has to be 'the right person'. Most of Roy's current entourage have been with him for thirty years plus. That continuity would not have been possible without a bit of give and take… a vital necessity for creating a successful team.

Roy continues, 'We rehearsed and got back on the road. I did all of the slapstick I'd been used to in the bands and Terry did the more straight type of comedy with his impressions. I think he had about half a dozen or so.'

Roy and Terry kept the name of Allcock and Brown but with neither of them acting as a straight man, the show looked more like two gladiators battling to see who could get the best laughs each night. Roy continued to write new material, generously penning one song that would bring in Terry's comedy impressions. Roy had always been happy to let someone else get the laugh if it was better for the act. Roy would perform some of the quick-change routines that had been perfected for his earlier shows.

'It was working quite well for a time, but the longer we worked together, the more I realised it wasn't working.'

Let's not go into detail, but it was one thing after another.

Roy resigned himself to the fact that him and Terry weren't right for each other and after about six months or so Roy says, 'I was trying to get round to telling Terry that I couldn't work with him anymore.' But he came to me saying that Brenda, his girlfriend, had suggested to Terry that he was a lot better than I was, that he was carrying the show and he should go on his own. He said, 'I'm thinking of going solo, Roy.' I said, 'When are you going to do that?' He said, 'Well I've booked myself out next Sunday.' I said, 'What about me?' I'd been playing the banjo, ukulele, drum solo, as well as my comedy while he did a few impressions. He said, 'Oh, you'll manage.' So we went our separate ways and I was taken on by Brian Findlay, a Middlesbrough agent.'

Roy hadn't told Terry, or anyone else for that matter, but he had applied to appear on the top TV talent show of the day, Opportunity Knocks, hosted by Hughie Green. It had uncovered a wealth of talent including Freddie Starr, Bonnie Langford, Frank Carson, to name but a few. Roy travelled to London to attend auditions for the show. He says, 'I didn't tell anyone I was going. I'd applied at a time when I was leaving the group, before me and Terry had got together and didn't get a reply until months later. I just thought it best not to say anything and go on my own 'cos I didn't know how it would go. At the audition I bumped into the likes of Les Dawson and Little and Large, who had all been doing the same circuit of social club as I had. We were all looking for that next step up the ladder of success. I waited quite a long time to do my audition, then had to perform in front of a panel of judges who would decide if I was good enough for the TV show. Hughie Green himself wasn't there. After the audition, one of the judges came to me and said, 'Roy, you're a very funny man, but you just can't say 'arse' on the telly.' Well, you couldn't then, so unfortunately opportunity didn't knock for me on that day.'

Brian Findlay, having taken up the reigns of arranging Roy's bookings, helped him get back on the road.

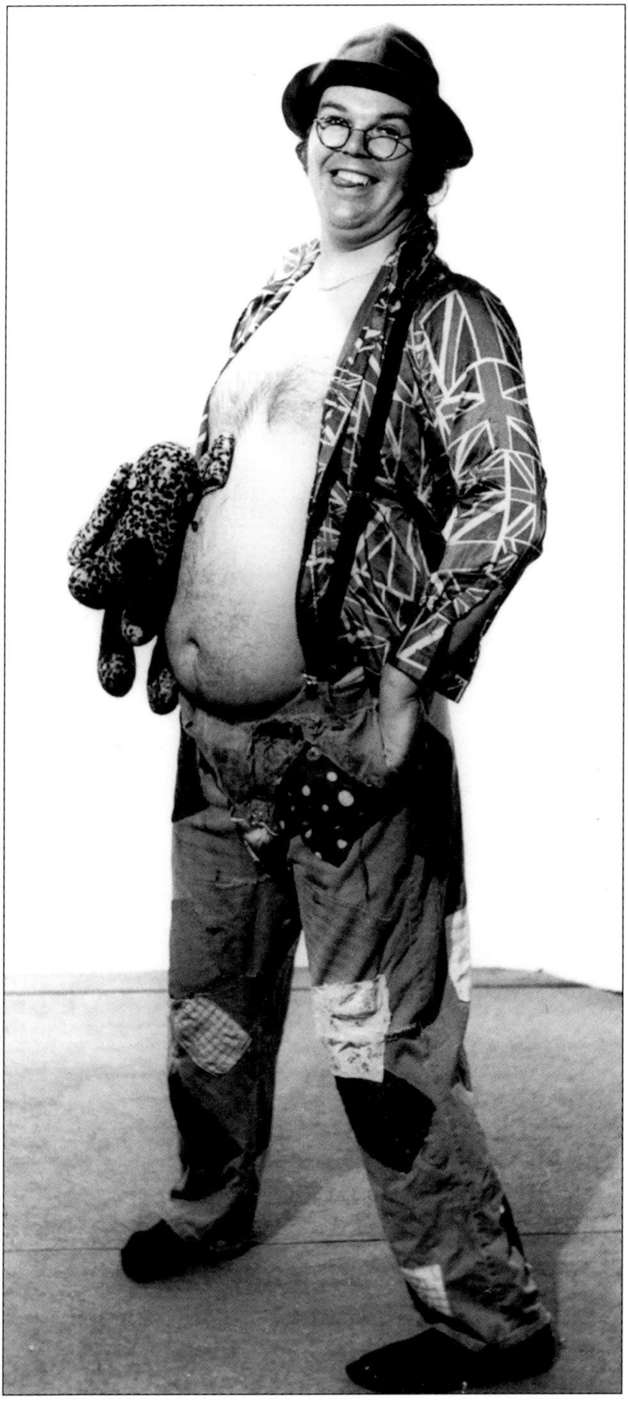

'My first gig was at West Denton Social Club in Newcastle, but when I turned up at the club and looked at the poster advertising the night's show, I got the shock of my life, I was only on with Terry fucking Harris guitar vocalist. I couldn't believe it. We said fuck all to each other. It had been booked through a third party so Brian wouldn't have known who the other act would be. Terry went on first, so I stood at the back to watch his show. He did all of my jokes, all of my routines. I said to the chairman, 'It's pointless me going on, mate.' He said, 'Why?' I said, ''cos that twat up there's just done my act.' He said, 'All of your act?' I said, 'Yeah, we were together as a duo for six or seven months and he's obviously remembered every routine.' The chairman said, 'Well, what're you gonna do?' I said, 'I'll just go home.' He said, 'No, no, go on.' Anyway I went on and fucking tore 'em apart. I just told gags. Pointless doing any of my routines… had a great night so that was one up his fucking arse, wasn't it?'

The reality was that Mr Allcock had jettisoned from the cockpit and from that date on Mr Brown was destined to fly solo. With even Roy totally unaware of where he was going, the only thing for certain though was that there were bound to be a few crash landings on the way.

28

Under Brian Findlay's wing, Roy was now getting plenty of work appearing as Roy Brown, still doing mainly social and workmen's clubs predominately in the North East. Though, still being without a full licence and proper transport, he was finding it difficult to get to gigs, Roy would ask mates for a lift. Jim Rudd, who'd been the roadie with Pipeline and Dek Vasey's Band for a while, would help out when he could, but was unable to do it permanently as he had a full time job.

Brian's sister, Val, was married to Steve Pinnell, and Brian asked him if he fancied doing a bit of driving for a new act he had on his books. He said to Steve, 'There's a new comedian working for me but he hasn't got a driving licence and needs someone to run him to his bookings, do you fancy doing it?' Steve said, 'Who is it?' Brian replied, 'Roy Brown, have you heard of him?' 'Bloody hell,' said Steve, 'that's the bloke we saw at The Coronation. He's dead funny.'

Steve says, 'We'd been to my wife's uncle's funeral recently and had all arranged to just go for a drink on the night deciding to go to a local pub, The Coronation Hotel on Acklam Road. When we arrived at the pub, we noticed there was entertainment on in the function room upstairs. There was a poster in the window advertising Roy Brown, local comedian. We'd never heard of Roy Brown before, but needed cheering up so we all went upstairs and found ourselves a table. Roy was on his own as a stand-up comedian, and when he came on, he had everyone in the room absolutely rolling about laughing. I thought he was the funniest person I'd ever seen, so when Brian asked if I fancied driving him to gigs, I said yes straightaway.'

Brian Findlay, sadly, another no longer with us, was a larger than life type of bloke, always called a spade a spade and created a 'presence' wherever he went in his own likeable way. People enjoyed being around him, especially club committee men who would expect a pint or two to be bought for them for allowing Brian to put his 'turns' on in their club. Brian was very likely just the man

Roy needed at that time, having broken his ties with earlier manager Vince. Brian and Roy worked together on trust, with nothing ever needing to be in writing and it worked well. Roy's association with Brian Findlay became more like that of a mate.

Steve was only too happy to take Brian's request on board, probably regarding it as no more than a second job to go with his bread deliveries. Little did Steve know that this part-time job of running Roy Brown to his bookings would be the start of a string of events which would dramatically change the rest of his life.

Roy thrives on the company of others, and it had been the case that up until this period of his career, he always had someone else to travel to gigs with him, and then not leave his side throughout his act… a bit of a comfort blanket, you might say. So, without the safety net of being in a band or a duo, whoever became associated with Roy would become more than just a driver, as long as he was the right person for the job, almost a non-performing straight man, if you like.

Steve's first job with Roy was picking him up at Beryl's house in Norfolk Close. Roy was still living in the flat above the hairdressers but spent a lot of his time at Beryl's house on the Lakes Estate in Redcar. Steve drove Roy to a club in the Newcastle area and had a great night. Only ever having seen Roy the once before, Steve thought the show was hilarious and by the end of the night, having dropped Roy back off at home, they were both getting on so well it was agreed that he would become Roy's regular driver.

Steve and Roy

Steve was also working as a bread delivery man, driving a van throughout the Teesside area, so, although it sometimes meant quite long days, running Roy to his gigs fit in well with his deliveries being early mornings.

Steve had been happy enough with his lot up until then, having only recently married Val and didn't really think too far into the future, but the friendship he was about to strike up with Roy would eventually lead to an encounter that would change his life forever.

Steve's second night with Roy was a bit different. They were to go over to Brough, which is just off the A66 on the edge of the Lake District. Dek Vasey came along as he would sometimes accompany Roy on keyboards if there was no backing provided, though he didn't play that night.

Roy was introduced and started his show and was going down quite well with the crowd, but there was a drunk sat with his mates that insisted on shouting out right at the end of some of Roy's jokes as he was about to say the punchline.

Steve said that even though they'd got on so well on that first night, he still didn't really know too much of Roy apart from the reputation that came with him from Grangetown.

After Roy had finished his spot, Roy asked Steve if he'd go over and bring the lad who'd been shouting out into the dressing room. Steve says, 'I never thought anything about it, so went over to the lad and said, 'Roy wants to have a chat with you.' 'Oh,' he said, 'great,' then followed me back to the dressing room. I went in first and he came straight in behind me, but as he came through the door, Roy hit him so hard that he went straight out again backwards. I'd never seen anything like it before, certainly the hardest punch I'd ever seen, but then I'd led a very sheltered life in comparison.'

Steve still portrays a shocked look on his face even now as he finishes the story. 'Roy stood over this chap on the floor, half in and half out of the dressing room and said, 'If you and your fucking mates are still out there when I come out, you're all gonna get it, now fuck off.' I was shocked thinking fu-u-ucking hell, then turned to see Dek, who was still sitting in the dressing room with a look on his face as though he'd seen it all before.'

Steve says, 'Even though I'd been brought up in the centre of Middlesbrough, I'd never seen anyone like Roy in action. I knew who were the hardest lads in Boro and the ones to avoid, but Roy was from a different neck of the woods and it was pretty obvious from day one that he wasn't going to let anyone mess him around. Roy was always happy to oblige with autographs, photos and a bit of banter, but anyone who crossed him or annoyed him would have to be prepared to face the consequences. Anyone would have to be a fool to upset him.' Steve adds, 'Roy was the man, no doubting, he was the man.'

On a more personal note, 1976 saw Roy lose his father and, even though he had a tough upbringing at the hands of his dad, Roy absolutely worshipped him, crediting him with handing down the hard-working ethic that he still carries today. It was a sad time.

THE GREATEST MAN IN THE WORLD MY DAD xxxxxx

BORN 1909
DIED 1976

I WAS FOURTEEN ON HOLIDAY IN BLACKPOOL 1959

From the first time Steve got to know him, he says that Roy was fantastic with his family. Steve recollects, 'Mam was very prudish but she loved Roy and would stick up for him if anyone complained about him being crude or anything, but wouldn't go to see any of his shows. Dad loved him too, but it was the fact that my straight-laced mam could see beyond the act and into the fellow behind the mask, seeing what he was really like. Roy was always so nice to them both.'

Steve adds, 'Roy was always generous to a fault, bringing Christmas presents and the like for my three children. I'd never known anyone who was so genuine. Even now, when you say that you've had mates in your life but you've had maybe four or five max that you could call real mates who you'd die for and could trust them with anything, Roy is what I've always been able to call a real mate, probably from day one.'

Steve had a desire to play the drums, with his dad having been in a big band. His dad had sold his kit when he got married, leaving himself with an old snare drum which Steve walloped from time to time, nothing too serious though, just annoying for the neighbours. But meeting Roy had rekindled Steve's passion for drumming, with Roy saying, 'Why don't you take it up properly?'

Roy would practice the piano on a daily basis in his flat, and he encouraged Steve to buy a practice pad, which was a quieter version of a snare drum that gave a muffled thud instead of a loud bang, to play along with him. After bookings they would regularly go back to the flat with a Chinese meal and listen to some of the great albums Roy would play, such as George Benson, and George Duke who was a brilliant American keyboard player.

Steve says they had some fantastic times but also, inevitably, got into a few scraps along the way. In fact, Roy's appearances in the social clubs of the North East became an indication of how determined Roy was to fight his way to the top.

There was one night when Brian had booked him into a club further north through another agency. The way that agencies worked was to swap acts with each other in order to give their venues a greater variety. It was the agent's first booking in the club and if everything went well they were going to let him send acts there for the next three months… a big deal for any agent in the North East.

Steve says, 'When Roy went on stage, the room was almost empty, apart from a large table right at the front which was occupied by a group of lads.' Roy's act was a mixture of his own material with the odd standard gag thrown in, and these lads were being a bit rowdy and disruptive.

Steve continues, 'Roy was having difficulty being heard and started to become agitated but continued with his act until one of the crowd started to shout out what he thought was the ending to a few of Roy's jokes. That was it… Roy just walked off the stage, approached the table full of lads and whacked the offender over the head with his microphone. He then, quite calmly, disappeared into the dressing room, leaving the enraged group of lads looking at each other in utter disbelief as to what had just happened then, as a unit, they stood up and headed toward the side of the stage in the direction of Roy's dressing room, obviously not looking for an autograph. I wasn't far from the dressing room so I managed to reach it and get inside and lock the door before they got there.'

'Almost immediately there was banging on the door, together with angry voices intimating that they wanted to get their hands on Roy. Roy said to me, 'Let 'em in!' which I didn't. He'd probably have flattened the lot singlehandedly, but after he'd said it there was a lighter knock on the door with a timid sounding voice saying, 'Let me in, I'm the Club Secretary.' I opened the door slightly, letting him squeeze in through the gap, with the baying lads right behind him, and pushed the door closed, locking it again for safety. 'We're going to have to give you an escort out of the club. They're all waiting for you 'cos you've hurt one of their mates. A few of the committee are going to make sure they leave the club, but they could be waiting for you outside."

'It went quiet,' says Steve, 'so the secretary and a couple of his mates sneaked us both down some fire escape stairs at the back of the club and out into the car park where our car was. We got in it and sped off away from the club.' Steve says he's pretty sure that the police had been called but they managed to get away before they arrived.

It was never established if the club had been impressed enough to give the agent the three months' worth of bookings he'd been hopeful of getting… somehow I don't think so!

Roy would regularly take his own backing with him on bookings if there wasn't going to be any provided or sometimes just to make sure the right notes got played in the right places. As well as Dek, other musicians who would go along were Billy Jarrett and Alan

Anderson, and their memories and stories of their time are very much the same as Steve's. They had many great nights but the ones that really stick in the mind are when Roy whacked someone over the head with his microphone, which appeared to have happened more than just the once.

Seaham Knack Social Club jumps into Steve's mind as a memorable night, where on arriving at the club, having to walk the full length of the concert room to get to the dressing room, they couldn't help noticing that the place was predominantly filled with male members who looked almost glued to their chairs as if they hadn't moved from them in a long time. In these clubs, members often had their own regular seats and woe betide anyone who might come in before them and nick it.

Steve and Roy were already wondering how his act was going to go down with these people when something quite astonishing happened. Steve says, 'Roy was just about to go on being around 8.30pm, the chairman had the microphone in his hand ready to introduce him, when suddenly the main door leading to the concert room burst open and a chap with a flat cap shouted at the top of his voice, 'THE PIGEON'S ARE BACK!' The whole audience turned round with the male members, who were obvious pigeon fanciers, jumping up and rushing for the door, leaving just a handful of people for Roy to entertain.' Steve says, 'It appears that the men in the room had all come in for a few pints while they waited for their pigeons to return after a race. I'd heard about stuff like this happening from different acts thinking they were just pulling my leg, but now having seen it for myself, I could tell it as one of my club tales.'

After about a year having practised solidly under Roy's guidance and tuition, Steve was ready to take up the reigns and started to back Roy on certain gigs with Dek still playing keyboards. It was at a club in Bishop Auckland where they were both due to support Roy, backing him on such ditties as Jollity Farm, amongst others. The lads had been busy setting up on the stage, Steve setting his drums up and placing Roy's props out which included his imitation dog, complete with flying helmet ready for the show, when he noticed someone at the side of the stage digging at Roy with his index finger, having a right old go at him.

Steve says, 'I went over and I could see that Roy was getting to the point where he'd had enough. We'd worked together long enough now for me to be able to see in his eyes when he was about to blow. It appeared that this chap was the Club Secretary and was insisting on Roy doing two spots. Comedians rarely did two spots and Roy was refusing to do so at the same time as the secretary was insisting he did.' Steve carries on, 'I could see the signs and decided to squeeze in between them, facing the secretary and practically begging him to let it go, when BANG! Roy's arm came from nowhere and his fist landed firmly on the secretary's chin. Roy then calmly instructed both Dek and myself to pack all of the gear away saying, 'Fuck 'em, we won't be going on here tonight.' Expecting to be in a load of trouble, there were club members coming over, saying that the secretary was right up his own arse and he'd been asking for something like that for years. Dek and I packed up as quickly as we could and got it all in the car because we knew that not everyone would have the same view, and the police could be turning up any minute. Returning to the concert room to tell Roy we were ready to go, he came out of the dressing room carrying his suit bag and we all left the room via the main door. It was quiet at the top of the stairs and Roy noticed an industrial hoover standing on its own in a corner. He pointed to it and said, 'Grab that, it's going with us.' I said, 'We can't do that, we might get pulled up on the way home,' to which Roy replied, 'Look, we aren't going on so we're not getting paid, that'll pay for the petrol we've used.' So we humped it down two flights of stairs and made a clean getaway. Didn't hear any more about it.'

It has been a difficult task putting precise dates on some of these events but Steve particularly remembers a night when he dropped Roy off at his flat. He was driving home along a stretch of road at the base of the Cleveland Hills, known as the Parkway, when Elvis Presley's death was announced on the radio… 16th August 1977. He said, 'It was such a shock that he nearly had to stop the car and pull over.' For those of us who were around and having been brought up with the King, I think we can all remember where we were when we first heard of his death. It certainly gives us a fix on one date during the period that Steve was working with Roy.

29

I had been working in Guitarzan, which was a music shop in South Bank at the same time as Roy was getting his bookings through the Brian Findlay Agency. Brian had been looking for an extra hand to help out in his office, and Roy asked me if I fancied it.

Although Roy and I were now not working together on stage, we were still buddies and regularly socialised together. I'd had enough of working in the shop. Teenagers were coming in who knew more about the guitars we were selling than I did, so I asked Roy if he'd put a word in for me. He did just that and I started working in Brian's office, arranging bookings for his acts, which included Roy himself.

Mick Boothby and myself were still doing the clubs as a duo, getting our bookings through another agency, so it made sense to have our gigs put through Brian's office. I was fixing our jobs as well as Roy's so it would be a regular occurrence that we were on the same bill together. He would often join us after he'd done his comedy set, playing drums for our second half dance spot using the club's drums… just like old times.

I enjoyed my new role as theatrical agent but by then Roy had become a bit of a hot potato. We still didn't know who his audience really was. He'd already been barred out of several clubs in the area, including The Dorman's Club in Middlesbrough, where, on the big opening night of the new concert room, during his act he inadvertently made a comment about the size of the Lord Mayor's wife's knockers. Then there was an occasion at the South Bank St Peter's Club when Roy made derogatory remarks about a local bag lady who used to roam the streets, only to find out she was related to one of the committee men.

That was without him being booked for the local police annual ball at the Marton Country Club where his opening gambit was, 'My wife's got two cunts, I'm one of them,' which was received in deathly silence. Roy still thinks the lads who booked him for that night only did it to get up the noses of the bigwigs and their wives who'd be there.

Roy had made his first saleable piece of merchandise in the form of a cassette tape from one of his shows. He would sell them from the front of the stage at the end of a gig. On a night at the Richardson and Westgarth's Social Club in Hartlepool, there was quite a demand for his tapes, and while Roy was selling them a thug pushed his way to the front and just took one. Roy said, 'That'll be five pounds, please,' but the lad just turned his back on him and walked away.

Roy says, 'I followed him back to his seat where he was with a few of his mates. I said again, 'You owe me five pounds for the tape.' He said, 'I'm not paying you,' so I asked his mates who were with him, 'Did you lads get a tape?' They answered, 'Yes we did.' I said, 'Did you pay for it?' They said, 'Yes we did.' So I said, 'Then why does your fucking mate think he doesn't have to?' then I whacked him so hard he flew backwards over the table behind him, scattering the drinks everywhere. I picked up the tape that he'd stolen off me and went back to packing my equipment away. It wasn't long before the entertainment secretary came over to tell me that I'd just thumped a member of the roughest family in Hartlepool and if I had any sense, I'd pack my gear up and get out as quick as I could 'cos he'd gone off to round up his brothers to come back and sort me out.'

It was during my time at Brian's office that a disaster happened while Roy was on holiday in Malta. Norman Wales worked part-time in the office, drawing posters, and he was also entertainment secretary at the local Acklam Garden City Club, responsible for choosing acts to appear on his club, and during Roy's time with Brian's office he had struck up a friendship with Roy. Norman and his wife – Louvaine, know as Lou – went on holiday to Malta with Roy, Beryl, Marty Miller, from the fruit and veg stall, and Marty's wife, Susan. They'd been to Malta before and enjoyed it so much that it became one of their favourite places to visit.

I can remember it like it was yesterday… it was a Sunday morning and I was at home getting ready for football – I played Sunday League for South Bank St Peter's Club – when the phone rang. It was Davy Rich. He said, 'There's been an accident in Malta involving Roy.' There hadn't been much information available at that time so Davy was only able to tell me that they'd all been in a car when it was swept away in a flood. I was shaken, didn't really feel like footy anymore but not wanting to let the team down, I played, but I can't really say I was there in spirit with my sole thought being, 'I hope Roy's okay, as well as everyone else.'

As the day went on, more information was coming through and it appeared that on the island of Malta it was unusual for them to have any rain at all, but when it did happen it could often cause flash floods. I found out from Roy later that the storm had been forecast – and they'd seen it hovering the night before over Sicily – but no one could have expected what happened.

They had been out in two cars – Marty, Susan and Beryl in one, and Roy, Norman and Lou in the other. The first car had set off before hand and got back to the hotel safely, while the other car was some time behind and felt the full force of the storm. It appears that the storm was the worst the island had endured in eighty years, and caused the reservoir at the craft village of Mosta, which was at the top of the bank they'd just come down, to burst its walls. It caused a deluge of 1,000,000 gallons of water to rush down the bank straight toward the car they were travelling in.

It was so bad that it started coming into the car, which was in danger of being swept away and, with no time to spare, Roy thought it would be safer to get out and find something sturdy to cling on to. There were trees alongside so very quickly it was decided that if they could each get behind a tree trunk, they'd be able to hold on until the worst had passed.

It proved more difficult than they thought with the strength of the water rushing past, but Roy and Norman helped Lou get to a safe point when there was a sudden extra surge and she lost her grip on the tree she'd been holding onto. They were helpless to respond as it happened so quickly with Roy remembering that within a split second Lou had disappeared over a dry stone wall, and didn't stand a chance. As you can imagine, they were devastated, as we all were back home, when Lou was found later in the sea a few miles away.

Roy and Norman returned to Malta at a later date when a memorial was erected onshore near the spot where Lou had been found. Roy had no option but to get back to work, but how do you recover from an incident such as that? I know it will stick in my mind forever and I wasn't even there. Roy said that a few years later they visited the site again to find that the plaque that had been erected in remembrance of Lou had been removed. It had been transferred to a section in a nearby graveyard where others who had suffered similar tragedies were laid to rest too.

Getting back to making people laugh for a living was tough for Roy but never was the old motto 'the show must go on' to become much more fitting than it was then.

Brian Findlay secured Roy a spot on the huge TV talent show of the day, New Faces, and Steve Pinnell went along with them to support Roy. It was a cross between Britain's Got Talent and The X Factor, and had followed on the tails of Hughie Green's Opportunity Knocks. Acts had to audition just to get on the show, so to be chosen to appear was already a huge achievement for Roy in itself.

Roy's New Faces Audition
With Tubby Ayton on bass and Paul Smith on drums in the background

Steve remembers what a great experience it was. I watched it on telly. We were all excited to see Roy for the first time on the box. There was a panel of 'experts' who would give their opinion on the performances in front of them and with it still being a time when Roy was trying to entertain workmen's club audiences, his script was quite tame from the material you would hear today.

He had his dog with him, stood by his side wearing an old pilot's helmet as it always did. Roy did a few cracks, finishing off with one of his comedy songs on the piano. He wouldn't have got away with Dolly Parton's Tits or Santa, Where's Me Fucking Bike, so again he had to keep the tone of his lyrics down.

The judging panels on New Faces were renowned as a tough lot with Tony Hatch (The Hatchet Man) being particularly hard to please. The judges had three categories that they could award up to ten points for: talent, performance and star quality. One of the panel on that day was Tony Blackburn, who gave Roy quite a good score, but likened Roy's comedy song and piano playing to being quite similar to the Tigger song from Winnie-The-Pooh… somehow I don't think he'd be thinking that of any of Roy's current comedy songs.

Roy came second on the show to a country and western band, leaving TV as probably not the medium that would turn him into a superstar. If Roy was to achieve his goal of becoming the best in his business, he was going to have to do it all by himself without the help of television exposure… their loss.

Steve Pinnell worked as Roy's driver, occasionally accompanying him on drums for around two and a half years from mid-1975… the best part of Roy's early solo career. Eventually, prompted by Roy's encouragement, Steve started getting some top drumming gigs so had to curtail his professional involvement with Roy. Although sad to be losing Steve, Roy was only too happy that he'd been able to help him follow his dream.

Steve says, 'I had a fantastic time working with Roy, even though we did get into quite a few scrapes along the way.' Then adds, 'I'll always be indebted to Roy for helping me achieve a lifestyle I could have only dreamt about in the days when I was delivering bread.'

New Faces

30

This was a time of experimentation for Roy and he was writing more of his own material, pushing boundaries even further, which from time to time got him into trouble with the more prudish of venues, sometimes to the point where he might even get barred from appearing at that venue ever again. Roy already had a number of clubs under his belt that refused to have him on. We are talking about mainly north east social clubs here and Roy was getting a bit of a reputation for sailing a bit to close to the wind. In many ways, the reaction Roy was getting from some clubs with his no nonsense style of comedy was similar to the reaction Elvis got from American puritans when he introduced rock 'n' roll to the masses… though without Roy having to swivel his pelvis or put a rolled up sock down the front of his pants.

Roy would say, 'It used to be all rock 'n' roll', nowadays it's all cock 'n' dole.'

In those early solo days, the further north Roy ventured into Geordieland, the harder it became to sustain the attention of audiences. It was almost as though the Newcastle and Sunderland audiences refused to laugh at anyone from the Boro, there having always being a bit of rivalry in the area… especially on the football field. There were quite a few Geordie comics doing the club circuit, including 'The Little Waster' Bobby Thompson, Bobby Pattinson, Bobby Knoxall and Alan Snell amongst others, and if audiences laughed at a Teesside comic, it was as if they were being unfaithful to their own. It was more likely that, with Roy bringing his own material with him, which his home area of Teesside had already warmed to, it would have been a bit of a shock to the system for anyone else.

At Roy's first ever solo visit to the Doxford Park Club in Sunderland, not going down very well and getting some abuse from a table at the front, Roy admits that, having had enough, he simply just walked off in the middle of his act. The entertainment secretary followed him into the dressing room, not best pleased, and said, 'The family on the table at the front that you upset are the hardest lot in the area so watch yourself when you leave the club.'

Roy said, 'I just walked off, didn't say fuck all to them.'

Secretary said, 'Just watch yourself, that's all.'

Roy says that he had been warned by a couple of his comedy friends not park his car directly outside the club, so he'd parked a couple of streets away. Now he had the task of getting to his car so far away without being tackled by the family.

Roy got changed and packed his suit away, then left through a back door leading straight into the car park. When he opened the door, he noticed there was a white van with no wheels standing on bricks.

There was a group of big lads standing nearby and one of them shouted, 'You won't get very far in that, will you, fatty?' while the others were laughing.

'No', Roy replied, 'you're right, I won't, and neither will the bloke it belongs to either,' then legged it across the car park, before they realised what was happening.

There were a few personalities at the time using the name Chubby who were doing very well with it so, after looking in the mirror, realising that was a good description of himself, decided give himself a middle name, and Roy Chubby Brown was officially born.

Roy says, 'I was sick of people calling me fat cunt, so I thought if I gave myself a fatty type name it would stop, and it did, for a while, though now 'You Fat Bastard' has become something of a trademark. I do remember one well-to-do girlfriend taking me home to meet her posh parents, who were ever so pleased that she'd got herself a boyfriend with a double barrelled surname. 'I don't think we've met the Chubby-Browns,' said her snooty mother.'

Roy adds, 'One of my first gigs as Chubby was at short notice, standing in for someone who couldn't make it that night, so there wasn't a poster up advertising me. The chairman came into the dressing room and looked at me with a puzzled look on his face. I said, 'What's up?' 'Well,' he said, 'I hope you don't mind me saying, but I thought you were black, Mr Checker.' The dozy cunt had thought he'd been sent American singer Chubby Checker who sang Let's Twist Again... for fifty quid. I did sing the first line when I went on stage, but nobody was fooled.'

As well as expanding his stage act and enhancing his name to try and stand out, Roy was very conscious of the impact his visual image would make, not wanting to be yet another comedian in a two piece suit. From the early days of scouring second hand shops for the crazy gear we sported as Dek Vasey's Four Man Band to the tartan outfits we had made for Allcock and Brown, now, as a solo artiste, he wanted to make an impression from the minute he bounced onto the stage.

Roy had been collecting towelling beer cloths, the type that used to be placed on bars to soak up any spillages. They were supplied by brewers and were usually bright gaudy items with the brewer's logos emblazoned on them for advertising. I'm not sure Roy really knew what he was ever going to do with them, but he'd collected a big black bag full and thought it would be great to have a stage suit made from them.

My mother, Emily, was a tailoress. She would make wedding and bridesmaid dresses, and made most of the clothes I had worn whilst growing up as money was tight in the 50s and 60s. Not like my trousers though… she wouldn't make me any drainpipes.

Roy asked her if she could turn this big bag full of beer cloths into a two-piece suit. She took up the challenge and got her sewing machine out. I say 'out', but it was always a permanent fixture on the dinner table. When the suit was complete, you can see from the photo that the result was quite effective. Roy would definitely have stood out in an identity parade.

Even though eye-catching and doing the job as it was intended to do by grabbing peoples' attention immediately, because it was made of towelling material, this suit was never going to have a very long shelf life. Roy says, 'It had to go anyway. I was sick of people throwing beer over me.'

Unperturbed, Roy had been collecting again. This time he'd managed to amass another large black bag full of what looked like somebody's discarded old rags. I can remember him tipping them out on my mother's living room floor and asking, 'What can you do with them then?' My mother was only 4 foot 10 inches tall and almost disappeared under the huge pile in the middle of the floor.

Roy explained what he wanted the end result to look like. He said, 'I want it to remind me of my agent... small cheques.' So with Mam having already got Roy's measurements from the previous suit and a simple glance telling her that he hadn't been on a diet just said, 'Leave it with me and I'll give it a go.' There was never any doubt that she'd come up with the goods but would be amazed, if she was still here today, to see that the result would turn out to be such an iconic trademark for Roy Chubby Brown.

Roy wearing his very first checked suit

A suit with so many elements in it would inevitably suffer from wear and tear considering Roy's hectic schedule and quick changes during his act. Eventually the baton was taken over by future driver Peter Richardson's wife, Lynne, in the mid 80s. Lynne took over the task of maintaining Roy's suits and also making new ones in the same vein, doing a fantastic job for thirty years until, only a matter of a few years ago, ill health forced her to pass on the huge responsibility of Roy's instantly recognisable suits to Ann Coulson.

The effect the suit has had on Roy's following army has been immense to the point that a number of his fans have had their own versions made and turn up at venues wearing them, although it has to be said that you need to be a certain shape to show a 'Chubby' suit off at its best.

Roy with 'The Chubbettes' in Sheffield

We even have a Teesside lad who puts his 'Chubby' suit on when he turns up to support the Boro on match days… watching the Boro always has been a bit patchy though.

Like the chrysalis turning into a beautiful butterfly, Roy's transformation was almost complete. Still yet to be crowned as Britain's bluest comedian, with his new middle name and unique attire to go with it, the Roy Chubby Brown that we all know and love today is almost within touching distance… all we need now are a few mucky jokes to go with it.

31

If you're in the entertainment business, whether a pub singer, club act or a big name, you will generally be asked from time to time to do a charity show. The first occasion will be when you approach an agent for work where, unless you are a well-known act within the business, he or she will say, 'I'll put you on a charity show so I can come and have a look at you'. For the social or workmen's club instead of 'charity show' read 'freebie', as this is definitely an occasion where charity begins at home.

Clubs would expect a charity show from agents in repayment for allowing them to put acts into their venue for a month or more, with the nominal entrance fee going toward their chosen charity plus anything from the likes of a raffle which would usually be items donated by associates of the club.

These occasions would normally attract a full house with the club's freebie generating massive beer sales. Committee men would get their usual beer tokens for 'helping out' and the agent would get his booking period in the club, everyone's happy. The club and often the agent would get a big slap on the back for their generous charitable gift, so the only ones not making anything from the 'Charity Night' were the acts who'd given up their valuable time and travelled to the venue at their own expense.

We all had our own chosen charities that we would regularly do bookings for but every now and then you were expected to contribute to a club's freebie to keep your agent happy. Roy would have been in the same boat certainly in the early group days, but once he became a solo act he would organise his own charity functions without being prompted by anyone else.

Roy is well known for his charity work, raising funds for numerous charities in his own Teesside area as well as helping with other deserving causes around the country. Cancer research, for his own reasons, is one of many that have benefited from Roy's generosity.

I'm sure if it hadn't been for the fact Roy holds the title of 'Britain's bluest comedian', he would have received an honour for his endless charity work in the same way as others have.

Even in his early solo days, Roy was so well respected by the local entertainment faculty that he could rally up musicians and entertainers to perform for free at these events. Roy would even organise charity football matches with some of the players who contributed to this book taking part in The Roy Chubby Brown team. I played in goal, Roy insisting that I wore a deer stalker hat with a duck fixed on top… I think the duck made more saves than me. There's still a team sheet kicking around from one of the games. I remember one of the Roy Chubby Brown charity matches was a freezing Boxing Day morning in Berwick Hills, Middlesbrough when it was so cold that nobody turned up to watch us. We did enjoy the après match drinks though.

Roy's involvement in raising funds is not just a recent thing though. He has been happily 'doing his bit', as you might say, from early in his career. A brainwave of Roy's was the creation of a show purely for charity that he would take to local clubs, putting on a full night of varied entertainment with all ticket and raffle revenue going to the chosen cause. It needed the co-operation of local musicians and Roy got it from the best in the area. They were only too happy to join in what were sure to be fun nights, as well as fundraising nights. This was indicative of Roy's pulling powers even then.

Chubby's Fresh Brown Eggs was an inspiration dreamt up by Roy while he was still working from The Brian Findlay Agency, in the late seventies, where he got some of the finest musicians in the area to perform for charity at local venues. Everyone knew what a good night they'd have and were always happy to give their services for free. They included vocal performances from Davy Rich, Art McArthur, Les de Souza and Jackie Summers… all top of their game, with backing supplied by Paul Smith on drums, Lee Vasey on lead guitar, Tubby Ayton on bass, Austen McLaughlan (Ottie) on percussion and Paul Flush and Pete Jackson on keyboard.

Over a coffee in a Stockton café, three of the ensemble look back at a time when doing anything with Roy was always going to be lots of fun. Jackie Summers, the only girl in the show, says, 'I met Roy through the band I was working with at the time. Together with Les de Souza, we were resident in a Stockton nightclub called Bentley's. We all got together for the show which was Roy Chubby Brown and his Fresh Brown Eggs. Thankfully I wasn't asked to wear one of the Fresh Brown Eggs t-shirts. Roy was always the perfect gentleman. He brought me flowers to every show.'

I think he used to take a short cut through the cemetery meself. Jackie's statement was met with howls of derision with Paul and Ottie, complaining that Roy never brought them any flowers.

Jackie continues, 'I used to sing vocals on the backing tapes for Roy's comedy songs that he'd sing on his shows. I took my ex-husband to one of Roy's theatre shows once… with him sitting there, arms tightly folded as if to say, 'Make me laugh'. When Roy started to sing Dolly Parton's er… er… parts…' They're not parts Jackie, they're tits… she still can't allow herself to say the word in public. 'Well, when Roy got round to singing that song, my ex-husband turned to me with a disapproving look on his face and said, 'Is that you?' I said, 'Yes, it is'. The thing was that when I was in the studio singing Roy's comedy songs I'd be concentrating so much on getting the words and harmonies right, I never thought about the actual words themselves, I could have been singing any filth… and probably was.'

Jackie would also sing on some of Roy's more serious recordings. She says, 'Roy would bring a small cassette tape recorder and we'd listen to the track he'd recorded himself before we went into the studio. Roy would always say, 'Get this right, Summers. Get this right or I'll wrap you round the nearest effing lamp post.' So I always made sure I got it right. I did the outro for the video The Helmet Rides Again but they got my name wrong, calling me Sarah. From that performance, Polydor had said they were interested in Sarah, but nothing came of it. I was also misnamed Jackie Fox on one occasion.'

Ottie comes in with, 'You could call the book The Other Side of Chubby, because everyone knows Roy from his comedy, but very few know him from his serious stuff. Roy's got a great musical knowledge and writes some fabulous stuff but doesn't get the opportunity to show it.'

Jackie comes back in, 'We all just had fun when we got together to work with Roy. They were just fun times.'

Paul Smith, also resident at Bentley's with Jackie, had known Roy from his days at Guitarzan music shop where he had worked giving drum lessons in the adjoining drum department, Bongo Bills. Paul is very well respected as one of the country's top drummers, having supported big name artistes such as Tony Christie, Joe Longthorne and many more.

Paul says, 'I got to know Roy more when he would come and watch a band we'd put together with his cousins Dek and Lee. Ottie played too, as well with Paul Flush on keyboards.' It was one of those outfits formed just to be able to play the type of music they liked and would do sporadic gigs around the area. Paul says, 'Roy just enjoyed what we were doing, Johnny 'Guitar' Watson and Gino Vannelli, stuff like that.'

Ottie was percussionist with local band, Rivers Invitation, who had won TV's Opportunity Knocks a few times and got to know Roy in much the same way as Paul had… through Dek and Lee, and from him coming to see their band, discovering how musically knowledgeable Roy was apart from his comedy image. 'I had a record shop in Middlesbrough at the time and remember Roy would tell me about his diverse collection of LPs. He was very much into the same type of music that we all were.'

They all remember performing on Roy's first comedy LP at recording studios in Pity Me, County Durham. Paul says, 'We spent the whole day just trying not to laugh, 'cos we were recording it live.' Ottie says, 'It had to be finished in that one day because of the availability of not only the studio but the musicians that were working on it.' Jackie was also there, accompanying Roy on his songs including er… er… Dolly Parton's Parts. She says, 'Roy was actually trying to make us laugh all of the time, it was impossible not to.'

Paul remembers travelling to The New Theatre at Hull when George Forster, Roy's manager at the time, took a full show to perform a 'shop window' in front of a collection of entertainment agents. Paul, who was one of the backing musicians says, 'We all went down in a bus together, there was Roy and George's other acts. Roy was told to keep it clean. I think the worst word he said was bugger. When I was talking to him after the show, Roy said, 'God, that was hard, just making sure I didn't swear, it usually just trips off the tongue,' but he was still dead funny.'

The Fresh Brown Eggs shows were a perfect combination of Roy's comedy and the band's brilliant sound, creating what was an extravaganza that Teesside clubs would normally have had to pay an arm and a leg for. Roy had, by then, become such a big name, especially in the North East, that most acts, musicians, artistes would quite readily drop whatever they were doing and join in if they could. Many of these clubs would never have experienced a night with so much talent on display before.

Chubby's Fresh Brown Eggs

Most performances were for charity. Jackie remembers doing one for the Heart Foundation, but Roy arranged one night at The Acklam Garden City Club where Norman Wales from Brian Findlay's office was the entertainment secretary. The evening was to raise funds to bring home the body of Norman's wife, Lou, following the tragic events that occurred during their holiday in Malta.

Roy's more recent charity work has seen him raise thousands of pounds for local causes including the cancer unit at James Cook Memorial Hospital in Middlesbrough, as well as the children's hospice Zoe's Place, Butterwick Hospice in Thornaby… these being just a few of them all.

  Roy raises funds in a variety of ways. One being the auctioning of signed comedy sketches drawn on A4 paper at each of his appearances. The lucky recipient – being the highest bidder – receives the sketches off Roy in his dressing room immediately after the show. Other methods of fundraising have included charity CDs of songs written by Roy and generally performed by his current driver, Keith (The Voice) Hammersley… or 'Fat Elvis' as we all know him.

Helping Roy raise the profile at most of his cheque presentations is Paul Gough (Goffy) from local BBC Radio Tees. Paul's connection with Roy goes way back to the mid seventies when he was a working DJ performing at clubs in his hometown of Hartlepool. He's pretty sure that the first time he met Roy was at the town's Corporation Club where Paul had a residency. He recalls, at the time, the club would often book comedians for their regular concert nights, with some being relatively big names who'd 'had their day' appearing and who saw doing the workmen's club circuit of the North East as effectively 'on their way down' from the limelight. Some of these artistes, comics included, could be quite aloof and unapproachable with their showbiz attitude.

Paul's recollection of his first encounters with Roy though are very different, as rather than on the way down, Roy was on his way up and, as would happen with most people Roy met for the first time, they hit it off from the start. Roy had never been a prima donna – he's got the wrong shape for a start – but Paul was immediately impressed with his warmth and friendliness that came over right from their first meeting.

From my own experiences, I remember Hartlepool Corporation Club as no walk over for acts, even less so for comedians but, by this time, Roy was starting to draw his own audiences who would come especially to see him so, after having a good night at the club and with both Roy and Paul getting on together, they became good pals.

Paul progressed from being a working clubland DJ to secure a job with Century Radio, one of the top regional radio stations in the north of England, situated in Newcastle, where his listening audience became to know him better as Goffy. Goffy in the Morning was a sensation… everyone talked about it with the result that it topped radio ratings. Having such a popular programme, Goffy was always looking for people of interest to interview on his show, so having a connection with Roy, thought he'd be an ideal candidate. Goffy's boss wasn't so sure though. He was worried sick, said he hadn't slept all the weekend before the live interview. By then Roy had gained a reputation for being quite blue and, with the show going out live, he might say something that could get him the sack. Goffy says that he needn't have worried, Roy turned out to be the perfect interviewee, as he was sure he would be.

Roy with Goffy and hospital staff

Goffy tells of the time they were at North Tees Hospital handing over a large cheque. 'He did a feature for my radio programme and we met up with the specialist who'd saved his life. It was a lovely day when we got there, I remember quite clearly, the surgeon gave Roy a big hug, the staff were telling Roy how great he was, how he'd won them over and even at that level they'd seen a different side to him. There was quite a lot of the press around the area, TV national newspapers were there. After we'd had a coffee, we walked down and out of the front entrance where we realised Roy had left his car on double yellow lines. His sense of humour at that moment was brilliant, he said, 'I can't believe it, I've just handed over a wad of money, and got myself a parking ticket in to the bargain.' He was just about to throw his parking ticket away when I said, 'Don't do that, Roy, I've got my marketing head on here, my PR head.'

Away from the radio, Goffy has a very successful media company called Goffy Media, he'd quickly spotted the potential for a story which he was sure could go viral.

'I said to Roy, 'This is a great story, you've come here, chatted to all the press from around the UK about how good this place is, how you should support it and how they saved your life, handed over a cheque, then you get slapped in the face with a fine for parking on double yellow lines."

Goffy continues, 'I took a photo of him holding the parking ticket with a grim look on his face. The next day, I think it might have been against the wishes of the authorities, I put it out on air exactly what had happened. It was incredible, the story was great. It's still on Google even to this day, 'Roy Chubby Brown gets parking fine while handing over charity cheque'. You can't underestimate the power of radio. I was driving the following day, listening to Jeremy Vine on BBC Radio 2 and up pops the top story, 'Comedian making big donation to hospital receives parking fine'. It was on the BBC national news. It was picked up everywhere. I had people ringing me for that picture from every corner of the country.'

'I could see at that time that the story was gold. Funnily enough on the Jeremy Vine Show, it was the final story on the one o'clock news, and I could visualise the newsreader smirking. I knew when I was taking the picture it would go everywhere, sensing that it was a great story and so it was. People have their own perceptions of Roy but I just take people as I find them and historically when I've asked him for anything for charities, Roy's left parcels, given cash donations and signed memorabilia, together with opportunities for meet and great occasions. He's never been shy and again, most of the time he says, 'Give me no publicity', Roy's just one of the good guys.'

Photo by kind permission of Goffy Media

Goffy continues today as one of BBC Radio Tees's leading presenters, helping raise the profile and awareness to support many of Roy's cheque presentations in our local area.

Roy's first LP

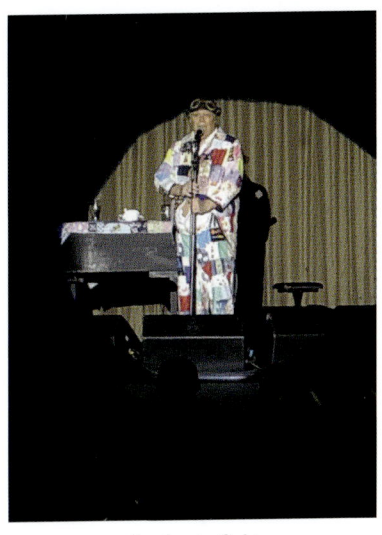

Roy with puppy   *In the spotlight*

Keep Fat

Roy at the piano

Fish and chips

Roy with the Redcar Lifeboat crew

Roy with a balloon model of himself

Roy at Comedy Carpet

Roy with a little horse

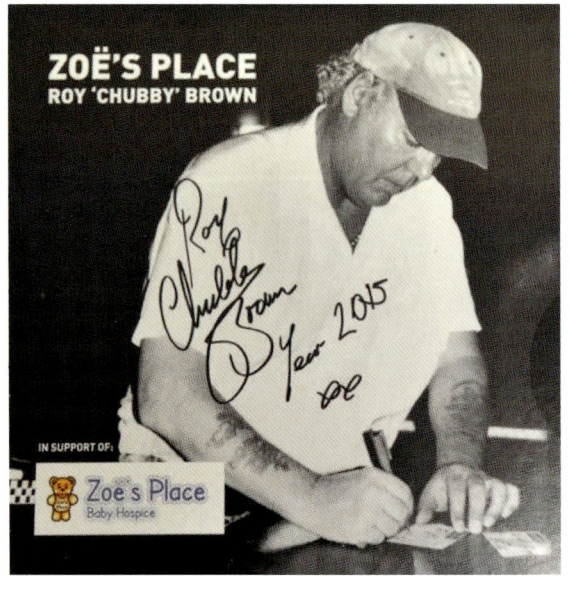

Above: Roy presenting a cheque to Zoë's Place

Left: Zoë's Place Charity CD featuring a song by Roy…
you can stream it now on Spotify and Apple Music

Roy with Ricky Tomlinson and Goffy

Roy presenting a cheque to Butterwick Hospice Care

Roy presenting another cheque to Zoë's Place

Roy at his baby grand piano

32

What's it like growing up when your dad is one of the most famous and funniest men in the country? Richard Vasey is Roy's eldest son and heir to his flying helmet and goggles and, over the years, together with younger brother Robert, has had to learn how to handle it… primarily with his schoolmates, then later into adulthood.

'I thought I was going up in the world when I became a roofer,' smiles Richard, a bit of his dad rubbing off him there. Yes, you can regularly see Richard plying his trade on top of a roof in our local Redcar area. Yet in the distant past if you'd ever seen a Vasey clambering across a roof, he would probably have been nicking the lead off it. But not Richard, having got the head for heights that his father doesn't possess, he runs his own successful business and is thought by many to be the best roofer in the area.

Robert is a successful property developer… buying properties, renovating them and selling them on or renting them out.

Richard, born in 1968, with Robert following just over a year later, are the offspring from Roy's first marriage to Judy, and although our story is about the transformation of Roy Vasey into Roy Chubby Brown, it might be interesting to find out just how the family coped with it themselves.

Richard and Robert's earliest recollections of realising what their dad did for a living were during infant school. Richard says, 'We would have been between seven and nine years old when me dad brought out his first Christmas card. It had on the front 'Chubby's Xmas Message', and when opened it said, 'Fuck Off'. There was a post box in the corridor at school and everyone could post cards to their class mates, and after breaktime the teacher would announce, 'Paul, you've got a card' or 'Stephen you've got a card'… like that. Our dad had given me a load of his cards, so I posted them to all of my mates. I didn't realise how bad it was for a Xmas message until I got summoned in to the Headmaster's office. He had a few of our dad's cards on his desk, he held one up and said, 'What is that?'

Innocently, I said, 'It's one of me dad's Christmas cards, he gave me a load so I sent them to my friends.' He said sternly, 'Do not bring them back in to school ever again.'

Robert was regularly asked by his classmates to tell them one of his dad's jokes. He says, 'It wasn't only the kids though, some of the teachers were Roy Chubby Brown fans, and they would ask me too, but our PE teacher was such a big fan that he got me to stand on a chair in front of the class and do a whole routine.'

They both admit that they've never known their dad be anything other than a blue comedian, having been too young at the time of Roy starting his career in the show groups.

Richard first got to see his dad in action when he was thirteen. He says, 'He asked our mam if he could take me to a show. Robert was still too young. I was as well I suppose but there you go. He was on a workmen's club in Leeds. Our mam said, 'Watch him, you know what your act's like, keep an eye on him.' Dad said, 'Yeah, yeah, he'll be alright."

'When we got there I was in the dressing room… I'd only been there about five minutes when two women walked in and started taking their clothes off. They were stark naked. I was gobsmacked didn't know where to look.' Bet he did! 'Our dad said, 'They're the strippers, son.' I said, 'Are they?' Dad said, 'Sit in the front row, I'll get them to rub their tits in your face.' I said, 'I'm not doing that'. So when the show started, I went and sat at the back where one of the regulars asked, 'Who's that lad there?' After being told that I was the comedian's son, he said, 'Go get him a pint.' I had two pints and I was leathered… only thirteen and never drank before. Dad said after the show, 'You'd better sober up on the way home or your mam'll kill me. I went to school the next day and told my mates about the fanny I'd seen the night before and they were all saying, 'Ask your dad if I can come next time.' That always stuck in my mind as being the first time I'd seen our dad on stage, as well as the first time I'd seen a fanny. I thought there was going to be trouble when a gang of lads set on him saying, 'You think you're funny? You're fucking rubbish.' I was only a kid, shit scared, but me dad just said to them, 'Yeah, I was like that after my first pint.' They started laughing and the situation was diffused. Then thinking to myself, phew, I thought there was going to be a fight there.'

Being a big Boro fan, Roy started to take Richard and Robert to the matches at the old Ayresome Park Ground. Richard says, 'We'd always get a cup of Bovril and a pork pie… they didn't serve alcohol then. Dad would wear his big Boro scarf and when he shouted, 'Come on, the Boro!' there would always be someone who'd belt out 'Chubby's shouting for the lads.' It was like he knew everyone.'

Robert says, 'After about seven games, all defeats, I told our dad I didn't want to go anymore so I stopped. After that they went on a winning run so I was banned from going again 'cos they said I was a jinx.'

Richard says, 'Dad would tell our mam that he was going to take us to the swimming baths and we'd get our trunks rolled up in a towel ready for him when he arrived. Me and Robert would be eagerly waiting for him, then we'd get in the car looking forward to playing in the baths in Redcar or Eston, but we didn't always get there. If we had to stop at traffic lights, there would be a good chance that me dad would get into some kind of road rage with another driver, then he'd chase them all over Redcar or Dormanstown.'

Robert says, 'He caught up with someone once and jumped out of the car and snapped his windscreen wipers off. It wasn't even raining.'

Richard says, 'If he wasn't able to catch up with anyone he was chasing he'd say, 'I'm dropping you back off at home, I'm gonna kill him,' and on those days we never got to the swimming baths. They're our early memories.' Richard continues, 'Dad had been seeing Pam, a girl from Stockton, at the same time as he was going out with Beryl. He told Beryl he was taking me and Robert away on our first foreign holiday to Majorca… I'd have been about 14, so we're talking around 1982-83. We had a flight booked from Teesside Airport and Beryl came and waved us off, but when we got on the plane, there was a woman sat alongside us who obviously knew our dad. Dad said, 'This is Pam. She's coming on holiday with us but keep it to yourself.' Quite a surprise, I must say, but it was our first time abroad and we were looking forward to it so much we just had to go along with it.'

'Our dad hates flying so to calm his nerves I think he must have drank a full bottle of whisky and by the time we arrived in Spain he was shitfaced. He had us both in headlocks, saying quite drunkenly, 'I love you two.' He was okay when we got off the plane, no dramas. He gave me and our lad a hundred pounds each and said, 'There you go… don't be asking for any more money during the week.' We went to the beach, and me and Robert got a pedalo together. We paid for an hour, but we decided to peddle out to an island that was just off shore, peddle round it and then come back. It took us two hours to get to the island, two hours to go round it, then two hours to get back. When we got back, our dad's stood on the beach at the water's edge with the coastguard alongside him, shouting, 'Where the fucking hell have you been, you little bastards? You were only supposed to be an hour. We all thought you'd fucking drowned.' He kept a close eye on us for the rest of the holiday after that.'

On leaving school at sixteen, Robert went on tour with his dad. He says, 'I'd go off with him each week for about three months. He'd do about three bookings a week – all theatres – and I'd go along with him staying overnight in a hotel room. After the shows it was comical to see grown men get off their faces on booze back at the hotel before crashing out for the night. I always wondered if that's what I'd be getting up to when I grew up.'

Richard says, 'Our dad's birthday was coming up and we didn't know what to get him. I was working with a roofing firm and I was telling one of the older blokes about it when he said, 'Why don't you get him a blow up doll?' I said, 'I wouldn't know how to get one.' He said, 'There's a sex shop in town… they're only about thirty quid.' I thought he seemed to know a lot about it! So I phoned our lad up and said, 'Shall we get our dad a blow up doll for his birthday? It'll be laugh, won't it?' He said, 'Yeah, okay, it'll be dead funny.' We bought the blow up doll, blew it up and put a pinny on it saying, 'Fuck me, Chubby', then placed it on his bed so that when he came in and went upstairs he'd see it. Our dad had a cleaner called Ellie who was getting on a bit and real tiny, only four foot something. Me and Robert were waiting in the house 'cos Dad was coming home through the day, having stayed in a hotel overnight, and we wanted to see his reaction when he saw the doll. Ellie came through the front door. I said, 'What are you doing here?' She said that our dad had asked her to pop round and give the house a clean before he came home. We never thought anymore about it 'til she came pounding downstairs shouting, 'There's a woman on your dad's bed!''

'I said, 'You what?' Me and our lad just looked at each other. Robert said, 'There's a naked woman on our dad's bed?' Then we ran upstairs, giggling like mad and brought the doll down saying to Ellie, 'You mean her?' She just said, 'You daft pair of buggers.''

'Dad came home and when he saw it, he laughed his head

off. He said, 'What a brilliant birthday present,' and had a good laugh over it. Dad had just started going out with Sandra and she would come to Redcar every now and then. The blow up doll was behind the punchbag in the garage and our dad said to Sandra, 'Have you seen what the lads have given me?' She went straight over to it and immediately accused him of having used it. She said, 'You've been fucking that doll,' with our dad pleading innocence 'cos it hadn't been used at all, it was bought for a laugh, but Sandra didn't give a shit… she just wouldn't let it drop. It should have been an early warning of things to come. I went to Blackpool one weekend when he was working there, staying over a few nights. I went to see some shows that other comedians were on and there'd be a couple of hundred people in each night, not many more. When I went see our dad, he was on one of the piers in a twelve hundred seater… it was sold out with people still queuing outside trying to get in.'

Boro got to the FA Cup Final in 1997, playing Chelsea, so Roy took them to Wembley. They flew to London from Teesside Airport. It was going to be a great day out. Boro had already narrowly lost in League Cup Final to Leicester and were battling against relegation but, with the likes of Juninho and Ravanelli, expectations for this match were high. Roy liked a bet so he gave Richard a thousand pounds, telling him to go to the bookies in the ground and put it on Boro to score first.

Richard says, 'It was getting near to kick off so I rushed down under the stand. There was a queue so had to wait, then I heard the players coming out and Abide With Me playing. I was getting closer to the counter… Dad would have gone mad if I hadn't got his bet on. Then the National Anthem… almost there… finally, I just got Dad's bet on seconds before the teams kicked off. The game had started while I was waiting for the betting slip. I finally got the slip in my hand and couldn't wait to show Dad that I'd managed to get his bet on when there was an almighty roar from upstairs. Roberto Di Matteo had scored from somewhere near the half way line after forty two seconds. Now, I had to go back to my seat and give me dad his betting slip which was now no use to him at all. I'll bet you could have heard the expletives loud and clear back home on Teesside.'

These stories are just a brief taster of what life has been like for Richard and Robert. There are many more tales but these give you a bit of an idea of what it must have been like to live in a small seaside town and be well known for not only being the sons of the bluest comedian in the country – Roy Chubby Brown – but also the sons of Roy Vasey, well known for very different reasons by the local constabulary.

The Vaseys… Robert, Roy and Richard

33

Roy's evolution was becoming more of a conundrum by the day. There would be people who would book him over and over again, having not experienced anything like him before with Roy already building up an army of fans, but we also had many venues that just weren't ready to accept the new Roy Chubby Brown. In the early confusion, the two would often get mixed up, with Roy regularly being sent to entertain unsuspecting audiences totally unaware of the style of comedy that was about to hit them between the eyes.

Where do we put him? Many of the clubs in the area were becoming too scared to get their fingers burnt by, as they saw it, inflicting the now notorious Roy Chubby Brown on their naive members. Then there were the more progressive types who couldn't get enough of him… although in the mid seventies those venues were few and far between.

Roy was coming to a crossroads in his career, and many of us thought that to succeed he was going to have to clean his act up. In fact, we thought he'd have to do that just to continue working the clubs. Brian Findlay put it to Roy that the agency was going to struggle to continue finding him bookings if he carried on down the path he was taking, with his act becoming more unacceptable to certain audiences. Roy was still nowhere near being 'Britain's Bluest Comedian' yet but was still very much too naughty for certain venues.

As said before, Brian and Roy were more like mates than agent and act, so I'm sure Brian had Roy's best interests at heart when he put the question to him as to whether he was going to clean his act up or not. Amid the debate though, waiting in the wings was George Forster. George of Fairworld Promotions was a shrewd businessman and wasn't one to let an opportunity slip through his fingers, especially one that was staring him squarely in the face.

George approached Roy about going on his books to find him the right venues for his comedy. He invited Roy to a meeting in his Newcastle office. Norman Pinchbeck remembers Roy asking if he would drive him there.

Norm says, 'I'd been helping Roy get to some of his bookings, driving his van for him 'cos he still didn't have a licence. By then he'd made other arrangements for getting to bookings and I bought his van off him for forty quid. He asked me to do one last job and that was to drive him to George Forster's office. He was having a meeting with him about booking him out, which I did and brought him back home. A few days later, there was knock on my front door. When I opened it, there were two policemen standing there. One of them said, 'Is this your van?' pointing to the van I'd just bought off Roy. I said, 'Yes it is, I just bought it off Roy Vasey the other day.' 'Roy Vasey?' questioned the other policeman, at which point they both looked at each other, shaking their heads as one of them muttered, 'Say no more,' then turned around and walked up my garden path, still shaking their heads. After having a quick look around the van, they just got into their police car and disappeared. It appears the van I'd just bought had been involved in a road traffic incident a few weeks earlier and they'd been looking all over town for it. What was funny though was that as soon as I said Roy Vasey, they both knew exactly who I was talking about. Roy was that well known to them.'

A new decade was approaching and, with it, new horizons. We would gradually see Roy moving away from the social and workmen's club scene. The contacts that new manager George Forster had would have Roy being peddled to the bigger and more lucrative venues. The eighties would see Roy turning more into the Roy Chubby Brown that we know today.

Roy says, 'The first job I got off George, he said, 'Go to Wallsend Labour Club and pick up a hundred and fifty quid.' I said, 'I can't do that, I can't ask for a hundred and fifty quid.' The most I'd picked up working for Brian Findlay had been seventy five. George said, 'No, go on, they've asked for you, they've charged two pound a ticket. It's a sell out, they'll give you a cheque… just put it in your bank account.' I said, 'I haven't got a bank account.' George said, 'You haven't got a bank account? I'll come to Redcar tomorrow and help your sort one out.' The booking at Wallsend was the following weekend and the next day after the show, George rang me – I was in my flat – he said, 'Did you get your money okay last night?' I said, 'No, I didn't. I didn't dare ask for it.' He said, 'For fuck's sake!' Anyway, he got in his car, drove to Wallsend, picked up the money then came all the way to Redcar to my flat and gave it to me in an envelope. I'd met him in Redcar town when we opened my new bank account so this was the first time George had seen my flat. He couldn't believe it. He said, 'What are you doing living in a tiny shithole like this? There's not enough room to swing a fucking cat?' I just said, 'I'll get a smaller cat.' George said, 'No, you should have your own house. You'll be on good enough money to afford one.' I said, 'But I won't be able to get a mortgage.' George said, 'I'll help you.' So I got a mortgage and bought a house on Corporation Road in Redcar, overlooking Locke Park. It was a bit of a mansion compared to what I'd been used to.'

Roy's reputation for his 'no holds barred' comedy and 'telling it as it is' was sweeping the country. No more so than in the north west where entrepreneur Roy Mozley was the proprietor of two of the area's biggest clubs, firstly Fagins in Manchester, followed by The Talk of the North in nearby Eccles.

Mozley was able to attract the top names of the day, including Bob Monkhouse, Ken Dodd, The Black Abbots, Bernard Manning, and Les Dawson, as well as international artistes such as The Drifters and Frank Ifield. Roy Chubby Brown had made numerous appearances at both clubs after initially being introduced as a relatively unknown quantity. The audiences would look forward to his appearances so much that he'd be asked to perform on some of the quietest nights of the week to boost attendances.

Roy Mozley says, 'I first booked Roy through George Foster, his then manager, for Fagins. He was the only person who could fill the club on a Tuesday and Wednesday, as most clubs had cut down to only three nights… Thursday, Friday, and Saturday. The business that Roy Chubby Brown created on the nights he worked for me was always outstanding. I had booked some of the biggest names in the entertainment business, but even they couldn't achieve the response and reaction that he would always get from my audiences. They would be in the palm of his hand from the moment he walked on stage. After I sold my shares in Fagins, I bought The Talk of the North and the first main attraction I booked was Roy Chubby Brown.'

Chubby has fond memories of appearing at both clubs. 'I owe a great debt of gratitude to the likes of Roy Mozley for initially putting their trust in an unknown comedian from further up north, who had been getting a reputation for being a bit different. Thankfully, Roy knew his audience and I had great nights at both clubs. The Talk of the North had an elevating stage that rose up through the floor in the middle of the dance floor, so my flying helmet would be the first thing to appear as I came into view. The first time I appeared there without anyone knowing who I was, the audience probably thought that Roy had booked Douglas Bader, the World War Two fighter pilot, to entertain them by mistake.'

With Roy Chubby Brown now making a name for himself in clubland, Roy Mozley said he had no fears over what seemed to be 'sticking his neck out' in booking him at three monthly intervals over the following year.

Chubby says, 'It was the opportunities like the ones Roy was giving me, to appear at venues away from my own area and out of my own comfort zone, that helped me to hone the comic skills which have given me such a successful fifty year career, and for that I will be forever grateful.' Chubby adds, 'Roy, being the generous man that he is, always paid me in advance of my performances, but I began to wonder if in those days, as I would arrive wearing blue dungarees, flat cap and Jesus sandals, I must have looked like I probably needed the cash up front.'

Right from Chubby's first appearance at Fagins, 'The Two Roys', as they were to become known, hit it off immediately and have been firm friends for the best part of fifty years to date.

Roy Mozley says, 'Chubby works at a hundred miles per hour and has a fabulous, outstanding memory… that's until it's his turn to get the round in!' Then Roy relents, 'Just my little joke, Chubbs, old mate. Everyone knows about his relentless generosity, and not only with the drinks.' He then continues, 'A lot of people don't know the real Roy Chubby Brown. I admire him in every way possible. He's such an honest lovely person. God bless him.'

Chubby recalls, 'Roy introduced me to many stars over the years, but in the earlier days, late seventies, I was appearing regularly with bands who had recently been chart toppers… huge names in their day like Freddie and The Dreamers, The Searchers and The Hollies. An amusing incident involving one of the chart topping groups, who will remain nameless, partly to keep the band's anonymity and avoid any form of

The two Roys

embarrassment, but mostly because I can't remember which group it was, happened around the same time as I was appearing at Roy's Talk of the North.'

'After the magnificent fanfare that introduced them, the group dramatically appeared from below on the rising stage, playing one of their biggest hits, only to find that the road crew had set up their equipment – drums, amplifiers and mikes – the wrong way round, so when the band had finished their rise, reaching the normal level of the stage, the lights came on to reveal that they were facing the wrong way and looking away from the audience toward the back of the stage. The audience, thinking this was part of the act roared with laughter, but I'm pretty sure there might have been a roadie who got the sack that night.'

Roy Mozley owned a restaurant in Worsley as well as The Talk of the North and the two Roys would often meet up there before a Saturday performance. Players and management from Manchester United and City would regularly be in the restaurant at the same time as Roy and Chubby, so you can see the type of clientele it attracted.

There was one particular night that Roy Mozley remembers, when he and Chubby were meeting up before going onto the club.

'It was around nine o'clock and I was running a little late,' says Roy with a smile on his face as he recollects, 'when, as I walked in, one of my employees, a Spanish lad, said, 'Mr Brown is already here so I have sat him at your table.' I said, 'Thank you,' then before I walked away, he said, 'Mr Brown brought you a brown paper bag so I took it off him to keep safe.' I nodded to show I'd heard him and walked over to the table to join Chubby. As I sat down the PA system which was playing in the background suddenly went up a notch and started playing Dolly Parton's Tits by Roy Chubby Brown. Chubby looked at me in embarrassment, totally lost for words – and you can't say that very often – before I quickly marched up to the music system and turned it off. Thankfully, before it got to Santa Where's Me Fucking Bike? When I turned to go back into the restaurant, the Spanish lad had come over to see why the music had gone off. I said, 'Why did you put that tape on?' He said, 'I thought Mr Brown had brought you some music to play in the restaurant so I put it on.' Roy had brought me a copy of his new tape and the lad, having not yet got a full grasp of the English language, had not noticed the titles of Roy's songs on the cassette cover, nor had he understood what was being played over the sound system, so while Dolly Parton's Tits was booming out, he had carried on serving my discerning customers as if they were listening to Vera Lynn. I re-entered the main body of the restaurant but, as I did, all the customers as one turned to give me a thunderous round of applause. One high flying big-wig stopped me in my tracks and said that he hadn't had such a good laugh in ages.'

Chubby has the last word on his old mate Roy Mozley as he says, 'It's a funny old business that we're in and genuine people can be thin on the ground, but with Roy Mozley what you see is what you get. He's one of the most honest, generous, friendly blokes I have ever had the pleasure to meet in show business and I thank him from the bottom of my heart for having enough faith to give me some of the earliest breaks in my career, and becoming the lifelong friend that he is still today.'

Roy would play many top UK clubs like Roy Mozley's during the eighties, progressing to finally breaking into the world of theatres under the guidance of George Forster. By the end of the decade, Roy had built up such an army of fans that wherever he performed, it would be in front of full houses… all without the help of any TV exposure.

Roy says, 'We were playing the Viking Hotel in Blackpool for a guy called Eric Slack – who's sadly passed away – but his son has a hotel in Blackpool and often dines out on the story about me being on his dad's place. I didn't go on 'til twelve o'clock and had a great night… tore 'em apart, they were standing in the aisles.' Eric said, 'You know, you should be on over there,' pointing at the South Pier which was directly opposite. 'I can only get eighty people in here. That pier seats twelve hundred people, you'll pack it out.' I did the Viking Hotel about ten or twelve times from 1984 to 86. I would take my family along and Eric would give us rooms for nowt. George talked to the people who were running the South Pier saying, 'Why don't you give Roy a go? Put him on at midnight.' They said, 'Okay then, we'll give it a try, see how it goes.' It would have been an extra show for them anyway, not interfering with any of the earlier shows that had already been booked.'

'I'd been performing in some of the top club venues in the country… Savvas, Blazers, Rooftop Gardens in Wakefield, Batley Variety Club among others, all big names in clubland at the time. They said they'd give me a try and put me at eleven o'clock. It was well advertised and after about a month I was performing to full houses, but by that time of the night the crowds that came in were all drunk. I started doing it every Saturday. We were getting rave revues so it was increased to Thursday and Friday as well. It was really hard work with the audience being half pissed and heckling. I usually only got away with telling three or four jokes, the rest was answerbacks and put downs. I spent more time practising my 'ad-libs' than I did my show in the end 'cos I knew they would probably take up the lion's share of my act. You feel like you've finally made the big time when you appear on the side of a Blackpool Tram… we'd been sat in a café having a cuppa when a bus went past with my picture and name all over it, that would have been 1986.'

Roy continues, 'George Forster was a good businessman. He was always able to get other people to pay for things… my name was on two or three buses, probably the best advertising you can get in Blackpool. They would say 'Live at The South Pier, Roy Chubby Brown… if easily offended, stay away'. I was the first one to use that phrase, 'If easily offended, stay away', then quite a few comics started to use it.'

Roy adds, 'After doing the South Pier, George said, 'We're going to start working the town halls throughout the country, they're already asking for you.' He said that I was in so much demand, it was hard to keep up with and thought we should also try and break into theatres.'

If George had said that to Roy just twenty years earlier, he'd have gone straight home to get his crowbar.

34

Roy's personal life with Beryl was going along quite nicely. He says, 'Me and Beryl were getting along well enough, and before George helped me to get a mortgage to buy my first house, I still had the flat above the hairdresser's, but would also spend a lot of time at her house. She did my washing for me and we always had a lovely Sunday dinner together.'

Beryl had a son, Gary, that lived with her from her former marriage. Beryl and Roy were together for such a long time while he was growing up that he regards Roy as his step dad.

Gary tells of a night when Roy came home to their house in a temper for some reason. He says, 'Roy was trying to get his briefcase open and it just wouldn't budge. After trying for a while and getting more angry, he flung it on to the table in a bit of a strop. The table was up against the front window and the briefcase slid along it at some speed, finishing up on the pavement outside having smashed through the pane of glass on the way. Me and my mam just stared at each other with our mouths wide open, with Roy immediately saying, 'Get on to the council in the morning and tell 'em someone's threw a brick through the window.' Mam rang the council and they said they'd send someone round to investigate. When the chap from the council came, he asked why there was no trace of glass on the inside, Mam replied that she'd hoovered it up. Then after going outside, he asked how come there was a pile of broken glass outside on the pavement, to which she didn't have an answer. The end result was that Roy had to pay for a new window.'

Roy and Beryl would regularly hold parties at her Norfolk Close house, one of which was for his comedian friends in the business. There were local comics there, as well as funnymen from further afield. Roy's driver, Steve Pinnell, remembers that Peter De Dee was one of the local lads at the party. 'Roy was hilariously funny that night,' says Steve, 'it was obvious from that evening of how much Roy was held in esteem by his peers.'

Gary says he was about eighteen when his mam moved from Norfolk Close to Lime Road in East Redcar. Lime Road was the next one up from Cedar Grove where ex-wife Judy was now living in the former marital home with Richard and Robert, who were now able to just walk around the corner to see their dad.

All seemed perfect from the outside but Roy admits, 'I was feathering me nest.' What Roy means by that was he had other ladies on the go at the same time. 'I had something like three girls I was seeing.' Awful when you can't keep count of them all, isn't it, Roy? 'Yes, I was seeing three girls, including Beryl at that time… and they all wanted me to put a ring on their finger.'

One of the girls was Pam, who lived on a housing estate in Stockton, where Roy would often call in after a booking. Gary's not sure how long it must have been going on but he confirms the same story that Richard had told about a summer in the early eighties when Roy had arranged two separate week's holidays to run one after each other in Majorca. He said, 'The first week was with Richard and Robert, the second week was with mam and me. When Richard and Robert got to the airport expecting to see me mam with their dad, they were surprised to see Pam, who they didn't know. I was to pick them up at Teesside Airport on their return, but when I arrived Roy had obviously told Pam to scarper out of the way before I got there so I was still unaware of her existence and certainly didn't know she'd been on holiday with them 'til later on. It was a quick turn around because he then took Mam and me off on the same holiday as they'd been on the previous week.'

Sure, it couldn't have been the same place or Roy would have had a Spanish waiter asking him where Miss Pam was this week.

'A year or so went by with things appearing to look normal until one night Mam gets a phone call… 'My name's Pam and I'm expecting your boyfriend's baby.' Mam was distraught and I drove her over to meet Pam in Stockton. I didn't go in, so I don't know what the conversation was about. I just know that she didn't say anything to Roy at that time.'

Beryl and Pam were saving it to ambush Roy at a later date.

Roy remembers it well. 'It was a Friday night and I was working at a club in Peterlee, no more than twenty minutes or so from Pam's house. I rang her and said I'd pop in on the way home, and that I'd bring some fish and chips. After the show on the way to Pam's, I called at the chip shop and bought fish and chips twice with mushy peas. When I arrived at Pam's and walked in shouting, 'It's only meee!' I got the shock of my life. Who's sat on the settee waiting for me but Beryl and Christine, the other girl I'd been seeing, with Pam stood arms folded in front of the fire.'

Pam looked Roy straight in the face, as they all were, and said, 'You've got some explaining to do!' with Roy replying, 'No, you have some explaining to do… I've only bought fish and chips for two,' then dashed out of her house with his heart beating ten to the dozen.

He didn't hear anything from the three girls immediately. He thinks they will have said to each that they were all finished with him. Then after a short break, one by one they each phoned him saying, 'You said it was only me you loved,' and Roy started seeing all three again.

Gary says that although Roy tried to regain his mam's trust and continue with their relationship, she never really felt the same after what had happened. Roy, having moved in to his new house on Corporation Road, hoped Beryl would come and live with him but it was not to be and sometime in 1987 they split up for good.

By then Pam had given birth. Roy says, 'Pam had a baby girl, calling her Lyndsey, who I agreed to financially support. I also bought household items for her… carpets, washing machine, hoover, telly… stuff like that.'

There was one day when Roy's mam was paying a visit to his house. Roy says, 'Me and me mam were just having a cup of tea, first time she'd been to my new house, so I told her about Pam and baby Lyndsay. She said, 'Do you see her?' I said, 'Yes, I do. In fact, she's coming over this morning. If you want to, you can hang about and meet her.' About half an hour later, there was a knock on the door. It was Pam. I said, 'Come in. Me mam's here.' Pam said, 'Does she know about Lyndsey?' I said, 'Yes, she does, it'll be okay,' so Pam came in. Lyndsay would have been about six months and Pam passed her over to Mam for her to hold. When Mam cradled Lyndsay, her face changed as though she had just seen a ghost, then she looked up at me and gurned, as if to say, 'There's something not right here.' When Lyndsey had gone, Mam said to me, 'That's not your baby.' I said, 'How do you know?' She said, 'It's got blue eyes and a pointy nose… all the Vasey's have these noses,' pointing to the hooter on my face, 'on top of that, it's got ginger fucking hair.' Mam always was one for getting straight to the point. Aunty Ivy, who'd come with me mam for a cuppa, joined in, 'There's no way that's your baby, our Roy. No way."

'A few days later I rang Pam up and told her I wanted a blood test. She said, 'You can fuck off! If you don't want this baby to be yours then it's not yours, so you can fuck off!' then put the phone down on me and, apart from the odd photo, I never saw the baby again.'

Even though Roy's professional life had taken a turn for the better, his personal life was still as complicated as ever. By then we had all come to the conclusion that Roy was never going to be satisfied taking the easy path through life, regardless of whatever it threw at him, but even he would never have guessed what was to happen one fateful night in West Yorkshire.

'I was doing Batley Variety Club,' remembers Roy, 'when an absolutely stunning young girl came in to the dressing room. I thought what a beautiful girl she was. Then she just came right out and said to me, 'You used to go out with my mother.' I said, 'Did I?' She said, 'Yes, Sandra Pallent.' I said, 'Is Sandra your mam?' She said, 'Yes, she's out front, she's watching the show. Can she come back?' I said, 'Yes, of course she can.' Sandra came back to the dressing room. I said, 'How are you doing?' She said, 'Oh, I'm going through a divorce with my husband, Geoff. I'm living in Pudsey, opposite a second hand car sales room. I've got a nice two bedroom house. Next time you're on in the area, why don't you come and have some tea.' I said, 'Well, I'm on here again in two weeks' time and I'm also going to be doing Harehills Social Club in Leeds. I called and had my tea with her, and she made a fuss of me. I said, 'Would you like to come and watch the show next time I'm down here?' So that's how it started back with Sandra again after all those years.'

Roy always had a soft spot for Sandra, right from her being his childhood sweetheart. Their previous relationship, so many years before, had been somewhat volatile, to say the least, but the people around Roy at the time of their reunion would not have been aware of that. Though it wasn't to take them very long before spotting the early cracks in what was destined to be a torturous few years ahead for 'unlucky in love', Mr Brown.

Roy and Sandra's new relationship picked up pace with Roy and Ronnie Keegan, his driver at the time, staying over in West Yorkshire most weekends, with Ronnie having latched on to one of Sandra's mates. Things got even more serious with Roy and Sandra eventually tying the knot around 1988… even Roy can't remember the exact date. Roy bought his dream home… Sunnycross House on Brass Castle Lane in Captain Cook's birthplace of Marton on the outskirts of Middlesbrough, for the newly weds to live in.

The house in Brass Castle Lane wouldn't have looked out of place on Downton Abbey… a smaller version, of course… but nevertheless, it had it all including a gated entrance leading you to a generous car park, and a massive rear garden with a large ornamental fountain. It was the sort of place that footballers of today would be only too proud to own.

From the outside, they looked the perfect couple, living the lifestyle that Roy's fame and fortune was able to provide. That was from the outside. From the inside, things could not have been more different. Quite quickly, Roy was beginning to realise how manipulative Sandra could be. She'd question him about his every movement, wanting to know where he'd been, what he'd been doing and who he'd been doing it with.

Roy says, 'I like to visit the gym on a morning and have a swim. One day, while I was sat winding down with a cup of tea, the girl off reception came over and told me that my wife had been on the phone, checking to see if I was actually there. I couldn't believe it. It was as though I wasn't allowed a private life. She had to know my every movement in every day. It was suffocating.'

Others have commented too.

Baz Francis and his family – big Chubby fans – became friendly with Roy and Sandra to the point of going on holiday with them – New York being one place they visited – and even spending Christmas dinner with the Vaseys.

'On one occasion Roy and Sandra came to us in Derby for dinner,' remembers Baz. 'They'd had a big argument on the way down. I'm not sure what about but we'd seen it before and weren't that surprised. I'd booked dinner for the four of us at a special restaurant in Derby, the Riverside, arranging for myself and my wife to meet them there. When they arrived, I could see they were not happy. It was a restaurant known for its ambience and there was soft music playing in the background. It should have been a beautiful evening with the finest of food. All of a sudden, Roy, without any warning, banged his fists on the table. The cutlery and pots flew in the air and he screamed a load of expletives at Sandra, most of which began with 'f', then he stormed out, heading for home.'

Roy says, 'Before I left, I whacked Sandra with a chicken leg.'

Baz carries on, 'He left us with Sandra and plates half full of uneaten food, neither looking that appetising anymore. We tried to contact Roy but his phone was turned off. We eventually got hold of him – having only got as far as Leeds – saying that he'd have to come back to collect Sandra 'cos we'd both had a drink and had no way of getting her home. Roy turned around, came back to collect her and took her home.'

I imagine it wasn't a very pleasant journey in the car, but that incident would appear to have been Roy and Sandra in a nutshell.

35

Steve Cowper had first met up with Roy whilst working as the resident sound engineer at The Floral Hall in Scarborough in the early to mid 1980s. He's pretty sure that this would have been Roy's first theatre booking – or certainly one of them – and he was appearing for one night. Steve's brother had come to know Roy from his regular visits to the town's rugby club.

Steve says, 'Ronnie Keegan was driving Roy at the time, as well as doing his sound and selling tapes.'

Steve remembers that the show's host was Kay Rossell, a north east club singer, who had a particularly frightening presence on stage when introducing the acts, telling the audience like an old school teacher would that when Roy came on they had to 'Shut up and listen!'

'The theatre shows were taking off in a big way, but Roy was getting more and more disillusioned with the sound at most venues which was totally out of his hands being produced by the resident sound engineer. Roy was determined to bring the show's sound and lighting more under his own control, desperate for his audiences to get full value for their hard-earned ticket money, wanting his voice to be heard clearly by everyone from the front stalls right up to the rear circle. With this in mind, he brought in Dimmer Blackwell, who was a top sound technician. So now with the show's own equipment and the best in the business to work it, Roy was ready to take on any venue in the country. This also let Ronnie concentrate on the sales of merchandise, which had become more of an important element with the addition of extra produce.'

Steve continues, 'Dimmer also had a successful recording studio and, with the Roy Chubby Brown show becoming more demanding, he felt he was beginning to neglect the running of his own business.' Dimmer had to make the tough decision to spend more time doing his studio work, thus leaving the Roy Chubby Brown show. Steve had become quite friendly with Roy and Ronnie, and it was Ronnie who approached Steve saying that Roy would like him to join the show as his soundman.

By the time Steve started working for Roy, he was seeing Sandra. Steve says, 'Ronnie was also seeing a girl in Leeds… she was married, so the least said about that the better, but it meant they could both crash out there occasionally without driving back to Teesside. We all knew about Roy and Sandra's volatile relationship, with Sandra wanting to know where Roy was at all times and often calling him and winding him up whilst he was working. We were all taken by surprise when he decided to marry her.'

Steve was on hand when Roy moved from Corporation Road to Sunnycross House in Marton. It came with quite a lot of land, having been several houses knocked through to make a larger one. Steve adds, 'It still needed a lot of work doing, but Roy turned it into an amazing home, and when the time came to move in, I was one of a few people to help, ferrying all of his possessions from Redcar to Marton because Ronnie was no longer driver/merchandise salesman as George Forster had him removed for making too many financial demands, no sentiment in business, George just sacked him, no messing, and he was replaced by Pete Richardson, who was Roy's own choice.'

Pete's first recollection of Roy was when he watched his show at the Guisborough Quoit Club back in 1978. A brilliant show he says, very funny and that he never stopped laughing all night. Pete bought Roy's latest album and asked the concert chairman if he could get Roy to autograph it for him. Roy obliged and wrote on it, 'Thanks for asking, Roy Chubby Brown'. Pete says that he still has it today. Pete tried, like we all do, to remember some of the jokes to tell his workmates on Monday morning, but it's the way you tell 'em, isn't it?

Pete went to see Roy many times after the Guisborough show, but it was one night at a club in Whitby and a chance meeting that would change Pete's life forever. He says, 'After the show I was stood in the gents having a slash when who comes in but Roy Chubby Brown himself, and we got talking.' Hopefully still pointing away from each other during the conversation. Pete continues, 'Roy's car had broken down and he had no way of getting back home to Redcar, so as I was going that way, I offered him a lift. He came to my house for a drink and to meet my wife before I drove him home to Redcar. We became good friends after that.'

Pete had a day job at ICI, as well as driving Roy to his gigs, so having secured a tour of clubs in the midlands, Roy asked him if he could put a week's holiday in and go with him, which Pete did. The first night in the midlands was at a venue called The Nightingale Club, which was a gay club. Roy went down a storm so it was a great start to the tour in a new area, which was usually a good sign of the things to come. However, the next night just outside Birmingham, Roy had just finished Dolly Parton's Tits, for which he used a giant guitar as a prop then. While Pete was putting the guitar away in the dressing room, the door flew open and Roy burst in saying, 'Put the gear in the car, we're off!' It appeared that a guy had come up to Roy at the front of the stage and wouldn't stop mouthing off, so Roy frog marched him out of the club and pushed him through a glass door. It was a quick pack of the cases before Roy and Pete beat a hasty retreat all the way back to Teesside with the rest of the tour being cancelled. Pete didn't really have to put a full week's holiday in for the two nights, he could have just thrown a sicky.

'From simply driving Roy and selling his merchandise, George made me Tour Manager,' Pete says. 'The scene from when I first met Roy had completely changed… gone were the workmen's clubs, them being replaced with much bigger venues to accommodate Roy's huge following. If I needed a reminder of just how big a star Roy had become I got it with one of the first bookings we did at the Oxford Apollo where two thousand five hundred people turned up to see a show which now included a brilliant three piece band called The Directors opening the show before Roy went on.'

Steve says, 'I first met Pete at The Civic Theatre in Bedworth where he confided in me about his worry of the Tour Manager tag. I told him not to worry as I'd help him any way I could, becoming close friends in the process.'

An ex-wrestler, Tony 'Banger' Walsh, also joined the team running security. The four of them, Steve, Banger, Pete and Roy became a closely-knit outfit and good mates, enjoying great nights socially, as well as professionally.

An incident that sticks out in Steve's mind was when they got their first booking at Savvas Cabaret Club in Usk, Monmouthshire. This was a big deal as George Savva had a huge reputation in the business, having originally run Blazers Nightclub in Windsor, which attracted big names such as Sir Cliff Richard. Savvas Cabaret Club was a smaller venue but nevertheless attracted popular TV

Tony, Pete, Roy and Steve raising money for Alzheimer's

personalities of the day in Michael Barrymore, Lenny Henry and Frankie Vaughan.

With George's reputation having gone before him, Roy was very excited about working the club and meeting the legendary George Savva. Steve recalls that when they arrived, Roy got out of the car and approached the front door of the club, wearing his usual blue denim dungarees and flat cap. A smartly dressed gentleman, George Savva himself, came out of the front door and approached Roy, but with neither having met each other before, and with Roy dressed the way he was, George beckoned Roy over, promptly saying, 'The bins are round the back.' Both had a good laugh when the mistake was realised.

Steve smiles as he tells of another time they were at Savvas. 'We were at Savva's and we were staying in some chalets the club had available for acts. We were going to be there a few days, so to fill in the daytime, Roy, Pete and I went to Bristol for a look around. Roy bought a few items, Pete and myself helping to carry the bags. On the way back to the car, we walked through an underpass where a guy was selling packs of socks and Pete could never resist a bargain so he bought a big plastic bag of white sport socks. He was so pleased that he persuaded Roy to buy some to wear on stage, but I refused saying they'd be cheap rubbish.'

Steve continues, 'All the way back to Savvas, Pete kept banging on about how I'd missed a bargain, but when he opened the bag and proudly pulled a pair of pristine white socks out and waved them in my face, I spotted there were no heels, so I asked him where they were. Pete said, 'Well, you expect an odd one pair might be faulty at that price,' so he pulled out a second pair. 'Look, the heels are fine in this pair,' but then he realised there were no toes.'

Steve carries on, 'Out of about fifty pairs of socks, there wasn't one pair that he could wear. I couldn't stop laughing, and suggested that we went to Roy's room to check his bundle of socks. They were the same! Pete ranted that he wanted to get in the car and drive all of the way back to Bristol to sort the bloke out! We didn't let him, with Roy bellowing out, 'Come on, Pete, put a sock in it!' Pete's face was a picture, but Roy and I just couldn't stop laughing at it for the rest of the day.'

Another occasion that brings a smile to Steve's face was on a trip to the South Coast. 'Roy was always buying clothes that were 'trendy', and Pete and I quite often took the piss out of them. Though it was always light-hearted, it became a standing joke. One time in Southampton, he bought a bright red coat, with Pete instantly starting to rib him over it, telling Roy not to stand with his mouth open in case somebody tried to post a letter.'

'We stayed overnight and the next day was another of those days when we went in to the town centre to kill some time. Roy was still getting ready in the hotel before we went out so Pete and I said we would wait for him outside the front door. As he came out, we noticed he had the red coat on – you couldn't miss it really – and said he looked like the hotel doorman, but just as we said it, a car stopped and a guy wound his window down, directly asking Roy, 'Do you valet park the car or is there a car park round the back?' The look on Roy's face was a picture, as he about turned and marched straight back into the hotel, changing his coat which we never saw again.'

While driving to gigs, Roy and Pete would find things to keep them occupied and pass the time away. On one trip, Roy said to Pete, 'See how many Beatles' songs you can remember.' Pete says, 'I've always liked The Beatles so the song titles just tripped off my tongue, probably didn't get them all but certainly quite a lot. Then, bugger me two days later, Roy comes up with a new song from the list of Beatles' songs I'd spouted out in the car. It was brilliant and he used it on stage. It was one song title after another. How he remembered them all I just don't know, but I still didn't get a royalty for providing him with the lyrics.'

Pete's a big lad with a similar body shape to Roy and every now and then people they hadn't met before would get them mixed up. It could happen as they arrived at a hotel where a receptionist might say to Pete, 'Did you have a good journey, Mr Brown?' Roy would always find it funny and would go along with it right up until Pete would ask for his Gold Card to make a payment, at which point Roy's answer was the usual, 'You can fuck right off.'

One night, travelling home from a gig, they stopped at a Chinese Takeaway, bought some food and sat in the car to eat it. Pete says, 'We were in Roy's car with his personalised number plate. There were a group of teenagers, about fourteen years old… should have been in bed… riding around us on bikes. One spotted the number plate and came up to the driver's side window and asked, 'Are you Chubby Brown, mister? Can I have your autograph?' At which point, Roy, still tucking into his Chinese, said, 'Course he is, son… give him your autograph, Chubby. There's some photos in the back of the car.' So it was my turn to play along this time, I had to put my Chinese down to go cold while Roy finished his off. I dug some photos out and signed them for about six lads with 'Roy Chubby Brown, now fuck off.'

Roy had decided he wanted to bring out another book covering some of the stories that had been left out of his autobiography and asked Steve to help him produce it, with the final product being a successful paperback called It's Funny Being Me, covering many hilarious stories from throughout Roy's career.

Steve remembers Roy always being on the look out for fine things for his new home. 'We had a booking in Southend and on the way there, we passed a large garden centre. We were in plenty of time so Roy asked us to turn around and go back so he could have a look inside. It was something that we would do on regular occasions if the time allowed. He bought some statues and I put them in the tour van to take up to Sunnycross House. On a different occasion I was with him when he chose a large concrete fountain with a pineapple feature. He thought it would look amazing in his garden, which it eventually did, buying it there and then, and saying, 'Put it in the van.' I told him I couldn't as it was much too big and heavy. So the decision was made for us to come back down with Pete on a day off – bringing an empty van – which we did, and by the time we got it back he'd had a stand built to place it on with all the plumbing and electrics installed. Pete and I managed to get it in position and his handyman connected it all up. Needless to say, it didn't disappoint…

standing as a magnificent focal point in what was now turning into a beautifully landscaped garden.'

Steve says, 'Sunnycross House was always a work in progress, with many additions over the years. It was very much Roy's pride and joy.'

But, with the Vasey's relationship now on a very slippery slope, it wasn't going to be too long before Roy had to let go of the one thing he had grown to love so much… his beloved house.

36

It was Roy's friendship with Steve Pinnell which led to Smokie and Roy combining to create their smash hit record, Living Next Door To Alice.

Steve, Roy's ex-driver/good mate/drummer, was now working with 70s rock band Smokie. Steve and Roy socialised regularly when they were both at home. Steve says, 'We have to go back to 1991 where whenever the DJ in Blooms Hotel in Dublin played Living Next Door To Alice, and the audience would all together shout back 'Alice, Alice, who the fuck is Alice?' Having come to the attention of one or two DJs on the continent, the song got mixed and bandied around a couple of times until, having come to our attention in 1995, our lead singer Alan Barton, and original member of Smokie, said to Steve, 'Why don't we bring it out and get Roy in to sing it with us?' It was something that the band wanted to do but it just didn't sit right with Smokie's image, but Alan thought Roy would get away with it.'

'So, I asked Roy if he'd like to do it and Roy said he'd love to.' Steve continues, 'I'll never forget the day we recorded… it was a Monday. I picked him up quite early and drove through to the recording studio at Castleford, a brilliant studio with a great producer. We already had the backing track so all that needed to be added was 'Alice, Alice, who fuck is Alice? Roy did six versions of it between 11am and 2pm, most of which were hilarious with Roy having us all in stitches. But by the end of the session, we got exactly what was needed.'

When released, it wasn't an immediate success and tragically, only a few weeks later, Alan was killed in a motor accident while on his way to the airport after doing some concerts in Germany.

The band were devastated to lose Alan, who was not only a bandmate but a great friend, and thought that was the end of the road for Smokie. But, after about six weeks, their management told them that they had sacks full of letters sent to them by their fans from all over the world. They all said the same thing… that they wanted the band to carry on in Alan's memory. They brought in a new singer, Mike Craft, who had done some work with the band in the past and he fit in like a glove.

Alice had to be rerecorded owing to contractual issues with Mike doing the vocals, and it didn't do very well at first, and things went quiet… it got forgotten about. Then the distribution company contacted them and said they'd been inundated with people asking, 'Where the fuck is Alice?' I'm sure they didn't actually say it like that but it would have been funny if they had. Still there were people out there who wanted to know how they could get hold of Alice. Apparently holidaymakers had heard the song while they were away and were asking for it when they came home. It was decided to re-release it at the band's own expense after the distribution company convinced the lads it would at least break even.

After three weeks their manager rang and said, 'You'll never guess, Alice is going in the charts at number twenty eight!' Then rang back and said that Top Of The Pops wanted them to go on with Roy.

Steve says, 'After that, it just got bigger and bigger. At that time you could get a number one with 20,000 sales and Alice sold about 800,000 yet still didn't make number one, being held at number three by Simply Red's Fairground at number one, and Mr Boombastic by Shaggy at number two. Fairground, Mr Boombastic and Living Next Door To Alice were the three highest selling records of 1995 and they all had to come out at the same time, stopping us getting to the top slot.'

Following the success of Alice, it was decided that even though it had to be re-recorded with a new singer, Alan's family would receive all royalties from any sales.

Steve wanted to tell of his first weekend home after Alan died… he was having a lie in on the Sunday morning, and the accident had been reported in the Sunday papers when the phone at his bedside rang. Steve takes up what happened next… "Hi Steve, it's Roy.' I wasn't surprised that he had rang when the news came out, and it was good to hear his voice, but what followed is something that will stay with me forever. Roy said, 'I've just been thinking, Steve, I want your bank account details.' Puzzled, I asked, 'Bank account details?' Roy said it again, 'Yes, your bank account details.' I'm just laying in bed thinking, 'Why?', but couldn't speak. Roy carried on to explain, 'I've just heard what's happened and can't handle it." Steve starts to

Roy on Top Of The Pops with Smokie

get quite emotional whilst trying explain the reason Roy wanted his bank account details. 'Roy wanted to put money in my bank account because he thought I couldn't work.' Steve, finding it harder to get his words out at the thought of Roy's generous gesture, continues, obviously very moved by the memory. 'Roy's first thought about me, having heard the news, was what was I going to do? How was I going to live? He wanted to help me get over what was sure to be a tough period. That's the sort of guy he is. I said to him, 'I'm okay, mate, I really don't need money. Your friendship and the thought means more to me.' It was a huge thing to happen in anyone's life with Roy immediately wondering what the rest of us were going to do. I knew I could get drumming jobs but it looked like the end of the road for the band, and I'll never forget how Roy's first thoughts were of how he could help. That story alone, by no means the only one, goes to confirm what I've said before that the bond which Roy and I have toward each other… it feels more like a brotherly relationship than even the best of mates.'

Roy and Steve would go and play squash and tennis at Tennis World in Middlesbrough. Steve says, 'As big as he was, Roy was incredibly fit and so light on his feet.' They also started to play golf together after Roy had been bought a top golf set that only professionals would dream of using.

Steve was a member of a local golf club and said to Roy, 'I'll try and get you in as a member.' Steve put Roy's name forward but they wouldn't let him join because one of the six member committee had blackballed him, saying, 'Why do we want him turning up in his flying hat and goggles?"

Steve says, 'I knew who'd blackballed him so I went up to him and said, 'Are you stupid or what? Roy is the nicest guy, my best mate. Do you really think he's going to turn up on the first tee with his flying hat and goggles? You must be thick if you do.' They still wouldn't let him in, then had me up in front of the committee three times for complaining.'

Steve adds, 'I owe a lot to Roy. It was Roy that got me into drumming properly and, through my introduction to Paul Smith – a Billingham lad and probably the best drummer I've ever seen or heard – I would never have got the lucky break to play with Smokie. Paul was filling in with Smokie but couldn't take the job on full time, so he recommended me and I've now been with them around thirty years. When I was playing all over Europe, Roy was always so pleased for me, ringing up regularly and asking, 'How's it going? Where are you? What are you doing?' and you could tell in his voice that he was always dead chuffed for me, having been there with me right from the start.'

37

Richard Hoyle, or Ritchie as he's known, has been Roy's tour manager since November 1989. Ritchie first met Roy in Blackpool when he was working as Stage Manager at the Opera House, and would also help cover the theatres on the piers as well, as they were all owned by First Leisure Ltd. He'd previously been tour manager with The Nolans, accompanying them on many trips to Japan as well as venues around the UK. It was during this period Roy started his long-term relationship with Blackpool's South Pier. George had also started booking Roy into theatres around the country, after his popularity had outgrown the capacity of most clubs.

After meeting at the South Pier, Ritchie and Roy got on so well that before he knew what was happening Ritchie had said farewell to First Leisure and was on tour with the Roy Chubby Brown show. It was a gentleman's agreement with a handshake, as they both said they'd see how it went over the next three months. It was obvious from the start that they trusted each other, even if Ritchie did check to see if he was still wearing his wristwatch after shaking hands with a Grangetown lad. To say that it's gone quite well would be an understatement and their mutual trust has lasted to this day with neither of them feeling the need to make it fully official.

Ritchie's job as Tour Manager has him performing many tasks to make sure the well-oiled cogs of the Roy Chubby Brown show run without a hitch. He is calmness personified on show night, settling Roy into his dressing room and allowing him time to compose himself for the night's entertainment, while Ritchie co-ordinates the behind the scenes preparations. Whenever Roy has any personal guests at the show, Ritchie is the guy who will meet them at the door, always creating a friendly atmosphere. If they've arranged to see Roy backstage beforehand, he'll escort them to the dressing room but always asks that Roy is left for a whole one hour before the curtain goes up, for him to concentrate on his material. He'll then come back to ensure that Roy has his sixty minutes of solitude.

Ritchie will occasionally be asked to do other duties like helping Roy erect a new prop he might want to use on stage. This happened not too long ago when it was decided that a blow up doll would enhance one of his comedy routines with Roy asking Ritchie to inflate it for him, which he did without hesitation. Roy reckons that Ritchie seemed quite good at it.

Ritchie's existence with Roy has been like many others… he has found himself in some

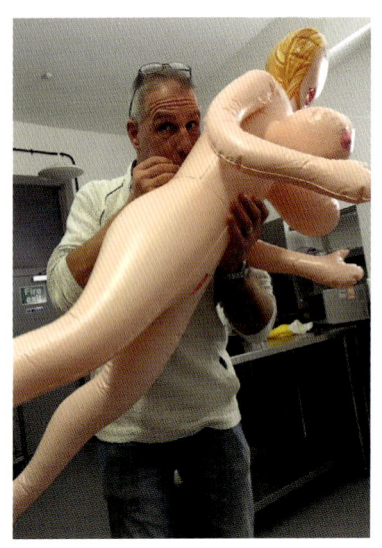

Ritchie finally manages to get fixed up

odd situations. One in particular that brings a smile to his face was when they were driving through Birmingham City Centre. Ritchie was in the back of the car with Roy in the front. Pete Richardson was driving. Ritchie says, 'As we came out of a multi-storey car park, a young lad punched the bonnet of Roy's car and then jumped on a double decker bus. Roy, as you can imagine, wasn't too happy about this and the air was blue, so he told Pete to chase after the bus and catch up with the little toe rag when he got off. We chased the bus through the busy streets of central Birmingham, getting caught in heavy traffic, but every time we got close to the bus at a stop or junction, it would pull away from us. The only thing missing from our escapade was some Benny Hill chase music. The young lad hadn't bothered finding a seat and, as it was an old style bus with an open platform at the back, he just hung on there facing back towards us, laughing and making obscene wanking gestures.' Ritchie admits that if Roy had caught up with the youngster he would have been laughing on the other side of his face… 'Thank God we didn't catch him!' admits Ritchie.

On another occasion, where self-control went out of the window, Ritchie was waiting with Roy and the rest of the team in the business lounge of an airport. They were going on their first Australian tour. They had both had a few too many in the airport lounge so decided between themselves that when boarding the plane they would both be ever so quiet so as not to attract any attention to the fact that they'd had a good drink and might not be allowed to board.

However, just as they were crossing the threshold from the steps to the plane, 'Roy let out the loudest fart ever,' Ritchie adds. 'It was a bit like the sonic boom of a fighter jet breaking the sound barrier, thankfully without the vapour trail, followed by, 'Fuck me, I've just farted,' from Roy in a typical knee jerk reaction.'

Their pact had obviously been blown apart quite literally, but thankfully the English 'Carry On' sense of humour kicked in with the air stewardesses and passengers creased up laughing. So, with all in the plane still giggling, they were both shown to their seats as Roy apologised to everyone as he passed them. I don't think they will be approached by MI5 for undercover work anytime in the near future.

Roy says, 'When we first went to Australia, our hotel was in an area of Sydney called King's Cross which was well known for its abundance of prostitutes. When we arrived, there were two police cars standing at the front door. We went in to reception, and the manager came over, little fellow with a 'tash, and said, 'Is this the George Forster party?' George said, 'Yes it is, is there a problem?' The manager said, 'No, no, I just want to give you a word of advice, please don't go out after nine o'clock. We have a madman roaming the street, they're trying to catch him. He's chopped two heads off this week with a samurai sword.' I turned to George and said, 'Could you not find a rougher hotel for us to fucking stay in?''

Whenever Roy visited Australia – they went twice in the nineties – the first night would always be a warm-up for the bigger venues to follow. Roy says, 'On our first trip, the warm-up was at a small venue called The Sit-down Stand-up Club. It only held about eighty people, I had a great night… tore them apart.'

The second trip, though, is one of Ritchie's favourite stories. 'The first show was the usual warm-up night for the larger two thousand seater venues which were to follow. It was in a club directly beneath Sydney Harbour Bridge with Roy continuously harping on about how his dad helped build it at Dorman's Iron and Steel works back in the day. We had a job to do and it didn't look like it was going to be an easy night. If you said that the crowd Roy was going to entertain were a bit on the rough side, then you would have actually been paying them a compliment. Even with Roy's vast experience of audiences, after peaking out through the dressing room door, he commented that they looked like one of the hardest mobs he'd ever come across. Sure enough, a small fight broke out between two tables while Roy was on stage and soon erupted into complete mayhem with just about everyone joining in. I'd never seen anything like it. The only way we were going to get out without being lynched ourselves was to have a cab pull up in the alleyway at the back. All of the corridors leading to the back door were full with what resembled the 1066 battlefield, so it was decided that the only alternative was to climb out of the window in Roy's dressing room… a feat that Roy hadn't had to perform since his early workmen's club days. There was only the three of us in the dressing room The other lads were all out front, so able to escape out of the front door. Unfortunately the window in Roy's dressing room was miniscule so the next scenario was like the train scene from Disney's Dumbo, with everybody squeezing one by one through the small aperture.' Ritchie says, 'I can still visualise the image of Roy, partway through the window, George pulling him by his arms from the front while I was pushing him from behind after his arse got stuck in the window.'

I guess that's what you call an 'arse in the pane'.

Ritchie says, 'I'm still not sure how we did it but we got out unscathed, sped our way back to the hotel and, over a welcome drink, breathed a sigh of relief, eventually all having a good laugh at the night's escapade, but wondering in the back of our heads about the rest of the tour… what on earth lies ahead?'

Roy says, 'John the agent rang the next day and said, 'Roy, Roy,' he always said your name twice, 'I hear you got them a bit excited last night.' I said, 'Yes, John, there's no dancing while I'm on.' If it had been one of my club agents from back in the seventies, I'd have been called all the useless cunts in the world for walking off regardless of what was going on in the audience.'

Thankfully, the worries for the remainder of the tour were unfounded as, after the traumatic introduction to the country's club culture, the venues that followed were full to the rafters and all huge successes, gaining Roy a massive following into the bargain.

Roy had done so well that further trips were arranged with the show travelling to Sydney, Brisbane, Melbourne, Adelaide and Perth, as well as taking in New Zealand, Hong Kong on the way out and Bahrain on the way home with a detour to perform at the Henry Fonda Theatre in Los Angeles… all complete sell outs. Ritchie says,

'On one of the trips, the DVD Down Under was recorded with a camera crew following Roy's every movement.'

Roy's annual DVDs had started as far back as 1990 with From Inside The Helmet, then a Universal contract started the following year releasing The Helmet Rides Again. The DVDs were always recorded at one of Roy's live shows and Chubby fans would eagerly look forward to their scheduled release the following Christmas.

An old newspaper cutting from 1991 shows his second DVD outselling all other comedy DVDs at that time, topping the comedy video charts even though Roy was still not getting any TV exposure. He has now amassed as many as thirty DVDs in total.

The nineties hadn't started off too well for Roy on a personal level with his mother sadly passing away in the November of 1990, but his professional career was very much on the up. As well as topping the DVD charts, he was also officially declared Comedian of the Year for 1991. The Club Mirror Award was handed over at the Lakeside Country Club in London. Previous winners had included Bob Monkhouse, Cannon and Ball, and Jim Davidson. Roy was so proud to be awarded such an accolade, even though he still hadn't been regularly seen on the telly.

Roy's DVDs had become so popular that in 1992, Universal found themselves with an excess of funds in their Roy Chubby Brown pot. They approached George Forster with options of what they could do with it… one was the making of a film, for which a plot and a script had already been written. Roy was appearing in the south of the country somewhere when George telephoned him and told him the script for the new film was being sent by courier for him to read before making the decision to go ahead.

Roy says, 'The parcel with the script arrived and I read through it. Afterwards I got straight on the phone to George. I said, 'It's not funny.' He said, 'What do you mean.' I said, 'Exactly what I've just said, George, it's not funny.' He said, 'Can you make it funny?' I said, 'Not without a re-write.' George said, 'It's too good an opportunity to miss, Roy. Have a look, see what you can do.'

Roy explains, 'It needed some comical scenes in it, so I thought back to our early band days and the sort of things that had happened. I put in the time I pissed through the telephone box that had no glass in it, and things like that, eventually coming up with what I thought was okay, and I got a credit as one of the writers. The cast was amazing… Roger Lloyd Pack, who'd been Trigger in Only Fools and Horses, Shirley Anne Field, Sue Lloyd, Kenny Baker, to name just a few. It was decided because of the plot being about aliens we'd call it 'UFO', no innuendo intended, I'm sure.'

'It was tough filming as I was still doing my stand-up theatre shows. Straight after each show, I would have to get in the car and drive to Pinewood Studios ready to start filming at 6am the next morning, though I'd never realised how much waiting around you do when making a film. It was a great experience… something that I never thought I'd be able to do when I was watching Johnny Weissmuller as Tarzan back at the Lyric cinema in the fifties.'

George Forster was thinking big now and in the UK, you just don't get any bigger than the London Palladium. Not the largest of venues Roy would perform at, but probably the one with the most prestige. You can actually book the place yourself and put your own show on, which is exactly what George did. The Roy Chubby Brown show performed for two nights, both packed to the rafters. Roy says, 'The star dressing room was tiny, I couldn't believe it. The manager came in while I was sat in there and said, 'Who do you think has sat in that chair?' I couldn't really think, I just said, 'Chubby Brown.' He came back with, 'Frank Sinatra, Judy Garland, Tom Jones, Cliff, just about every top act in the world has sat in that chair.' The show couldn't have gone better, the crowd where brilliant. Another one crossed off my bucket list, just need a fucking bucket now.'

Roy with The League Of Gentlemen

The conclusion to the nineties would give Roy one of the proudest accolades any man could get… he had a town named after him. The fictional town of Royston Vasey came onto our screens in 1999 with the introduction of The League of Gentlemen.

Reece Shearsmith, Steve Pemberton, Mark Gatiss and Jeremy Dyson created the surreal comedy series that followed the lives of the strange inhabitants living in Royston Vasey, and chose Roy himself to appear as the town mayor.

Roy says, 'It was a real honour to have this comedy town named after me. It has to be something really special to have anything named after you. I know my Uncle Stanley was dead chuffed when they named a knife after him.'

38

Life on the road with the Roy Chubby Brown show sounded like a great time, all fun and frolics, but less could be said of life back at Sunnycross House where things were deteriorating rapidly as time rolled on. Roy had been getting some bookings abroad. George had secured some work in Spain, and Sandra insisted on going along, taking with her a friend. They'd been booked into a lovely seafront hotel not far from the venue Roy would be appearing at.

All was going well until one evening when, standing at the bar, Sandra said to Roy that George had been eyeing her up. Roy knew that Sandra was a flirt and said, 'Nah, can't be.' 'No,' she said, 'he's been saying suggestive things to me.' Roy says, 'I was fuming. I shouted over to George, 'Get over here, you mucky little twat.' He came over saying, 'What's up?' I said, 'Sandra's just told me that you've been coming onto her.' He said, 'I've done no such thing,' and walked away. Later he came to me and told me I was not to bring Sandra with me anymore, and that he'd booked flights for her and her friend to go home the next morning. So Sandra and her friend went off home, leaving us behind to get on with the show… she was never allowed to come with us again, even to shows at home. I'd been quietly seeing a girl while I was away working in Blackpool. She asked me if I could give her £8,000, said she wanted to start a business. I said, 'I can't just take that sort of money out of our joint bank account without giving a good reason.' She said, 'Well, that's what I've been offered by a Sunday newspaper for my story about me and you.' I told her to fuck off and never thought any more about. A few weeks later, on a Sunday morning, I sat down on my comfy chair with the newspaper and when I opened it there I was, a full double page spread of how I'd shagged this girl but insisted on keeping my flying helmet and fucking socks on. I never keep me socks on… maybe my flying helmet, but never me fucking socks. I was at home with Sandra so I had to hide the newspaper. I jumped up as she walked in the room, quickly hiding the paper behind my back. As she came closer to me, I managed to stuff it down the back of my trousers, then I said I needed to go to the toilet, walking backwards towards the door. She wasn't taking any notice of me anyway. I didn't go to the toilet, I went straight outside to the bin and shredded the paper best I could then went back into the house, knowing full well it would only be a matter of time before one of her family would ring her and tell her about it.'

I remember it well… at the end of the story, it said, 'Have you slept with Roy Chubby Brown?' and a contact number to go with it. I was going to ring in because while we were on the road together staying in pro digs, as they were called, they would regularly only offer one double bed instead of two singles so we'd have no other option but to share… a bit Morecambe and Wise like.

Roy continues, 'One day after we'd had the most enormous fall out, she just grabbed her coat and went off to her mother's. While she was out, I phoned a locksmith to come and change all of the locks. He said he was busy so I phoned Pete, asked him to go to a hardware store and buy some locks then come over and change the locks on my doors. Pete said, 'No problem, Roy. I'll be over straightaway.' After about an hour Pete arrived and started changing the locks. He said, 'Why are you changing all of these?' I said, 'So that fucking bitch can't get back in the house.' Suddenly Pete said, 'Fucking hell, she's here! What am I gonna do?' I said, 'Quick get out of the other door,' so he ran out of the front door and came straight back saying in a bit of a panic. 'I can't get out she's parked right across the drive blocking the way.' I said, 'Six foot one bloke like you, seventeen stone, frightened of my fucking little wife.' He said, 'You are too.' I said, 'Just push her fucking car into the hedges.' So she's at the back door where we'd already changed the lock, with her mother and I can hear her trying to get her key in which wouldn't fit. She shouted, 'Roy, Roy, I know you're in there. Open this door.' I replied with, 'Fuck off! Go rot in hell, you poxy bastard.' Then another voice came, 'Roy, it's Sandra's mam, I'm gasping for a cup of tea.' I said, 'There's a café up the road.' Sandra said, 'If you don't let us in, I'm going to get the police.' I finally let her in and when she said, 'Was that Peter Richardson?' I said, 'Yes it was.' She said, 'Well, he's never allowed in this house ever again.' I said, 'But he's my driver, I'll have to let him in.' She said, 'If he sets foot in this house, I'm going to get the police on him.' When Peter rang me the following day, he said, 'What time am I picking you up, then?' I said,

'Can you pick me up at the end of the lane?' I had to walk to the end of the lane with my fucking suit over my arm, she wouldn't let him in the house. We had to meet at the end of the lane every time he picked me up after that. I got a letter from the Salvation Army saying that a young lady had been looking for me saying I was her father. I rang them up and said, 'I don't have a twenty seven year old daughter.' They told me that according to her, my name was on her birth certificate as her father. I knew nothing about it. Her mother was Barbara, who I'd had a fling with while her boyfriend was doing time in prison. We arranged to meet up at the Copthorne Hotel in Newcastle. I went with George, my manager, and she brought a friend. She told me who her mother was and once I saw her I thought, Bloody hell, she's the spitting image of her. She introduced herself saying, 'I'm Allison, I have reason to believe that you're my father.' I asked, 'How has this all come about?' She told me that she'd been brought up by a couple in Jarrow who told her early on that she was adopted. She said, 'I knew your name was Royston Vasey from my birth certificate and tried looking it up on the internet, then one of my friends said, 'You know who he is, don't you? It's Roy Chubby Brown, the comedian.' I didn't even know I'd been named on a birth certificate, it was news to me. Barbara must have done it without me knowing.'

Roy continues, 'Allison had also been trying to trace her mother but she didn't want to know anything about her. I said, 'Your mam might have a husband and kids now and be in an awkward situation, raking up the past might put her in too difficult a position for her to accept you coming back into her life.' I was trying desperately to soften the blow of her mam not wanting to know her. But I didn't turn my back on her. I did what I could for her but, by now, I had another life too, I was working twenty-four hours of the day, writing, performing and touring. I was married to Sandra, who didn't really want anything to do with the family I already had, let alone someone else turning up out of the blue. I did work up the courage to tell her that I'd had a letter from the Salvation Army, but she didn't want anything to do with it. She went ape shit, telling me I should have told her before, even after I'd explained that I didn't know. When it came to birthdays or Christmas, Allison and I would swap cards and there was always a present. She's been to see the show a few times, and we still keep in touch on the phone, texting regularly. She's living out in Saudi Arabia now, her husband's a fireman.'

Just after Allison came back into his life, Roy had stopped doing social clubs but was performing on a charity night at his sister's club, North Ormesby Institute, where Barbara and husband Norman were steward and stewardess. Roy had been a regular visitor, calling in to see his sister, so he knew quite a lot of the members and was socialising before doing his act.

Barbara came over to him and said, 'Roy, there's a lad at the front door says he's your son.'

Roy asked, 'Richard or Robert?'

'No, neither. Someone else,' said Barbara,

'Can't be. I haven't got another son,' said Roy.

'Well, you'd better come and have a look. He's your double.' Barbara took him to the front door where the lad was waiting.

Roy says, 'I got the shock of my life. I knew straightaway… he did look like me. I asked him who he was. He said, 'Martin.' I said, 'Who's your mam?' He said, 'Maureen, but she's married now, didn't you know about me?' I said, 'I knew she'd had a baby but I didn't know I was your dad.' I didn't know what else to say. It took the wind out of my sales, I must say. This lad Martin would be just about the right age from when I'd been seeing Maureen in Redcar. I brought him in so he could watch the show. I sort of got to know Martin after that. I would never dream of turning my back on him even though up until then I didn't know he existed. We didn't see much of each other, I was working hard trying to make something of my life, but if I was on anywhere locally, he might turn up at the front door, with a mate and they were always allowed in for free.'

'My life was already complicated, having married Sandra who didn't want to know anything about my past. I couldn't even mention the names of my kids, Richard and Robert. If I did, she'd just fly off the handle so I wasn't able to tell her about Martin. Well, not at first anyway. When I finally did, she just said, 'Fucking hell, how many more are there out there?'

'Sandra's lack of understanding, constant wittering and general behaviour was affecting my ability to concentrate on work. Without beating about the bush, it was soul destroying. I didn't know what I'd be coming home to after being away doing shows. In fact, the only time I didn't feel under pressure was when I was away from her. It got to the point that when I had to walk to the end of the lane to meet up with Pete, I'd be kicking my heels and shouting as soft as I dared, 'I'm free! I'm free!' I hadn't been able to say that since my late teens. Somehow the time I'd spent in borstal didn't seem to have been so bad after all.'

Roy continues, 'The inevitable split happened… I'm still not sure of the date but probably in 1996. We'd been together a mere eight years, felt like more. Thankfully, I'd been given time off for good behaviour, with the expensive divorce eventually coming through in 1998. The divorce wasn't a pleasant experience. I had to fight tooth and nail just to hang on to my beautiful baby grand piano, but the result was Sandra was finally out of my hair and I could now get my life back in order.'

Roy was probably thinking, I wonder what's around the corner?

For once, he needn't have worried.

39

When someone marries into the Royal Family, it goes without saying that their life will change in a way they could never have imagined it would. I'm guessing that, in a similar way, anyone marrying into Comedy Royalty might have to cope with the same life-changing effects. When the young Helen Coulson introduced herself to the larger than life Roy Chubby Brown way back in 1997 she could hardly have been aware that her life was never going to be the same again.

In 1997, Helen Coulson was working in the accounts office on a farm in her home county of Lincolnshire. She got on very well with her colleagues and they would regularly socialise together. One of the nights out that had been arranged was to go and see Roy Chubby Brown at Skegness. Helen didn't really know much about Roy at the time but, after getting an invite, agreed to go along. Their nights out were usually enjoyable… whatever they got up to.

Helen says, 'It was fabulous. I'd never laughed so much in ages, but didn't think of it being anything more than another great night out with the girls.' The next day at the office, John, the farmer, asked Helen where they'd been the previous night. Helen said, 'We went to see a comedian, I've never laughed so much in my life.' John had a girlfriend and said to Helen, 'He sounds good, we'll go next week. Would you like to come with us?' Helen said, 'Yes, I would love to.'

So the following week, the three of them – Helen, John and his girlfriend – went off to see Roy at Skegness. While they were standing in the foyer, Helen went over to Peter Richardson, who was driving Roy and selling the merchandise at the time. She asked if she could get to meet Roy and have a photo taken, also telling him her boss and his girlfriend would like to meet him too.

'I got talking to Roy after the show and we instantly seemed to get on, having our photograph taken together. It's hard to believe that was twenty four years ago. I still have the photo, which is very precious to me. Roy probably looks at it and thinks, That's the fateful day that has cost me a hell of a lot of money. Only joking, though Roy is the most generous person I've ever met.'

'Roy was appearing at the same theatre the following week and he asked me if I would like to come back, which I gladly did. I got there early and was taken straight to Roy's dressing room. Roy had done his soundchecks and was just sat drinking tea, killing time until the start of the show which was still a few hours away. There was a café just across the road from the theatre so I asked him if he would like to go over for a bite to eat, something he never does before a show, but he agreed and off we went. We talked about all sorts of things, with one of the main subjects being Blackpool. He was doing the summer season, appearing on one of the piers every week, and invited me to go there to meet up with him. I said that I'd love to but I'd never been to Blackpool before so I went on the train with Peter Richardson meeting me at the station. I'm not sure of what kind of impression I made on Peter after getting off the train because while I was walking toward him, I tripped and fell flat on my face, a bit Norman Wisdom like. Peter probably thought what the hell have we got here, clumsy bugger, although he did manage to stifle that giggle we always get when someone falls over. After spending the weekend together, I think we both knew in our heart of hearts that there was something special happening. I can just remember thinking that I was going to spend the rest of my life with this man.'

Roy and Helen

What Roy didn't know yet was that, in the very middle of an acrimonious divorce, his 'unlucky in love' handle, which had haunted him all of his life was about to be banished into Room 101, never to raise its ugly head ever again.

Helen continues, 'Roy had his own place in the countryside of North Yorkshire, not far from his roots on Teesside, where he did all of his work writing new material and songs. My family were based in Lincolnshire, so we agreed to buy a second property there that I would live in together with Roy when he wasn't travelling. It has been like that from day one and still is. One thing led to another and it wasn't too long before we started talking about raising a family of our own, with Reece being born in March 2001. We decided to take a break, going to Las Vegas being one of our favourite destinations, having already been a couple of times. Reece was still only one month old but my brother Andy's wife, Debbie, said she would take good care of him and we should go on our trip. We'd been together about two years by then and the subject of marriage had cropped up, but I kept saying to Roy that he probably wouldn't want to get married again having been 'down the aisle' twice already. Unbeknown to me though, on this Las Vegas trip, Roy had already decided he was going to ask me to marry him while we were there.'

Helen suggested that Roy could explain more about the Las Vegas trip so it's over to Chubby to fill in the details.

Roy says, 'Yes, we'd talked about marriage on a few occasions, but Helen was convinced I wouldn't want to take the plunge again, so I thought I'd surprise her by popping the question in Las Vegas. I wanted to find out how much it would cost first so after arriving I made a few discreet enquiries finding out that for $70 we could get married with the price including a ring and a best man. I thought, fucking hell, I'm in here, then.'

Roy adds, 'I'd already given it a lot of thought beforehand… we'd been together a few years and never argued, she'd do anything for me, but what Helen gave me that I hadn't had with previous relationships was space. That gave me the freedom I needed to concentrate on my work without being busybodied as to where had I been and what I'd been up to, which had happened in my last marriage. Helen's so laid back. I don't think she's got an enemy in the world, even though, as her husband, I'm likely to say that, but I honestly think it's true. We booked into the Mirage Hotel, only to find out it wasn't really there (just a joke), and on the first day we had a look around, seeing the sights and visiting one or two of the comedy clubs. The next day we got a taxi down to Fremont Street. The Fremont Street Experience is a pedestrian walkway offering free live music on several stages with casinos, bars, restaurants and a lightshow displayed on a giant canopy over head. It's incredible. We'd been before but not from this hotel so we asked how far away it was and, being told it was eight blocks down, we decided to get a taxi, because in America when they tell you somewhere's two blocks away, they actually mean about five miles. And we were glad we did. Mo Farah would have been out of breath by the time he fucking got there. Because Fremont Street is pedestrian, we were dropped off at the end, in front of an old building where there was a long queue waiting outside the door. I said to Helen, 'I wonder what that long queue's for, might be a show on.' After asking someone, it turned out to be the registry office… the queue was full of people waiting to get registered so they could get married in Las Vegas.'

'It hadn't been explained to me that in order to get married for $70, you had to first get registered, so I turned to Helen and said, 'Do you fancy getting married then?' She said, 'Honestly?' I said 'Yes.' Helen said, 'I'd love to marry you.' I said, 'Right.' So we stood in the queue, filled all the forms in. Question one: 'Have you been married before?' There were fifteen separate forms to complete, it wore my Roy Chubby Brown pen out, and we booked the wedding to take place in two days' time. I'd already told the lads in my team that I would never get married again, so I was sort of going back on my word. I phoned George Forster up the next day, the day before we were going to get married, and had to make a bit of a joke about it. I said, 'George, you'll never guess what happened last night… I got so pissed I asked Helen to marry me.' George said, 'Congratulations, Roy. When's the wedding?' I said, 'Tomorrow at half past six.' He said, 'So, what if I send…' I butted in, 'Don't be sending anything!' He said, 'Not for you. Flowers for Helen.''

'What I didn't know,' Roy continues, 'was that George and his son, Michael, were playing golf with some Welsh lads… I can't remember whether they were in Portugal or Spain, one or the other. One of the Welsh lads asked, 'What do you do?' to which Michael answered, 'We look after Britain's bluest comedian,' He said, 'Who?' Michael said, 'Chubby Brown.' The Welsh lad said, 'Oh, our dad loves him, he listens to him all the time in the tour bus when they're touring in Europe… the Netherlands, Germany and places. He thinks he's brilliant. Where is he?' Michael said, 'He's just been on the phone, he's in Vegas, told us he's getting married tomorrow at half past six.'

'The Welsh lad said, 'Our dad's in Vegas. Do you think they might want to go and see him?' George said, 'Why? Who is he?' His mate said, 'Tell them who your dad is, Mark.' He said, 'Tom Jones.' George said, 'You are fucking joking.' He said, 'No, my dad's Tom Jones.'

'Mark rang his dad in Las Vegas and arranged for me and Helen to go to his show after the wedding. We didn't know anything about the conversation on the golf course or the involvement of Tom Jones's son, Mark, when the phone rang in our hotel room. I answered it and asked who it was, the voice on the other end said, 'I'm Tom's PA.' I think he said his name was David. I said, 'Alright, David.' He said, 'Tom's found out that you're here.' I said, 'Tom who?' I still didn't know who he was… he said, 'Tom Jones.' He told me that Tom had arranged some tickets for his show as a wedding gift and he'd send someone to pick us up and take us to the MGM Grand where he was performing. When I got off the phone, Helen said, 'Who was that?' Off the top of my head, very nonchalantly, I said, 'Oh, it was just Tom.' She said, 'Tom who?' I said, 'Tom Jones, big mate of mine is Tom,' lying through the back of my teeth, 'when we used to do the clubs in South Wales, Tom used to come and watch the band. He thought we were great, became big mates.' She didn't believe a word of it, so I told her what was going to happen.'

Helen says, 'We got married on the 30th of April 2001 in The Little White Chapel of Flowers, which was beautiful, although the wedding itself was not what you would call lavish, just the two of us walking down the aisle on our own. I was wearing a white trouser suit, with Roy also sporting a smart two-piece suit. There was no photographer booked so we asked the vicar to take some photos. He took about four or five. We then went back to our hotel without too much fuss. I remember thinking how good it felt to be called Mrs Vasey at last. I wouldn't change anything about our wedding day for the world. We always said we'd have a bit of a do when we got home, but still haven't got round to it yet.'

Roy says, 'When we got back to the hotel after the wedding, the car which was sent to drive us to see The Tom Jones Show arrived bang on time, dropping us off at the door of the MGM Grand. On arrival we had been told to go straight to the box office and collect our tickets where we were met by a man in a white suit who gave us an envelope that had written on it, 'Mr and Mrs Vasey… Congratulations'. I said, 'That's a Cliff Richard song… we've come to the wrong place.' Helen just said, 'I can't believe it.' Then he escorted us straight out the back into what appeared to be a 'green room' where artistes meet up with their guests before they appear on stage. There was a huge spread on… fish paste sarnies as far as the eye could see, just joking, it was probably caviar but I'd never seen so much food spread out on one table in all my life and Champagne to go with it. 'Here's my boy,' came this voice in a strong Welsh accent. It was Tom Jones. He came over and put his arm round me. Helen, a big Tom Jones fan, was in a right state. She was nearly crying. He said, 'Congratulations,' and gave her a kiss, then said, 'This is my sister.' His sister was there for the show with her husband. Tom had a huge entourage around him.'

'The room was full of beautiful women… Miss Oklahoma for one, there'd been a beauty competition during the day. I could see Tom talking to them but he kept coming back over to us and telling me some of my own jokes. I said to him, 'Did you put this spread on just for us?' he said, 'Of course we did.' We knew he hadn't, he was just winding us up.

'We were then taken out front to watch the show and seated at a table right in front of the stage. We'd only been sat there a few minutes when a chap came and sat at the table next to us and, I'm not kidding you, he was the double of Tom Jones. Helen said, 'Look there's Tom.' I said, 'Where?' She said, 'There…', pointing to this Tom Jones lookalike. I said, 'It's not him.' Helen said, 'It is him. I know what he looks like. I've just been talking to him.' I learnt afterwards that Tom is this bloke's idol and he turns up every night to watch him.

'When Tom came out to do the show, he was outstanding, brilliant, and his band were unbelievable. I love my music and didn't know who to look at next… the drummer, bass player, guitarist, whoever you chose to look at were absolutely fantastic, so put them together with Tom Jones and you just had one incredible show.

'After the show, we were invited backstage again. You wouldn't believe the amount of top quality food that was laid out, lobsters galore, the sort of stuff you would pay the earth for. So we had a bit more chat, filled our bellies then said our goodnights and went off back to our hotel, which wasn't that far away. You can imagine with all the excitement we'd had, Helen couldn't sleep, and I was phoning everyone back home saying, 'Guess who was at our wedding?'

Helen says, 'We returned home, settling in to married life as Mr and Mrs Vasey. After being together for four years, being married and having a son together was a cementing of our relationship. Two years later in 2003, we had another addition to the family… a baby girl we called Amy, after Roy's mother. When Roy isn't touring, his daily routine starts between 7am and 8am… never having a lie in or breakfast in bed, saying it would make him feel lazy. Roy has to be busy; he's just that kind of person. Even on holiday, it's not long before his writing pads come out for him to write down any new material he can come up with. On mornings when we are together, I will sometimes do porridge for Roy's breakfast though, being quite domesticated, he often does it for himself as well as washing up and pushing the hoover around occasionally. As for DIY or fixing things around the house… you can forget it. For one birthday he even bought me a tool box. Luckily for Roy, I immediately saw the funny side of it.

'Roy regularly goes to the gym where he enjoys a swim, and has a walking machine that helps him keep fit enough to perform his energetic theatre shows. In his younger days, he would do weights as well but not much these days as he gets a few more aches and pains but still does very well for a seventy six year old… don't tell him I said that. For relaxation, he likes to play his piano or drums when he's at home.

'Whenever we go to the local shops, he gets recognised a lot but it doesn't bother him too much because he's always happy to give anyone his time. He isn't too keen if someone shouts 'You Fat Bastard' while we're both shopping in the supermarket. He always makes a joke, turning to me saying, 'You must lose some weight, pet', as though they were shouting it at me.

'We do have our favourite restaurants both in the North East and in Lincolnshire, but the truth is we probably eat in more often than out, with Roy working away so much. Either way, we don't really mind. Having the two houses works well for both of us, with my family all living nearby in Lincolnshire, and Roy's 'Fortress of Solitude' not far from Middlesbrough means he can get his head down and concentrate on his work without having to cope with any 'Dad's Taxi' duties, giving the kids lifts everywhere. It makes it that bit extra special when we both get together wherever it is. I bet you're all thinking that Roy would have some bad habits that constantly got on my nerves, as happens with most couples, but I have to say he doesn't really have any… I'd love to have told you he had. He does often burn food after putting it in the oven and forgetting it's there until the smell of it wafts around the house. Needless to say, most of Roy's cooking ends up in the bin.'

'Being out with Roy means you're never far away from him letting someone know what he's actually thinking about them, mainly about someone's bad driving. Roy's always been very punctual and can't stand it if people are late. He's certainly not afraid of complaining about having to wait too long for anything.'

'Amy was born in August 2003, making our family complete. The kids still remember the stories he would tell them when he put them

Amy and Reece

to bed, regularly asking, 'Is that a real story, Dad, or have you just made it up?' Good job their dad didn't tell them any true stories about him when he was growing up or they'd have had nightmares. Reece and Amy have been lucky growing up knowing how much their dad loves them. They have happy memories of playing games and going on family holidays, as well as many other occasions that we have all enjoyed together.'

'If I had to sum up what it's like being Mrs Vasey, I would have to tell you that my husband Roy is truly an inspiration of what you can achieve in life when you don't get the best of starts. He travels the length and breadth of the country, even going abroad, to spend one and a half hours on stage making people laugh.'

'My Roy is an amazing husband and dad, always being there for us when we need him be it, either in the flesh, or on the phone from wherever he might be working. Our marriage works because not only is he my husband but he is also my best friend, and even after twenty four years I still get excited when he comes home. I miss him so very much when he is away… I'm sure that's when you know you truly love someone.'

The Vaseys… Amy, Helen, Roy and Reece

Roy had finally found the person who could give him everything he'd yearned for throughout his life… love, a new family to enhance the one he'd already got with his two boys, and the space he required to carry on with his beloved work. Everything in the garden was lovely, all of the pieces of his life's jigsaw were neatly coming together, but 2002 was not far away and that year would prove to be Roy's 'annus horribilis', as Her Majesty The Queen once said, with worrying times for the Vasey family which would test their fortitude to its outer limits.

40

We're in the grip of a new millennium now, the dates we see on our daily newspapers read like something only Dan Dare, our sci-fi hero from the Eagle comic back in the fifties, would talk about, but now it was oh, so real. The birth of a new millennium isn't something everyone is going to experience, though, to the lucky ones, it's a bit like the start of the new footy season… it brings with it the expectation of a change in fortunes, turning over a new leaf, a brand new start.

But the start hadn't been so good for Roy. It was April 2000 when he got the shock of his life. 'I picked up the Gazette one day and the headlines said, 'Roy Chubby Brown's son gets ten years in prison'. I couldn't believe what I was reading. I knew Martin was a bit of a lad but had no idea it could come to this. Well, my phone never stopped ringing, with reporters asking me what he'd done. I said, 'I don't know him, I don't really have a lot to do with him.' I didn't even know his second name was Reilly until then. Maureen had got married and her husband adopted him, gave him his name.'

Even after such a shocking event as your son being sent to jail, life had to go on and it did for Roy in a much more positive way. The new millennium had already meant finding the girl of his dreams, getting married and starting a new family, as well as the chance to expand his theatre work to take in audiences around the world but alas, in the midst of so much at last going so well for him in his life, it was also to bring with it a new torment that Roy certainly could never have expected.

2002 and George told Roy he'd been offered three weeks work in Australia. 'It'll be ten grand a week.' I asked, 'How many shows?' George said, 'Three shows each week, maybe four… any more and you'll get extra.' He'd made a deal with an agent who used to be an opera singer, but was then running an agency in Sydney.

As the date approached for the new Australian trip, Roy had been noticing that after an hour and a half on stage, he was having difficulty talking, croaking a bit. He says, 'After an hour or so on stage it felt like I was losing my voice. George was at my house, having a cup of tea, when I said to him, 'I'm a bit worried about this Australian trip, George.' He said, 'Why?' I said, 'I keep losing my voice.' He said, 'Aw, you'll be all right when you get out there. It's just the cold here, getting a snotty nose and the like. You'll be okay, it's warmer there.' I said, 'Okay then.' Then George said, 'If you want to be certain though, Roy, to put your mind at rest, we'll get it looked at.'

George booked Roy into The Nuffield Hospital in Stockton to be examined. Roy says, 'When I went in to see the doctor, he started talking about nodules. I'd heard other people talk about them but no more than that. I told him I don't do much singing, mainly talking but plenty of it. He asked, 'Have you been working where there's lots of people smoking, pubs and places like that.' I said, 'Just about every job I do… by the time I go on, sometimes 11.00pm, the room's usually full of smoke, you can hardly breath. On top of that, I often have to strain, shouting out loud at the top of my voice just to be heard. He said, 'We'll do a biopsy, see what we find."

Roy continues, 'He did a biopsy and two weeks later sent for me. I had to go and see Dr White. He phoned me and said, 'Roy, I want you to come in.' I said, 'Have I anything to worry about?' He said, 'No, no, I just want you to come in and see me.' I went in, I was trying to tough it out… I'd always been used to laughing things off. I'd say, 'If I ever had a leg off, I could still hop around.' Somehow this felt very different, I didn't feel quite so tough this time.

'The first words from Dr White were, 'Roy, I want you to come into hospital straightaway.' I said, 'What's up?' He said, 'You've got a cancerous patch on one of your vocal cords. We'll have to remove it.' I said, 'Fucking hell, I'm going to Australia next Monday. He said, 'You what?' I said, 'I've got a three week tour of Australia starting next Monday. It's all sold out.' Dr White said, 'It's not up to me to judge, Roy, but if you go to Australia they could be bringing you back in a box. That has to come out now.'

'Hearing the word cancer blows your mind, I felt like I was in the middle of one of those Alfred Hitchcock spinning special effects, a bit of a dream, no… a nightmare. Dr White was still talking to me but I couldn't hear him, he just sounded like a muffled voice. My vocal cords were my lifeblood, they were my living. I owed everything I'd got so far to them, how would I survive without them. It was only seconds but all of the important things went through my thoughts, Helen… we'd only been married a year or so… Reece, Richard, Robert. Would I see them again after the operation? If so, would I be able to speak to them? Would I ever be able to speak again? I came back to earth with a bit of a bump as Dr White finished off what he'd been saying. I never heard a word of it. 'I'll make arrangements for you to come in, Roy,' then he stood up and shook my hand, saying, 'Don't worry, you're in safe hands.' I don't think I said anything, just pushed out one of those false smiles you have to do now and then.

'I went into the car park and got into my car still dazed, not being able to comprehend what Dr White had just said to me. I phoned Helen straightaway. I said, 'I've got cancer.' There was a hush, then I heard her crying. It was uncontrollable, she couldn't say anything. She finally blurted out, 'I'm coming over.' Reece was still a baby so she got someone to look after him then jumped in her car and drove to my house. When she got there, she was heartbroken saying, 'I've only known you five minutes. We've just had a baby, I can't lose you.' We never slept for two days then she took me back to the hospital. I'd only been diagnosed the day before yesterday and there I was, two days later, back at the hospital having a major operation to take away part of my throat and one vocal cord.

'The nurse that looked after me was called Noleen. She was Irish… a lovely woman. She held my hand and said, 'Don't worry, Roy, we'll do everything we can for you.'

'We all ask that same questions when they say you've got cancer. I asked, 'How long have I got?' Noleen tightened her grip on my hand, and I said it again, 'How long have I got? I've got a wife, kids and I'll have to tell them.' She said, 'I can't see into the future but I'm hopeful and you should be hopeful too, think positive because we've caught it before it's got any worse.' Well I couldn't, it just doesn't sink in when you've been so able bodied all of your life… being able to climb, run, ride a bike then suddenly the rug's pulled from underneath your feet and you're having to adapt to a new way of life. All I could think about was, God, am I ever going to walk on stage again? Afterwards, Dr White came to see me in bed. He said, 'We've removed one of your vocal cords. It'll take you a little time to learn how to speak again.' I couldn't speak at all.

'After all of that, it did have its funny moments though. I was walking around Tesco when a lad came up to me and said, 'Hi

Chubbs.' I opened my mouth but could only croak… fuck all else would come out. He asked me how I was and, thinking I hadn't heard him, said again, 'Hiya Chubbs. How you doing?' I gave him another croak. His wife came over to see what was happening. He said, 'I just wanted to talk to Chubby but he doesn't want to speak to any fucker now that he's famous.' I started laughing, so occasionally it did have its funny side.

'Even though they had taken away part of my vocal cord, I still had to have radiotherapy which meant my throat was sore all the time. I was going to James Cook Hospital in Middlesbrough to see a voice coach. She'd stand in front of me saying, 'Ba-ba-ba', and I'd answer her back with a 'Grrr-grrr-grrr'… nearest I could get. It was true I had to learn how to talk again. I began to wonder what my first word would be. We're born with two vocal cords and I now only had one. I thought, Fuck me, I'll never be able to sing in stereo again. She came at me again… 'Me-me-me-me-me'. I thought, fucking hell, she's beginning to sound like my second wife. I was thinking up little jokes but I just couldn't get them out of my mouth. I had to practise these exercises to strengthen my vocal cord 'cos it's a muscle just like any other in our body. After a few sessions, the voice coach sat me down and said, 'Roy I want you to say the first word that comes into your head.' I gave a grunt to clear my throat then started, 'Ffffffff.' I tried again, 'Ffffffff.' It just wouldn't come. I could already see she had a worried look on her face when suddenly I blurted out, 'Ffffridge.' She gave out a nervous giggle and said, 'Phew, I thought it would be something like that.' So it did have its lighter moments.

'Though I have to admit it, the following weeks were quite depressing. I was on a complete downer, regularly coughing blood up over the sink. I wanted to die. I couldn't manage the normal food I'd been used to. I had to eat baby meals mushed up out of a jar. I was craving to get my teeth into a bacon sandwich… which I did try a bit too soon, only managing one bite after it felt like I'd swallowed broken glass as soon as it hit the back of my throat. I was at home writing material, I had my piano to play, but always wondering if I'd ever be able to do it again… it was constantly running through my mind.

'What was heart-warming and gave me a real boost though were the messages I received from people like the Only Fools And Horses team… Del Boy, Rodney, Trigger, all of them. Boycie sent me a lovely letter. Ricky Tomlinson. I got a letter off Bob Monkhouse, telling me not to worry and that the next time I was in Buckinghamshire to pop round his house for a natter. Doddie contacted me. I still keep in touch with Lady Anne, Doddie's wife. I write to her often. And whenever there's a function honouring his life, I always get an invite from her.

'Every Monday, I had to have a camera down my throat. I thought that Universal had never told me about this when I signed up to do them DVDs. I hated that, couldn't sleep on a Sunday night just thinking about it the next day.'

Helen was amazed how well Roy had coped with such an horrific situation. She says, 'The radiotherapy Roy was receiving made him feel so ill. It was a bad time and he really struggled with the treatment. He was so poorly and, because he could hardly eat anything, lost over two stone. He just generally felt shocking. As bad as he was, he went to all of his appointments, not missing even one. I admire him for that. If it had been me, I'm not sure I could have coped with it all.'

Roy had lots of time on his hands… not something he copes with very well but was able to resume his daily visits to the gym after recovering from the initial operation even though he was still receiving radiotherapy and unable to talk properly. Roy enjoyed his swim and meeting up with the usual suspects one of which was Mick Monroe, a local comedian. They'd struck up a friendship, with them having a shared interest.

Coincidentally, Mick, real name Mick Shearing, used to live next door to Davy Rich back in 69/70 when Davy was involved with The Nuts show group, so knew of Roy at that time without actually knowing him personally. Mick had loose connections with Roy since then, even attending his fortieth birthday party at Stamp's Nightclub in South Bank where Tyne Tees Television presenter Paul Frost did a 'This Is Your Life' on him. I remember Stuart Stamp, who owned the club, was about the same shape as Roy, so he came on stage with Paul wearing a Chubby suit and flying hat… it was hilarious, probably the first time we'd seen anyone else wearing Roy's stage outfit.

Mick says, 'Mine and Roy's paths didn't cross very often for a number of years, with him travelling the length and breadth of the country, then I joined a gym in Stockton and Roy was a member and we would talk every day over a cup of tea. By that time, I'd become a stand-up comedian and Roy was so generous in offering me material that he'd written. While recovering from his throat cancer, he would often come to the gym and even though he couldn't talk, he still wrote gags every day, giving them to me. He'd regularly bring in a few sheets full of new gags for me to use in my act.'

Mick was friends with Keith Hammersley, a vocalist working the North East clubs. Keith says, 'I'd moved to Great Ayton so was using a gym nearby in Stokesley. Mick said, 'Roy's started using our gym, why don't you come over? We have a cup of tea now and then.'

Keith continues, 'I'd met Roy years earlier but had lost touch. Mick told me when they'd be there so I went over and met up with them. Roy was talking to me in a very husky voice, it was just after he'd had his operation to remove his vocal cord, but I was able to pick up bits of what he was saying. I was gutted to hear of what he'd had to go through but pleased to see that he was looking so good. We'd always thought and hoped that Roy would get through it all okay.'

As much of a concern for his own well being, if not more, was the fact that the people around him were unable to work too, leaving them out of pocket, so Roy wanted to get back to work for their benefit as much as his own. The crew had to become self-sufficient during this period with Tour Manager Ritchie getting some work through the connections he'd built up while he was Stage Manager at the Opera House in Blackpool, with Steve Cowper helping out in George Forster's office. Roy says, 'Thankfully they all had supportive wives who were in full time employment, so they would never be completely on the breadline.

'I'd been worried sick because they'd all been with me for so long. Ritchie's been with me for thirty one years now, and most of the others have been with me a long time too. I was worried sick that they weren't going to manage. It wasn't the fact that they would go off and get another job and not come back… I knew they'd come back because we were a team, a good team and we'd been all over the world together: America, Australia, New Zealand.'

Peter Richardson had taken a full time job and was now not available to drive Roy to his bookings, so he asked Keith if he fancied doing it. Keith continues, 'On one visit to the gym while Roy and I were on our own, he said to me, 'How are you doing these days, Keith?' He knew I was still doing the clubs and I told him I was getting a couple of bookings a week, sometimes only one… clubs aren't what they used to be. Roy said, 'Hopefully I'll get my voice back and be back on the road properly. How would you like to come along and help me? Do some driving and generally help me out? I'll see you're alright. You'll have to realise that, as opposed to doing what you're doing now, you'll be on the other side of the curtain. You won't be the one onstage… that'll be me. Could you handle that?'

'I said 'Roy, I'm very honoured that you've asked me.' Roy said, 'I'll look after you.' I said, 'I'm not bothered about that, it's just great. I can't believe you've asked me to be with you.' Roy said, 'It'll be great. You'll be away from home a few times, but it'll be great.' I said, 'I'd love to."

'Roy continued, 'The plan is to start back at Blackpool… it's coming up quite soon. Now, I don't know how it'll go, I don't know if I'll be onstage very long but the press have got hold of it and it's all going to be out that I'm back onstage at the North Pier in Blackpool. Now, you don't have to come with me on that one, I'll just go on my own.'

'I'm not sure how he got there – whether it was Steve or even George that took him – but Roy had given me his mobile number and I knew what time he was going on so I rang him before to wish him good luck and again afterwards to see how he'd got on. He was quite croaky but managed to say that he'd done okay, only managed half an hour but everyone understood.'

It had been six months of treatment before Roy was given the good news that his cancer was now in remission, and the signal that he could start working again. The hospital said they didn't need to see him for another year. Roy says, 'They'd told me I could return to work but I had to be careful. I couldn't wait to get back, and where better to make my first performance but my old stomping ground… the North Pier in Blackpool. My opening line was, 'I've been to the medical centre and the doctor said, 'I'm sorry, Roy, you've either got Alzheimer's or you've got cancer.' I said, 'Well, thank fuck I haven't got cancer.' There was a huge cheer from the audience and I just thought, 'I'm back.' I only lasted thirty minutes, my voice disappeared, just vanished, nothing would come out. I was able to apologise and everyone clapped. It was a wonderful warm response. At least I knew it was still there. My old mate Johnny Hammond came along to support me and, later at the bar, he said, 'How can you make fun of what's happened to you? That was amazing… you were as funny as fuck.' I just said, 'It's what you do, isn't it?' I've always looked for the funny side of any situation and I wasn't going to stop now. It's what has always got me through.'

Roy wondered if he'd come back too soon but tickets had been sold for future bookings. There had already been a collective decision that the regular five nights a week would have to be reduced to two or three. Having only managed half an hour onstage at his return to Blackpool, Roy was forced to rest his voice for a week before giving it another go. 'Everyone who had been working with me prior to my cancer treatment were immediately available to come back, agreeing that the reduction in the number of weekly performances would be a necessity to ensure a successful return. I understood why Pete could no longer drive me but we still socialised and continue to be really good friends to this day."

After the enforced week's break, Keith was installed as Roy's driver… the first stop was at York, The Opera House. Roy says, 'All of us, even the management team, were sitting with our fingers crossed for each of the following nights. Would I get through it? That was always the initial worry, as well as having the right material. With so much time off, your mind starts to think, can I still make them laugh? You write something and you wonder if they'll find it funny?

'We took it as slow as we dared, being careful not to overdo it but also conscious that we needed to give the audience value for money. By doing the two to three gigs a week, having plenty of rest in between, it wasn't too long before I was able to do fifty minutes to an hour. Audiences were brilliant. They all knew what I'd been through and that I was still battling with the after effects.'

It was pretty obvious when talking to Roy the morning after a gig that his throat was still taking some stick. Recovery from such a traumatic operation can take a long time to get over, but it was his and others' livelihoods at stake so Roy was certainly prepared to go through the pain barrier when he needed to. A full year after his operation, Roy had to attend hospital for a check up to make sure it had healed well and there was no sign of the cancer returning. It meant having the dreaded camera down his throat again. This time though, it was all good news… everything was looking fine.

'I felt like I was floating on air,' says Roy. 'Overjoyed! I wanted to kiss every nurse in the hospital. With the help of everyone around me, I'd beaten the cancer. I couldn't believe it.'

At this point, Roy wanted to pay special tribute to the doctors and nursing staff at The Nuffield in Stockton and James Cook University Hospital in Middlesbrough for helping him overcome the biggest hurdle in his life. Without their expertise and patience, Roy insists that he might not be here today. I think we've all got them to thank.

The naughties, as we'd been encouraged to call the first decade of the new millennium, had so far been a mixed bag for Roy but, with his cancer problems seemingly behind him, there appeared to be so much more to look forward to.

41

Coming towards the end of 2003 with Roy having returned to the stage in a full time capacity, albeit with a reduction in days per week, George informed Roy that the cancelled Australian tour was now back on for the following year. John the Antipodean agent had arranged a three week tour of dates in Australia and New Zealand, but starting with one on the way in Hong Kong.

On one of Roy's visits to the gym, during a conversation with Mick Monroe, Roy said, 'I'm going out to Australia next year. Why don't you come?' Mick says, 'I had a think about it and told him later that me and my brother would go on holiday to New Zealand, stopping off at Singapore for a few days on the way and we'd meet up with him in Wellington.'

Roy says, 'I was still worried about my throat holding out for the full length of the tour. I'd got back into my old routine of working every week, though now had to spread my bookings out in order to give my voice time to recover, but I wouldn't know unless I gave it a go. The day came and we all set off for Australia, stopping at Hong Kong for the first booking. On arriving at the Waterside Theatre, I saw that they'd had John Cleese on the week before, so I thought they were in for a bit of a shock here, but we'd sold about four hundred tickets for the show and we were sure everyone knew who they were coming to see.'

'George came to see me before the show and told me I had to sacrifice a pig. I thought it was a wind up. I said, 'Fuck off, George.' He said, 'No, it's got nowt to do with me… the manager said you have to sacrifice a pig. It's a tradition. It's to bring good luck. He said the last person who wouldn't do it was Leo Sayer… he fell off the stage and broke his leg. It's supposed to be a bad omen if you don't.' They brought me a silver salver with a pig's head on and an orange in its mouth. I was told I had to go to the four corners of the theatre and offer it to the gods… hold it up and say something like, 'Hello, my name's Roy Chubby Brown. I'm a comedian from the UK. Would you please make tonight's show as good as you can… my offer to you is this pig.' I reluctantly did as I was asked, but at the last corner where no one could see or hear me, I said, 'Now then, you cunt, I'll ram this pig right up your fucking arse if you don't pack this theatre out and make me some money, you little twat.' I thought no more about it, got back to the dressing room and lost me voice – my fucking voice just went off – so they got a doctor out. He gave me a steroid injection in my throat and my voice came back enough to get me through the show. I didn't dig any trees up, got a few laughs but not much. I had too much on my mind… worrying about the cancer, how I was going to pay the lads if I suddenly couldn't work, even what if I died so far away from home and Helen had to get my body back. My mind was in a bit of a muddle, and losing my voice like I did didn't help at all.

'We flew from Hong Kong to Perth, where the agent rang and said there'd been a mistake, Perth was to be our last gig, not the first. He said he knew it had been our first gig on our previous tour but this time your first night is in Sydney. We got to Sydney, went to the hotel and when I got there, I couldn't speak. I tried but nothing would come out. We were scheduled to do Sydney then go out to Wellington in New Zealand to perform there with another city thrown in as well, before coming back to Adelaide, then Brisbane before finishing in Melbourne, but I had to cancel New Zealand.'

Mick Monroe was already in Wellington with his brother, waiting for Roy to arrive. Roy had told Mick, 'I'll meet you there, I'm on at the Queen Street Town Hall. There's a bar opposite called Peter's Bar, go in there and order twelve steaks and twelve seats for us all on my opening night.' Mick says, 'Roy would have only just arrived in Hong Kong when I ordered the steaks and seats, so having done that, we just got on with our holiday. After a few days I thought we'd look the Town Hall up and see what kind of a place it was, only to see a sign over Roy's poster saying, Roy Chubby Brown Show Cancelled.

'With no explanation as to why, I gave Roy a ring to find out that he'd lost his voice in Hong Kong and had to cancel a few shows with New Zealand being one of them. We stayed on in New Zealand for the next three or four days then we flew to Sidney, staying at the Star City Hotel with Roy and his crew. After Roy had rested his throat, we went with him to a few of his gigs – Roy would be picked up, taking us along too. They were all sold out. We then flew home via Singapore with Roy following one day behind.'

Roy says, 'We stayed for a couple of weeks in the hotel until I managed to get my voice back for the last four shows in Australia… Adelaide, Melbourne, Brisbane and Perth.'

Roy continues, 'The shows were nicely spread out, giving my throat enough time to recover after each one and while in Adelaide, we had a few days to spare. We were told Henley Beach was a good place to visit. It was only a couple of miles away and if we went down to the harbour, there'd be a boat that would take us there. When we got to the harbour, it was more like one of our bus stations. There were dozens of fifty seater boats lined up all with their destinations displayed on a board alongside. Most people take a boat to work rather than join the traffic jams that occur on the roads during the rush hour. We had to look for the Henley boat.

'On the busy quayside there was an Elvis impersonator busking. He was an aboriginal with a little grass skirt, but he had a white jacket and a black wig, sporting the biggest pair of Elvis side burns I'd ever seen. When he started singing, we were crying laughing, he was so funny. He's famous there… everyone knows about him, my face was aching. I don't think he realised how funny he was.

'When we got to Henley, we went straight to the beach. It was packed but we managed to find a small patch of sand to put our towels on. Aaran, our soundman, was down at the water's edge, paddling among the small waves as they came in. We were about ten yards away, talking about the show and what we were going to do when a suddenly large wave came in and hit Aaran on the chest. The force of the wave made him fall backwards and the current dragged him into the sea. He screamed and shouted, 'Help, I can't swim!' Ritchie jumped up before we had time to move and ran down, grabbed him and pulled him out. He nearly drowned. I said 'Can't you swim?' He said, 'No, I've never learnt.' We were all shocked by the event. I just said, 'Fuck me, you could have drowned if Ritchie hadn't pulled you out.'

'In Brisbane, the hotel we were booked into was in the middle of a jungle. It was just like I'm A Celebrity Get Me out of Here. Proper thick undergrowth with string bridge walkways leading to your log cabin room. During the day, cleaners come in and check all the nets on your windows – there's no glass in them because of the heat – and they're looking to make sure nothing has come through them like snakes or spiders. Well, you know what I'm frightened of? Moths, fucking moths. When I was a kid, I must have been in a room where a moth resembling a pterodactyl had flown round the light bulb.

'The hotel had an outside bar, a bit like a Tropicana bar with a piano playing. It was great way to wind down while we weren't working but when I went back to my cabin, I said 'Is someone coming back with me?' They said, 'It's only over there!' I said, 'You'll have to come with me, I don't like the look of them fucking moths.' Ritchie said, 'I'll walk back with you.' The moths were gigantic, looked more like fucking bats some of them. They were tropical moths. Ritchie said they were harmless. I said, pointing to one that was circling around us, 'That cunt could pick me up.'

'One morning while we were in Brisbane, George said, 'Do you fancy a game of golf?' I'm not a good golfer but I like to play, so I said, 'Go on then, why not? It'll kill some time.' So we went to the local golf course about ten miles from the city… a beautiful course but it was jungle all round and on the first tee, it said, 'Beware of Snakes'. I snapped, 'What the fucking hell are we doing here? You might just hit a ball and hear sssssssss… a snake. Fuck this for a lark!' Then I spotted another sign saying, 'Please do not retrieve your balls from the water because of the crocodiles'. And there was loads of fucking water, more water than fucking dry land.

'We were walking along… George was there, and, Michael, George's son was there, carrying our clubs as we walked past one of the lakes… a massive, enormous lake it was. Suddenly something emerged very slowly from the water. Well, we all nearly shit ourselves. It was an Aborigine! They dive in, retrieve your golf balls and sell them back to you. They must be fucking mad. I nearly took his fucking head off with my five iron. I said, 'You fucking idiot… fucking frightening the shit out of us like that.' He just smiled, a grin as wide as the lake itself but with no front teeth, and said, 'You want your ball?' 'You're lucky your balls aren't all over the bank, you cunt,' I spluttered. Fuck me, he just came out of the water, frightened the fucking life out of us all. I thought my heart was going to stop. Right where he'd walked out of the water there was a big sign saying, 'Don't retrieve your ball because of the crocs'. I was beginning to feel like an old croc myself now.

'We'd been on the course about an hour and a half when the club staff came out, driving little carts with drinks and snacks, oranges,

Mars bars, things like that. A guy came round the corner and said, 'Are you playing on the ninth next?' I said, 'I think so. The ninth's just round the corner, isn't it?' He said, 'Well, you might have to wait, we've got a pack of kangaroos.' When we walked round towards the ninth where there must have been seventeen kangaroos just sitting on the fairway, looking straight at us, as if to say, 'What the fuck are you doing here?' It's just so funny, even the baby ones just sat there looking. I said, 'How we going to get past them?' George said, 'I think we'll have to wait until they go home.' I said, 'I think they're already home, but I'm not hanging about 'til someone puts the fucking kettle on.' They just sat about like they didn't have a care in the world. Some of them were eating the grass and walking round, some must have been at least six foot six. They were starting to look a bit restless, and I know kangaroos can be a bit dangerous so I said, 'Get on the cart now, just in case.' As I said it, one of the ground staff came, made a noise and they all ran off. They must have been frightened by the particular animal noise he was making so they left in a bit of a rush. If you drive out of Melbourne, through the traffic lights and head towards the coast, you arrive at another large built up area with the feeling that you'd driven into another city because it has everything… it's only about three or four miles away and another part of Melbourne but it felt like driving out of Birmingham directly into the centre of London. The Concorde Theatre and Assembly Rooms, where we were playing were on the high street, they'd had tribute bands on the previous nights with Abba and two nights of Freddy Mercury. When I got there, a bloke said to me, 'Can I help you?' I said, 'I'm Chubby Brown.' He said, 'God, you look nowt like him.' I said, 'Well, I don't walk round wearing my flying hat and goggles.' I said, 'My crew's here. How do they get the stuff in?' He said, 'We'll get it in for them, just tell them to go and get a cup of tea.' I told Ritchie and the lads and we went across the road to a café. The waitresses had tight little shorts and tops and I just thought, 'Wow, there's some fanny here then.' On the right, there was a garage with old cars… old American cars like Chevrolets with the wings on the back, like you see on the TV show, Happy Days. I said, 'Just look at them fucking cars.' There wasn't just one or two, there were fifty or sixty of them with one right up in the air, sticking out of the upstairs window of the garage.'

'Back at the theatre, the manager came to see me and said, 'You must be very popular, your tickets went within two hours, that's never been known here.' He said, 'I've never known it, it always takes six or seven days for a celebrity to sell out of tickets but yours went like that!' snapping his fingers as he said it. 'What do you do? We've just been told that you're a suggestive comedian.' I said, 'I'm known as Britain's Bluest Comic.' He said, 'No wonder then.' So I asked, 'Have you got any inhibitions here?' He replied, 'Oh no we're very open-minded.' The theatre seated fourteen or fifteen hundred. It was a great night. There was a lot of hecklers in, they must have seen my first or second video and thought I liked to be shouted at. I had to say, 'I don't mind you shouting but not all at the same fucking time. If I wanted to be shouted at, I'd had brought the wife.' Brilliant night. At Perth, we were on with a jazz four piece that had a girl lead vocalist. When we were in the dressing room, I said to her, 'Have you been on with a blue comedian before?' 'Oh,' she said, don't worry about us, we've done them all… the Albert Hall, Ronnie Scott's Jazz Club.' They were piano, bass and drums… she sang jazz, a bit like Cleo Lane. The audience were all blokes and when she was introduced, the band behind her went into some complicated jazz riffs and as she came to the front of the stage, someone out of the audience just stood up and shouted, 'Show us your fucking fadge!' The piano player looked at her, then the bass player with them all walking off. I said, 'I did try to warn you.' She didn't say anything to me but George said that she told him they would never work with Roy Chubby Brown ever again. It was while we were in Perth, sat on a wall at the side of the beach and just about to go into the sea for a swim when a helicopter flew overhead and boomed out, 'White shark in the area! White shark in the area! Please leave the water!' Ever so calmly, without a fuss, everyone just came out of the water. I said, 'Fuck me, a white shark in the area, that doesn't happen on Redcar beach. The worst injury you can get in the sea at home is if you accidentally catch your big toe on a discarded old shopping trolley.' I don't really need to tell you that I didn't get my swim that afternoon. From then on, I just stuck to the hotel swimming pool. I didn't fancy offering Jaws the decision of whether to go for a skinny one with no meat on its bones or sink his teeth into the fat limey bastard, with the prospect of having some left over for supper later on. Shark bait… no thanks.'

Roy continues, 'Rugby's so massive in Australia that their clubs seat anywhere around a thousand people, they're massive like theatres. They've got restaurants, bowling alleys, you can play five-a-side football… they're just like massive leisure centres. I supported Paul Young at a rugby club on one of the nights. Paul was the headliner, having had huge hits in the mid-eighties with the likes of Every Time You Go Away and Love Of The Common People. I was on at 9.00pm and had one of those nights you just never forget. They were laughing from the moment I walked on stage. After I'd told a joke, I had to wait for the laughter and clapping to die down to tell the next one. It was fantastic, but it does knock you out with the timing a little bit. By the time they'd stopped laughing and clapping, I'd forgotten where I was in my act. It was a brilliant night. The owner came to me after the show and said, 'We've never had a response to a comedian like that before. Can you come back tomorrow night?' It would have been great, I'm sure, but I had to tell him that the agent had me booked out elsewhere. There's a motto, 'Always leave them wanting more,' and on that occasion, I think I did. We worked Australia on three separate occasions. The last one being after my cancer treatment had finished. After so long, it's hard to remember which story happened during which visit but I brought back with me lots of good memories from each visit… apart from the giant fucking moths that is.'

42

It had to be around 2004, just after the Australia tour, when Roy and George Forster parted company. It's rare that an act and a manager would stay together forever and Roy will always be grateful for George's assistance in turning him into Britain's Bluest Comedian. Without George, he might still be doing the club circuit, picking up cherry bobs. The fact was that their relationship was not as tight as it had been and Roy decided it would be better for him to move management. Roy signed to Handshake, with Stuart Littlewood becoming his manager. Stuart had managed some of the biggest names in the business… Little and Large being just one of many, so Roy was as sure as he could be that he was in good hands.

After coming home from Australia, apart from the changing of management, life started to get back to normal, but doing only two or three gigs a week meant a considerable reduction in Roy's income. He was never going to be destitute but had the likes of Keith, who had recently started driving for him, to consider, as well as other members of his crew. Over a cup of tea at the gym one day, he was talking to Mick Monroe. Mick says, 'Roy asked, 'Have you done any after dinner speaking? I wouldn't mind getting into it but I don't know how it works.' I said, 'Yes, I have. It's simple really. You just get up and talk about your life and do a questions and answers session.' Roy said, 'Why don't we do a few together? See how they go?' So we did, with Keith starting the show up, singing a few songs, then I get up and crack some gags, finally Roy with forty five minutes of questions and answers about his life and career. We were able to take it back into working men's clubs, even the odd pub. It was good for Roy because he could fit extra gigs in without putting too much strain on his voice.'

Keith, having been brought in as driver then becoming merchandise salesman, had now becoming part of Roy's Q and A Roadshow. Keith says, 'The Q and As were always something that Roy really enjoyed doing. They were usually at a nice venue or bigger working men's club, top hotels like the Holiday Inn… it all depended who the promoter was at the time. We don't do them anymore but often talk about them and Roy loved them. We all got a little bit of credit and most of them were for charity anyway.'

HAVE YOUR PHOTO TOOK WITH CHUBBY HERE

Keith continues, 'When the audience arrived, those who wanted to would queue up for a meet and greet plus a photo with Roy at a cost of £5, with everything going to charity, Zoe's Place or Cancer Research. I'd keep an eye on things, do a soundcheck then keep an eye on it throughout the night. The equipment we used wasn't the main show gear. We'd bring a PA system, though some of the promoters provided a PA and Sound Engineer.

'I would go on, introduce myself, sing five or six numbers and then bring Mick on to do twenty minutes or so. We always planned for Roy to not go on too late, but occasionally we had no choice and the audience could get a bit silly, having had a few beers. Mostly the evenings were really good with everyone behaving themselves. They'd paid their money and just wanted a good time. We tried to have it all done and dusted by 10pm. We had to think of Roy's throat, especially if we were working the next night. Roy's part of the night opened up with the TV screens we'd brought along showing him playing his drums, then it would display 'Please welcome… Roy Chubby Brown' with Roy coming into view and I would referee the questions being asked by the audience, as well as interviewing him in between questions.

'Roy would just wear his normal clothes – civvies if you like – and would never sit down. He wasn't comfortable sitting down. After the introduction, telling everyone of how he started in the business with a few funnies thrown in, I would ask him a couple of questions. I always knew when he'd finished talking 'cos he gave me the look that meant he wanted me to say something. I would chip in with a bit of banter then I would take questions from the audience. We'd often have somebody going round with the microphone to make it easier. The audience would regularly get an answer from me before Roy, with me being on the receiving end of a glare from him in to the bargain. There were always a couple of funny questions with Roy answering somebody back and the whole place laughing uncontrollably.'

The Q and A sessions, as few and far between as they were, became a regular part of the Roy Chubby Brown show, gaining him a headline in our local Gazette of 'Chubby's returning to the clubs'. It was deemed as quite a big thing for those clubs who remembered him from the beginning of his career… even the ones that had barred him out wanted him back.

Life continued in that vein for the years immediately following Roy's cancer scare and the Australian tour, with Stuart Littlewood handling the theatre gigs while Roy, Keith and Mick did their own thing with smaller Q and A bookings.

Keith had become an integral part of Roy's team, but we have to go back to the mid 70s for the first time they came across each other. Keith and a few of his friends had decided to form a group and with Keith being lead singer, he was given the job of buying some speakers for the PA system. One of the lads in the band was good with his hands so said that if Keith managed to get some speakers, he would make the cabinets to house them.

Keith bought some speakers from Guitarzan musical shop in South Bank but they weren't compatible so he wanted to exchange them or get his money back. When he took them back to the shop, he noticed a large figure standing near the counter, dressed very unusually in blue denim dungarees, flat cap and Jesus sandals. Not having seen him before and thinking this chap must have come to read the lecky meter… unbeknown to Keith, he was staring straight at Roy Brown, as he was then. Keith looked twice at Roy's dungarees, thinking that he hadn't seen anyone dressed like that since Pa Clampett off The Beverly Hillbillies telly show.

After explaining himself to Alan, the manager, there appeared to be some dispute over whether he was going to get his money back. Keith said, 'I'm out of work. I've had to get this money off my Nanna. I just want some replacement speakers.' Alan told Keith he didn't have any other speakers and walked out into the back of the shop.

Keith takes up what happened next. 'This fellow in the dungarees looked over to me and asked, 'What happened there?' So I told him we were forming a group but the speakers I'd bought weren't the right ones, they didn't fit. He immediately shouted, 'Alan!' Alan came back into the shop. 'Give this lad his money back.' Alan said, 'What?' 'Give this lad his money back, they're trying to form a group.' Alan went straight to the till, took out the money and gave it to me saying, 'I was going to give it back to you anyway. I was only out the back looking to see if we had any replacements.'

'When I got outside, my mate, who'd been with me said, 'Don't you know who that was?' I said, 'No, I don't.' He said, 'It's Roy Brown, the comedian. Swears like fuck, he's great. I've got one of his cassettes.' I just said, 'Bloody hell.'

Keith and his mates formed their band, The Rick Davis Road Show, an Elvis tribute band, and worked the North East clubs for a few years, with Keith picking up his nickname of Fat Elvis, owing to his portly shape. During this time, Roy and Keith didn't come across each other. The band eventually split up and Keith decided he would like to work the clubs as a solo act.

Keith had been rehearsing his new solo act at the Embassy Social Club in Thornaby, which was just up the road from where he lived. The drummer was a mate of his and the keyboard player wrote Keith's musical parts for him to take to venues where the resident musicians would back him. The two lads would come into the club to occasionally back Keith on quiet afternoons so that he could rehearse his new show.

As a thank you for letting him use the club for rehearsing, Keith offered to do a free show. Keith thinks it would have been around 1980-81. The night that Keith was doing his free show coincidently turned out to be a night when Roy Chubby Brown was booked to appear… this would be the very first time he had worked with Roy, and says he was very excited at the prospect. By then

Roy had become a huge draw, bringing in full houses wherever he appeared.

Keith had a job working for an electrical company, delivering and installing televisions, which came with a company van that he used for carrying his gear around to his bookings. With the Embassy being close to where Keith was living, he set up his PA equipment on the afternoon so he could walk to the club on the evening where he met up with Roy and Ronnie Keegan, Roy's driver at the time, who Keith knew quite well. The club was packed, Roy was dead funny, had the crowd in hysterics, and they had a brilliant night.

Keith, who was working under the stage name of Rick Davis remembers, 'Roy came into the dressing room after my first spot and complimented me on my singing, which was a huge thing from such an established act. He said that he'd never heard anyone sing Walk A Mile In My Shoes before, which Keith had taken from a live Elvis concert.'

Not long after the Embassy night, Ronnie said to Keith, 'Roy said you can come to the show tonight if you want.' Keith says that he was dead chuffed to be asked and only too happy to go along, which he did on a few occasions after that.

Those nights would generally end up at The Europa in Middlesbrough, a favoured late night restaurant, or Roy would pull up outside a fish and chip shop, buying them all supper on the way home. Keith recalls that Roy had a Ford Sierra, but only ever saw him driving it even though Ronnie was supposed to be his driver. Keith remembers Roy driving the car one snowy winter's night to a club in Scarborough, before driving back through the stormy weather.

Roy asked Keith if he would do some harmonies on a new song he'd written. They were recording it at Dimmer Blackwell's studio. Dimmer had been working as Roy's soundman at the time. Keith admits, 'I was real nervous about this, having never been in a recording studio before, and to be asked by someone as high profile as Roy was immense. I remember turning up at the studio with top class musicians including Paul Smith and the likes. I was speechless, didn't know what to do. Roy gave someone a few bob and sent them out to get us all bacon and sausage sandwiches, which is typical of Roy even now.'

Keith says, 'The song we were recording was I Just Called To Say I Fucked You, a parody on the Stevie Wonder hit, and Roy kept having to stop because he was laughing. Roy would look over to me and I felt I should have been laughing as well, but I was rigid to the spot, so nervous thinking I'd done something wrong. I'd never been anywhere like it before with all these brilliant musicians. After it had been produced, I noticed that on the back of the disc's sleeve, it said, 'Thanks to Rick, which was my stage name, for not laughing.' I've got a copy of that somewhere at home. Afterwards he dropped me off and we just went our separate ways.'

Ronnie Keegan got sacked from driving Roy around by George Forster, Roy's manager, after complaining about a few things. Ronnie had been getting on to Roy about stuff, and Roy, not feeling he should get involved, told Ronnie that if he had any grievances to take them up with George, which he did with the result being that George, who was a businessman and not one to stand on ceremony, just sacking him, saying that he'd had enough.

With Ronnie now out of the picture, there was a lengthy period when Keith didn't have any contact with Roy at all. Keith carried on with his own club and pub work, where agents often advertised him by saying, 'You've seen him with a pint in his hand, now see him with a mike in his hand.' Roy was never far from his thoughts, always wanting to know how he was doing and going to see his shows when he was on Middlesbrough Town Hall.

One coincidence that came up was with Keith's uncle Billy. 'I'd been going with Roy and Ronnie when I mentioned it to my uncle, who told me that he'd been at sea with Roy.'

'Uncle Billy was about five years older than Roy and he told me that he took Roy under his wing a bit. He said, 'He was a handful, you know.' He said, 'Roy wouldn't take any crap, any shit off anybody.' Evidentially what Roy had been doing on ship was getting stuff out of the fridge, like booze or anything they wanted… nobody should have been drinking and Roy shouldn't have been getting it for them. They all got him to do it, even my Uncle Billy, because they thought nobody would bother him, but someone spragged on Roy and the captain punished him by stamping his card, and amassing too many stamps means you got side-lined for sailing jobs.'

Keith says, 'I carried on doing the clubs without really any contact with Roy but always liked to keep up to date with how successful he had become… doing theatres rather than clubs… producing videos. We all couldn't wait to get our hands on each one as they came out. I've got quite a large selection to date. I remember when I used to go with Roy when Ronnie was driving him. After the shows there'd be long queues at his merchandise stall, buying cassettes and stuff. That's how popular he was even then. To get to the point where Roy asked me if I would like to become one of the team and drive him to his bookings was immense. I couldn't believe it had happened. However, George gave me two years, tops. Not long after I'd first started with Roy, Forster got me to one side saying, 'How're you getting on? Do you like the job?' Before I could answer him back, he said, 'I'll give you two years.' I didn't really know how to answer him. I knew him to be a ruthless businessman and I was still finding my feet so wasn't sure how to react to anything he said. I just concentrated on trying to prove the man wrong. So far, so good. I could never have dreamt that I would be flying round the world with one of the funniest men on the planet.' These days Keith probably spends more time with Roy than any other person and, like Peter Richardson before him, is effectively more of a personal assistant than anything else.

The next few years trundled along quite nicely, everyone was now used to doing only a couple of gigs a week, and if a third was ever thrown in, it would always be touch and go for the last one. There were still occasions when Roy was forced to rest, but the one thing he hated doing was letting his fans down, so cancelling any nights would certainly be regarded as a last resort.

After Roy and George parted company, even though things were going well for Roy, his brand of humour was never going to be everybody's cup of tea, and because of that he faced being banned from appearing in certain towns. These stretched the length and breadth of the country, from cities in Wales, Scotland, across England, before unceremoniously landing on his own doorstep when he was banned from appearing at the Town Hall of his home town of Middlesbrough, at which he'd performed annually for a number of years, causing quite an uproar from his local band of followers. The Middlesbrough ban has now been rescinded, though he has yet, as of mid-2021, to make his return due to cancellations because of Covid.

While Roy's professional and home life were ticking along quite nicely, he hadn't seen anything of his estranged son, Martin, who had been sent to prison at the turn of the century for a firearms offence. Keith knew Martin's family well and would keep Roy informed if there was anything to tell. It appeared that Martin had been living in a flat above Stillington Working Men's Club on the northern outskirts of Stockton-on-Tees, a club that Roy would have performed at in his early days. 2009 came along and another headline involving 'The son of Roy Chubby Brown' appeared in the local Gazette when Martin received yet another custodial sentence, being sent down for four years for drug offences.

Roy says, 'I never knew anything about it. Martin can't have been out of prison for very long before he went back again. He'd called in at the gym once since he got out and we had a cup of tea together. He did eight years for carrying a gun and shooting at drug dealers. I asked Martin what happened, he just said, 'Aw fuck him, he was horrible. I was gonna fucking kill him.' Now he was back behind bars for another four years.'

43

Roy continued to spread his wings and took in dates in Spain and the Canary Islands. Keith tells of a visit around 2015 to Marbella, organised by promoter John Carr, where they appeared at the Costa Hotel. 'It was a fantastic venue. I worked as supporting act for the shows, and I'd open the show, warming the audience for when Roy came on. Everything was beautifully set up, it was a class place, but while I was on there was a table of people being exceptionally loud. It was only Tyson Fury and his family, and I started to wonder who was going to be brave enough to ask Tyson Fury if he wouldn't mind being a bit quieter when Roy came on, so we sent John, the promoter.'

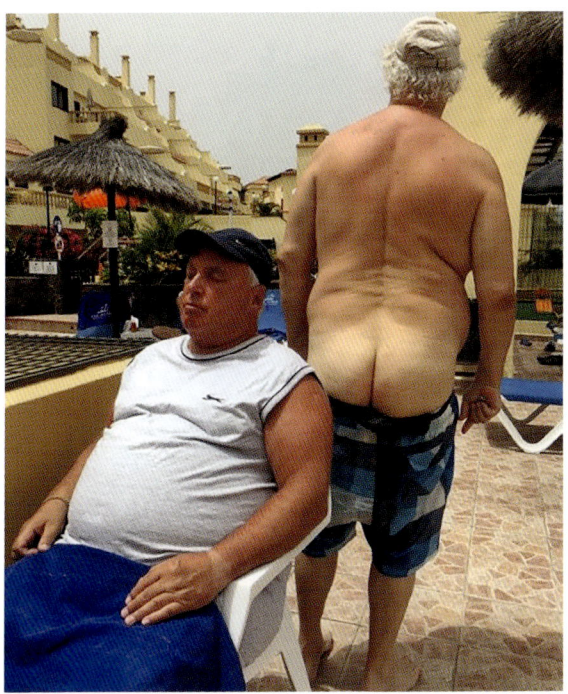

All work and no play for Keith and Roy in Spain

Keith continues, 'After John had a word, Tyson immediately stood up, bashed his fist on the table to everybody's shocked surprise and shouted out, 'I'm telling you now… family, sister, brothers, cousins make a noise when this man comes on and I'll batter the lot of you.' That was it, there wasn't another word all night long and they absolutely loved the show. And afterwards, I'm sure Tyson went back to see Roy.'

The Canary Islands became an annual visit with the show always going down well with the holidaymakers, but the majority of Roy's work continued to be the sell out theatre venues in the UK.

2015 saw Roy celebrate his seventieth birthday at The Blue Bell Hotel in Middlesbrough, where the entertainment was provided by Roy's brilliant guitar playing cousin, Lee Vasey… an original band member from the early days, as well as Keith doing a spot later on. Attending was a mixture of family, close friends and entertainment associates. Crissy Rock from the hit TV show, Benidorm, was there, with Roy and her having been friends for a number of years. Stuart Littlewood, Roy's manager, came along, though there would be a parting of the ways later that year. Steve Pinnell was there, myself and Mick from Hall, Cock and Brown, Davy Rich from The Nuts and Mick Monroe, plus loads more. It was a wonderful evening for Roy and everyone had a great night, meeting up with people they hadn't seen for ages.

Roy was still a regular at the gym each morning, swimming a few lengths in the pool. A regular visitor who would specifically come to see Roy was his son Martin, having finished his latest custodial sentence.

Roy says, 'Martin was still into drugs in a big way. I never understood it, to be honest. I know I'd had a chequered past but I didn't get the drug thing at all, but he still came to see me at the gym and I never questioned him. I gave him some money when he said his mates were all going to Benidorm and he'd like to go with them but couldn't afford it. Keith, not knowing what I'd done, just happened to tell me he'd seen Martin in Teesside Park shopping centre when he should have been away, so we'll never know what Martin spent the

Roy and Martin

money on, will we? Keith knew the family quite well, so he became a bit of a go between for us, letting me know if Martin needed me for anything.'

Keith tells of an occasion after a stop over. 'We were at Aldershot and I knocked on Roy's hotel room door to go for breakfast. He said, 'You go down and I'll follow you, I'm just on the phone.' Ritchie and a couple of the crew arrived and I said to him, 'I'm not very happy about Roy's face, it seems to be slightly droopy on one side.' Roy came down and nothing else was said but within ten minutes it had got worse. I said, 'You've got Bell's Palsy.' He said, 'Bell's what? Isn't that what Quasimodo had?' I said, 'It looks like a stroke… pray to God it isn't because you seem alright in yourself but your face is drooping on one side.' It was starting to look quite horrendous and getting worse, it looked like a dropped pie.' Although I'm not sure either Roy or Keith would know what a dropped pie looks like… catching any pie before it hit the floor if they were to ever let one fall from their grasp.

Keith continues, 'By the end of the breakfast, he could hardly talk. I said again, 'It's Bell's Palsy.' He said, 'What the fuck do you know, doctor fucking death?' I said, 'I know people who've had the same thing. George Barnes, the snooker player, he came to the pub one day looking just like you.' Roy said, 'What in a flying hat and goggles?' I said, 'No, with his face dropped like yours, and I asked him what had happened, he said, 'I've got Bell's Palsy.' It didn't last long, he's okay now.

'Roy was due go onstage later that day, so we found a doctor. Me and Ritchie went into the doctor's surgery with him… it was a lady doctor, she looked into his eyes and after about ten seconds said, 'You've got Bell's Palsy.' I clenched my fist and went 'Yesssss!' Not that I wished any ill on Roy but for once I had been right. I can't think of a time when I've been so emotional while I've been with him as I was that night to see him go on that stage and perform like that. He could hardly talk and he told the audience what was wrong with him and they sat there, they understood, they took him to their hearts. The tears were rolling down my face because I couldn't believe it. Had it been me, I would have wanted to be home. I'd have had a panic. It just looked horrendous, one side of his face had just gone down. I don't think he posed for any photos that night.'

As said earlier, mid-2015 would see Roy parting company with manager Stuart Littlewood and leaving Handshake. Roy said, 'For a short while this left us without anyone to fix the show's bookings. I said to the lads, 'We'll all have to stand by the phones now. I'll get some cards with the phone number on and we'll all have to take bookings. Do you agree with that, Ritchie?' Ritchie said, 'Yes, we'll do it all ourselves."

Roy continues, 'After a couple of months, Keith came along and said, 'I've got this lad, he's an absolute Chubby Brown fanatic. He's called Stephen Lloyd, runs an agency, he's worked Freddy Starr, and The Krankies, and he said he wants to work with you.' So I met him at the gym, and Steve just said, 'As from now, I'll take over, I'll look after everything.' I had no reason to think he wouldn't. Unfortunately, it didn't quite work out as we thought it would and after only a couple of years we decided to move on when Ritchie said to me, 'I know somebody who was an act… Tony Jo, he was one of the Grumbleweeds. He's got loads of acts on his books, he said he'll look after you.'

Tony Jo took on Roy's management, arranging bookings and looking after all Roy Chubby Brown dealings. Sadly, ill health has forced Tony to take a back seat, with Ritchie now taking the helm and steadying the ship. Ritchie is now not only Tour Manager but also managing the bookings and doing an admirable job with both.

While all this to-ing and fro-ing with managers was going on, there was still the serious job of making people laugh to be dealt with… so back on the road we go with Keith recalling a flight to Dublin. 'The pilot said, 'We're just about to head into a slight bit of turbulence. Could the crew please sit down… and fasten your seat belts.' In no time the plane started to rock 'n' roll beyond belief and there was no one more terrified than me. I was sat next to Roy. It was horrendous. I thought that was it. We all know that Roy hates flying, he'd actually gone green. When the plane got back level again, the pilot said, 'Air crew resume duties. ' The whole plane went quiet and the girls got back up with the trolley then came down towards us with the coffees. When one of the crew reached us, she looked at Roy and asked, 'Can I get you anything, sir?' Roy replied, 'Yes, a fucking bible.' Everyone on the plane heard him and the laugh came as a complete relief after the bumpy ride we'd just had.'

It was while on a booking in Scotland that Keith received some tragic news that he had to keep from Roy while he was still working. It was a night in March 2019 when Keith was waiting in the car while Roy signed autographs when his phone rang. He says, 'I knew Roy's son, Martin's, family quite well and it was a mutual friend who'd rang to tell me that Martin had been found dead. I thought, shit, I can't tell him that now and made an instant decision to leave it 'til later on before giving him the bad news.

'When Roy got into the car, he was still on such a high from having a great night that I still didn't think it was the right time to tell him. After about twenty minutes, I was still waiting for the correct time, but I said, 'I'm sorry, Roy, I've got something to tell you and I can't put it off any longer.' He said, 'What is it?' I said, 'Martin's dead.' He gulped and said, 'You what?' I said, 'They've found Martin dead.''

Roy says, 'We were told later by pathologist that he'd been having a drink and drugs binge with one of his mates, fell asleep and just didn't wake up. Whether it was accidental or not, we'll never know.'

Even though Martin appeared later in Roy's life and they didn't have a great deal to do with each other, Roy was always there for him if he ever needed anything. Roy's never turned his back on any of his children.

As you would expect, Roy was devastated. There were a further two bookings to do in Scotland which he cancelled, not being in the right frame of mind to complete them. Roy says, 'I cancelled the shows I was about to do in Scotland, came home and attended the funeral at Teesside Crematorium in Middlesbrough.'

When asked for a comment by reporters from the national newspapers Roy told them, 'Martin was a lost soul who has finally found peace.'

44

Ritchie and Keith typify the sentiments of the rest of the team as to how much they must like working with Roy by the fact that they have been with him for such a long time. The full crew are a dedicated bunch and Roy knows that they can be fully relied on to help him produce an enjoyable night's entertainment for the people who have dug deep into their pockets to come and watch the show.

The Roy Chubby Brown show attracts a broad spectrum of followers, mainly Chubby fans because they know the style of humour they're going to get before they arrive. I'm sure everyone turns up in good humour with the intention of having a great night out watching their favourite comedian though occasionally there might be one or two in the audience who think they can be part of the show. For these situations, Roy employs his own security.

Geoff Ormesher is the head of security. He started working with Roy back in the summer of 1989, around the same time as tour manager, Ritchie. In those days, Geoff and five others were sub-contracted from a security firm called Starguard, with a total of six guarding each Roy Chubby Brown show.

Geoff had been working in the security business for some time but Roy's show was so popular within the business that Geoff said, 'To get onboard was a bit like getting a prized job on the bin wagons... someone had to leave or, even more dramatically, die!'

Thankfully it was the prior... someone left. And, as there were still no jobs to be had on the bin wagons, Geoff was only too happy to step into his shoes when asked. Geoff's first shows were at the South Pier Theatre in Blackpool – which is no longer there, the theatre having been demolished in January 1998 and replaced with a steel roller coaster, The Crazy Mouse.

Geoff's job, along with the rest of the security team, was to take tickets at the door and search people as they entered the theatre. During the shows, they had to control any rowdy behaviour from members of the audience, and remove anyone that wouldn't tone it down, intent on continuing the disruption while Roy was on stage. The shows were being performed on Friday, Saturday and Sunday nights, and some of the crowd would have been out boozing for most of the day, so by the time they got to the theatre were well-oiled, to the point that they were often out of control and causing mayhem.

Roy has always been fully aware that his audiences pay with their hard-earned cash to come and see his shows so anyone that sets out to spoil the evening with their behaviour has to be quickly dealt with, usually to loud cheers of agreement from the rest of the crowd. Roy always has a bit of banter with hecklers, which is expected as part of his show. Throwing putdowns at them usually works and they would finally run out of things to say. Occasionally though you get the ones who've had a few too many drinks and refuse to be quiet, spoiling the night for everyone else… which is when Geoff and his boys step in and remove them from the auditorium.

Roy had become more comfortable using the same security team on his regular visits to Blackpool, so the lads, including Geoff, were asked to join the Roy Chubby Brown show full time on his tours throughout the UK. Around ten years later, Geoff eventually took over the contract with his own company GSO Security, and has now toured with Roy for over thirty years.

George Forster was Roy's manager when Geoff started at the South Pier and eventually changed the venue to the North Pier, where the theatre was situated at the far end, about a quarter of a mile out in the Irish Sea. Geoff remembers a day when Roy, together with his driver at the time, had arrived at the pier, and, whilst walking along toward the Theatre, they came across a Scottish bloke who started to shout and swear at Roy. Roy politely asked him to stop as there were women and children present. George asked that in future, on his arrival, Roy had to be met by a member of the security team and escorted from his car, along the pier and into the venue, a task they still perform to this day.

In the present Chubby era, Geoff still meets Roy as he arrives to make sure he gets into the theatre without any mishaps, together with any bags from the car that are required for the show. After making sure Roy is safely in his dressing room, Geoff puts on the electric kettle and makes him a cup of tea, after which Roy will go out on to the stage to complete his soundcheck.

Once the theatre opens to the public, the security lads monitor any bags that need to be searched, while also checking to see if anyone looks to have had too much to drink. Denise and John, the supporting act, go on stage at 7.30pm, coming off around 8.00pm, which leaves a twenty minute interval for people to finish their drinks in time for Roy to come on at 8.20pm. During the interval, Geoff helps to clear the bar and get everyone seated in time for the main event… Roy Chubby Brown.

Geoff is ably assisted by Paddy Christopherson and Neil Bingley these days and during the show, together they monitor the audience for disturbances. Approximately fifty five minutes into Roy's performance, Geoff collects a pint of beer from the bar and takes it up to the stage where he hands it to Roy for him to knock back in one go, even though Roy actually isn't that big a drinker. The action of Roy knocking back a pint of beer so swiftly always brings the audience to raptures, cheering and applauding the event in the same way we all would if England were to lift the World Cup.

Just before the end of the show, Geoff goes backstage to help Roy with his costume change for him to perform The Full Monty, then back into his patchwork suit for the finale.

After the show finishes, Geoff assists in taking photos during the meet and greet sessions that follow each performance. Then, once it's quietened down, he escorts Roy to his car to see him safely on his way to the next venue or home.

Geoff has travelled far and wide as security to Roy's shows across the UK and abroad in Gran Canaria, Benidorm and Tenerife, as well as running Roy's Facebook pages from Roy's instruction, and also co-hosting the website: *www.roychubbybrown.biz*

Geoff says, 'Roy is an absolute gentleman to work for and I regard him as a good friend, who always has time for his fans. He is a very generous and good-hearted man, whose fundraising efforts for cancer charities are phenomenal.' Then Geoff adds, 'When I was seriously ill in hospital, Roy drove the long distance from his home to Liverpool to visit me in person, which gave me a real boost in my recovery.'

Geoff ponders, 'Working with Roy Chubby Brown for over thirty years, as I'm sure you can imagine, there's never been a dull moment.'

A time that will stay in Geoff's mind forever happened in Blackpool around the year 2012. 'Roy had, by then, played every theatre venue in Blackpool that was available to him, every one but The Grand that was.' The Grand, a magnificent building, probably one of the finest Frank Matcham theatres in the country... Frank having been the architect on such famous structures as the London Hippodrome, Hackney Empire, as well as London Palladium and others throughout the country. Roy was excited that he was going to be performing in a theatre where so many famous names had tread its historical boards.

Geoff continues, 'Myself and the security team arrived about 3.45pm in order to meet Roy around 4.30pm. He arrived on time and was met at the stage door by the theatre manager, after which Roy, as usual, went straight on to the stage to complete his soundcheck. You could see how excited Roy was to be finally playing The Grand'. Once on stage, Roy just stood quietly for a while looking around in awe, staring at the stalls directly in front of him, then raising his head, turning from side to side to see the circle area, finishing off stretching his neck backward to take in the top tier gallery, known in theatre land as 'The Gods'. Then, once satisfied with the sound check, he went to his dressing room to relax with a cup of tea until it was showtime.'

Geoff continues, 'The support act went on and after their spot, the auditorium lights went up and everyone headed off to the bar. There was only a short interval, so I had to go and make sure the bar had been cleared which always closes while the main act is performing. As it is with the shows, quite a lot of these people who had come to see Roy had been in the bar since arriving without going up to watch the support act. Having successfully got everyone away from the bar area and into their seats, it was now time for Roy's show to start.'

At 8.20pm and with everybody where they should be, the theatre lights were dimmed. You could feel the anticipation amongst the audience when Roy's introductory salvo of 'You Fat Bastard' boomed out with everyone in the audience enthusiastically joining in. It got louder and louder, 'YOU FAT BASTARD! YOU FAT BASTARD!' as Roy appeared from the wings with the follow spot shining brightly on his patchwork suit. The follow spot is a piece of equipment which projects a bright beam of light onto a performer, some of you might have heard it called Super Trouper in the famous ABBA song.

Geoff adds, 'I was casually looking round the audience, making sure everyone was behaving themselves with half an eye on the stage. Roy came toward the front of the stage, then just as he was about to say, 'How did you know it was me?' Suddenly it wasn't him. The bright follow spot had been blinding Roy while he walked forward and as he looked for the front edge of the stage for guidance, he mistook the rail on the outside of the orchestra pit as the place he needed to be. Consequently Roy went arse over tit into the pit with a massive thump and a bit of a yelp… The audience, of course, roared with laughter thinking it was all part of the act.'

Geoff, spotting what had happened, raced over to the orchestra pit to find Roy rather dishevelled but actually trying to get up and back on to the stage. 'I ran into the pit,' tells Geoff, 'and guided Roy to the backstage pass door at the side of the orchestra pit which he went through, up the small flight of stairs and straight back on stage. He only had one of his moccasins on and his goggles were a bit skew-whiff, but you could see that he had the audience in the palm of his hand as he reappeared on stage to one of the loudest cheers I've ever heard.'

Roy went on to have a brilliant night, even though he was in pain. Geoff says that the next day, he was bruised to hell. Geoff smiles as he remembers, 'The theatre manager came over to me after I'd got Roy back on stage and said, 'That was great! Does he do that every night?' I explained not!'

Completing Roy's team are the brilliant sound and lighting skills of Phil Brown, who's now been with Roy for around six years, plus the fantastic Denise Danielle on vocals, brilliantly accompanied by musician John Todd, who have been supporting the show for nine years.

Left to right: Paddy (Security), Phil (Sound and Lighting), Geoff (Head of Security), Christine (Support Driver), Ritchie (Tour Manager), Roy, Denise and Toddy (Support Act), Keith (Roy's Driver and Merchandise Sales) and Neil (Security)

Together with Roy topping the bill and giving his fans exactly what they've come to expect with new material every time they see him, you've got yourself a full night's extravaganza that brings the audience to their feet as the show reaches its finale with Roy bidding his farewells and leaving the stage to rapturous applause and yells of delight.

A vitally important part of Roy's show is the brilliant musical backing tracks that belt out when he does any of his comedy songs. Roy demands perfection for every aspect of his show so it's pretty hard to believe that the fabulous sounds which accompany him on stage are reproduced in a small but fantastically equipped studio stuck on the side of a semi-detached house in Marske-by-the-Sea, a couple of miles from Redcar.

John Taylor, sound engineer extraordinaire, is the culprit… learning his skills from the ripe age of seventeen, working in a Scarborough theatre where he had access to a recording studio, spending his youth there as a tea boy, but also getting hooked on recording. John is a talented guitarist with a great voice. He says, 'I perform very little now. I'm a songwriter and only play my own stuff so we do an album and then maybe ten to twelve dates to promote the album.'

John continues, 'I first met Roy through music. It was through a mutual friend who's also a customer. He had a project that he was doing… a football world cup song, and he got the rights to an old 80s hit. A band called Tenpole Tudor did a song called Swords of a Thousand Men and he converted the lyrics, got permission from the writer, and his idea was to have it as a World Cup song but he was going to get celebs in on it. He got a couple of lads from Middlesbrough, Journey South – who did quite well in X-Factor – and the vet off Emmerdale, but also, he knew Chubby's gardener and you know Roy's really approachable for most things, he did the voice over. There was a video made with Roy doing some dancing and he voiced the famous Kenneth Wolstenholme words, 'Some people are on the pitch…. they think it's all over… it is now!' It's brilliant! He did the blue version finishing with 'It fucking is now!' Of course he had to do a straight one too. It did okay but it didn't get nominated for the official World Cup song. They called the band Alternative England, the song's called Hopes of a Thousand Men, the name was changed slightly to differentiate it from the original. I produced the track and Roy liked the sound so much, he asked, 'Who did the music for it?' He was simply told, 'A guy in Marske'. He rang and said, 'I believe you did the music for Hopes of a Thousand Men, and I really like the sound of it.' He had just finished filming his annual DVD and said he wasn't happy with the music content. He said, 'If I come over, do you think you could have a look at it? Roy came over to my studio – it was the first time I'd met him – he said, 'This piece of music is my own…' Because of copyright, he has to have his own original music on his videos. I said, 'Yes, I can do it. I'll get a couple of girls in to do the backing vocals,' and produced the song for him, with it going on his DVD. Roy was happy with the result and Universal, who he was signed with for his videos, were also happy enough to go with it. Now I produce the backing for his shows when he puts new songs in the show to freshen them up. I've done a lot of his songs and I've shot videos for him, though I didn't think when I first decided I wanted to go into recording that I'd be working with titles such as Songs In The Key Of Shite or Songs In The Key Of Fuck. Roy does write a lot of serious stuff though, which I've produced for him, sometimes singing on them myself. His Friends CDs, which we've done, are excellent. We bring professional musicians and singers in to work on them. They all come out brilliantly with Roy often playing the piano.

'I've probably recorded maybe about twenty or thirty straight songs with instrumentals as well for him but the vast majority of them is the comedy stuff for the show. We've started doing videos to the songs now and I do all his CD manufacturing for him, including his online stuff. I do all the analytics for his downloads. There's two albums and two singles on iTunes so I just take care of that side for him.

'Roy has his own label, RCB Records, an independent label, and out of everyone I know, bearing in mind I've been here thirty years so I've been doing a lot of recording with songwriters and putting lots of people on iTunes, nobody touches Roy for numbers. He streams a lot of music as far as New Zealand, Australia, all of the places he doesn't go to anymore, even Canada, South Africa… mainly English speaking countries.

'One of the funniest things that happened was he was in here one time doing some filming. He said, 'I'll have to get dressed up in the studio.' He came over for an evening session and got changed, and he said, 'You've seen my arse before, haven't you?' The next thing, he was hopping around behind the screen. I could see him balancing on one leg. I said, 'What is it?' He said, 'She's sewn my bloody legs up'. Apparently, the woman who makes his suits occasionally sews his trouser legs up as a joke. I wished I'd had the camera rolling because he was just jumping around with his trousers half up. It was hilarious. Apparently it happens regularly! We had to sit and unpick the stitching before we could start. The air was hilariously blue, but that wasn't anything unusual.'

Roy and John of Mirage Music

45

The empty pages that follow are where Roy wanted to lift the lid on some of the dodgy dealings he has had to endure throughout his career. We have been advised that it could lead to legal repercussions so we have left the pages empty so you can fill the blanks in yourself.

46

The year 2020 started off as any other year would… Auld Lang Syne… the lot… hopes, expectations, all positives. It turned out to be anything but. February saw Roy celebrate his 75th year of survival on this our planet Earth. As well as the usual family celebrations, Richard, Roy's oldest lad, arranged a night at The Sutton Arms in Faceby, not far from Roy's North Yorkshire house, for us old fogey friends to meet up for a meal. What a collection! We looked like a bunch of old time crooks who'd got back together to plan one last heist, much like the Hatton Garden mob.

It was a surprise for Roy and, as you can quite well imagine, reminiscing was high on the agenda, with lots of laughs to go with it.

Cake and pie… Roy's favourites

It was a fabulous night, the likes of which we wouldn't be able to repeat for a while because of the dramatic events that were about to unfold during that forthcoming year, namely the pandemic! One month later and we were living in lockdown… life as we knew it no longer existed. The best we could hope for was to meet our family on the drive or see them through the front window… at least we didn't have to put the hoover round every time someone said they were going to visit.

The lockdown included theatre land because Covid 19 had arrived, sweeping through the country, and was extremely contagious. Roy's shows came to a grinding halt again. As with his cancer lay off, Roy's immediate thoughts were for the team around him. How were they going to survive? It was thought at first it would only be a short break but here we are, late-2021 and just starting to get back to how things were before it all kicked off. Unfortunately, for some it will never go back to normality.

To start with, Roy was able to help out financially, but as the situation lengthened it became apparent that would not be possible to continue as long as there was no income coming in, but with the crew all being self-employed in their own right, it was hoped that the government scheme would help in some way. Geoff was still able to carry out his duties on Roy's Facebook, while Roy kept us all entertained for free with his daily blogs. The blogs were gratefully accepted by his fans who showed their appreciation with their Facebook comments, a collection of which speak for themselves.

That's better...just had me daily dose of Chubbs! Thankyou legend xxx
1h   Like   Reply

Hello again chubby love your daily blog's they keeping me going through all of this from start of reading your jokes to the end you have me in kink's with laughing , Love ya chubby X 😂😂😂👍
1h   Like   Reply

Fcuk me chubbs your still the greatest ever 😂😂😂😂😂😂😂😂😂😂😂
1h   Like   Reply

Watched the 50shades dvd last night! Brilliant!!
3h   Like   Reply   👍2

Brilliant as usual chubbs your really keeping everyone's spirits up keep going love ya pal
2h   Like   Reply

Thank you for your daily dose of gags. Must see you again as soon. You may remember you were in a hotel in Darlington about 12 months ago and a coach load came in with the Staffordshire Darts team. I was the driver…. Keep them coming and stay safe.
2h   Like   Reply

Ha ha cheers me up everyday chubby. Stay safe …..
40m   Like   Reply

Joe Longthorne and Roy had been friends for a very long time so when the suggestion was made for Roy to be the first celebrity to appear on Blackpool's North Pier, after it had been newly renamed The Joe Longthorne Theatre, in remembrance of Joe, he jumped at the chance, even though the North Pier hadn't been one of Roy's favourite venues in Blackpool. He used to complain, 'You can hear the sea under the stage, and in stormy weather it sways from side to fucking side.'

The performance was in the shape of a live stream and was scheduled to be staged on the 27th June 2020, slap bang in the middle of the coronavirus lockdown which meant an empty auditorium with everyone else involved respecting social distancing. The theatre was renamed after Joe's sad passing earlier in the year... Roy was a great admirer of the wealth of talent that Joe possessed. Roy says that Joe was one of the best all round entertainers of his day, being a fabulous singer, a great impressionist and dead funny, and could have made it big in America but, being a family man, he preferred to work closer to home.

Roy has a grin on his face when he tells of the first time he and Joe met back in the late seventies. 'I was booked to appear on the Jackson's Bakery Club in Hull and, on reaching the club, noticed there was quite a big crowd arriving for the show. I wasn't so well known in those days so I was pretty sure they hadn't come to see me.

Joe and Roy

As I walked in the front door, I made a comment to the doorman about the number of people coming into the club, to which he replied, 'Aye, our kid's on.'

'I continued into the concert room, where just about every seat was taken, with people still coming in through the door. I went straight to the dressing room. The entertainment secretary followed me in. I said, 'The doorman's son must be popular around here.' The secretary said, 'Who?' I said, 'The doorman's lad... he said, 'our kid's on'.' The secretary started laughing, 'That's Joe. Joe Longthorne's on with you.' I hadn't come across Joe before that day so I didn't know that being a local lad he was known as 'Our Kid' across the whole of Humberside, but we both had a good laugh over it when I told him.'

'From that first meeting, after watching Joe perform, you could see he was a star in the making, an obvious crowd puller, and we became good friends over the years, so when I was asked to be the first performer on at The Joe Longthorne Theatre, I was only too pleased to have been given the honour of reopening the North Pier in Joe's name. As well as at the same time making funds for my charities.'

On the streaming date, it was still not known when theatres would fully open to allow Roy to get back to doing what he loves, so this was an opportunity to give his loyal fans a much needed Chubby fix.

A technical glitch, which was completely beyond the control of Roy's management team, meant that some subscribers to the stream were unable to get a link on the night. I struggled, but managed to get on after about thirty minutes with the help of a family member, then watched the show in its entirety the following day as it was kept available for the next thirty days, so anyone that missed it could watch it later on 'catch up'. It appears the problem had been with the server of the company supplying the stream, who accepted responsibility and offered their apologies immediately after the show.

Regardless of the minor problem, most of the subscribers were able to make the link, with Roy and his manager, Tony Jo, who was doing the Michael Parkinson bit – not selling Roy life insurance plus a free pen – but as interviewer enjoying a terrific trip down memory lane with a few stories from Roy's earlier days on the road. The show was a complete success as Tony coaxed stories from Roy, as well as fans texting in with questions, together with some unseen Roy Chubby Brown clips from years gone by.

Before the show, Roy and Tony had an informal chat that was filmed and shown where Roy, armed with the day's newspapers, explained to Tony how he kept up with current events. Roy gave Tony a few stories from the day's papers that he was able to turn into jokes, a process he repeats on a daily basis to keep up to date with his material. The stream was a huge success with Roy's fans, who were only too happy to get a look at their hero on a live stage.

With the blogs, live stream and eventually monthly shows at The Joe Longthorne Theatre, albeit with a reduced audience after Covid restrictions were slightly relaxed to allow people in with social distancing, Roy has helped us all through the tedious months of lockdown. With restrictions being lifted totally in July 2021, it is hoped that Roy's shows will get back to normal. His first non-restricted night was at The Pheonix Theatre in Blyth, Northumberland on 24th July… having a great night with a standing ovation. The whole team were relieved to be back on the road again.

47

Throughout his career, Roy has always enjoyed the support received from his comedic comrades, especially during those dark days of his cancer scare, while he's selflessly offered the same to any who needed it themselves. And, although Ken Dodd will remain Roy's all-time comedy hero, a special mention must go to another character that he forged a great friendship with over the years… the legendary Bernard Manning.

Bernard and Roy talked regularly, with Bernard ringing two or three times a week, belting down the phone in his unmistakable gravelly voice, 'Now then, ya fat bastard. Have yer got owt for me?'

Roy says, 'I'd tell him the gag of the week or whatever, then he'd say, 'Did you hear the one about…?' carrying on to tell me his latest joke. We became firm friends and he called me his love child, 'Chubby's my love child, yer know,' he'd say.'

'In the early days, I worked with him at the Mayfair Suite in Newcastle. The crowd were shouting, 'Chuubbee… Chuubbee… Chuubbee!' Bernard said, 'They can shout your name all they like, as long as they don't get the fucking wage packets mixed up.' I'd have been on £150 at the time and he'd have been on about a grand.'

Roy continues, 'The really sad part though is Bernard rang me on a morning back in 2007. It was a Tuesday or a Wednesday. I was out at Tesco's so he left me a message with his same gravelly voice but much quieter, 'Roy, it's Bernard, I'm not very well, son. Thought I'd ring yer to cheer me up and put a smile on me face. Give me a ring when you can, mate.' After Tesco's, I went to the gym before I came home and never thought to listen to the answerphone immediately until I spotted the red light on it, which meant there was a message. I turned it on and listened to Bernard then rang him. His son answered the phone. I said, 'It's Chubby.' He said, 'I've got some sad news to tell you, Bernard's just died.' I got BT to put Bernard's last answerphone message to me on a disc and I've still got it today.'

As you can see, the comedy fraternity are a tight bunch, very much there for each other. But there was yet another challenge that Roy and his associates were going to have to cope with, when, in recent years, the new millennium heralded the 'woke' society, which had difficulty seeing the funny side of life, who then introduced us all to the 'snowflake'.

With them came 'cancel culture'. If there was anything going on that they didn't agree with, they said, 'We'll just cancel it.' Roy got caught up in the 'cancel culture' when this section of our society thought they were better equipped to decide how we enjoyed ourselves than we were… trying to dictate to us what we laughed at and what we didn't.

They didn't only stop there though. University debating societies found themselves being kicked off the agenda because the snowflakes didn't agree with the subjects they were going to debate, so even the toffs were being affected. 'Don't agree with you, we won't talk about it, never mention it again, na, na, na, na! I'm not even going to look at you, don't want to hear what you have to say. I'm putting my fingers in my ears!'

If you look at it, any joke is poking fun at someone, often yourself, but now if you have even the mildest giggle at any section of society, you immediately become labelled, when in reality you were just having a laugh. This labelling has caused Roy Chubby Brown to be banned from several venues over recent years, much to the displeasure of his fans, even though these venues would have been filled to the rafters at previous visits of the show.

It was amazing to see that at one point Roy's cancellations were on a par with the cancelling of kiddies school sports days because the 'woke' brigade thought that youngsters couldn't cope with coming second or getting beat. So, not only were these people trying to dictate what you could go and see, they were also robbing the next generation of a vital character building lesson in going out there to win but being magnanimous in defeat by taking it on the chin and moving on.

TV are putting out warnings at the beginning of just about every programme that goes out now, even our beloved soaps. Though I did think it a bit much when they announced, 'This programme might have scenes which could cause some viewers a certain amount of distress…' just before Match of the Day came on.

Most of our favourite sit-coms would never have been allowed airtime today because of narrow mindedness and fear of upsetting some snowflake. Fawlty Towers and Rising Damp get warnings before they dare show any repeats. There are many others. The likes of Love Thy Neighbour and Till Death Us Do Part will probably never be aired again. Roy and I have spent over two years writing a sitcom starring Roy himself… we called it Smoggies, being about a pub in our own area of Middlesbrough. But, because of the PC brigade, it's very unlikely that it will see the light of day.

I was going to leave it there but even while theatres, clubland, festivals, and all those connected including artistes and technicians, are at last starting to recover from the effects of the global pandemic, Sheffield City Trust came along and stuck the boot in, deciding, 'He's not our cup of tea, so we aren't going to let you see him!' It's the sort of thing we cringe at and 'thank God that's not us' when we hear similar things happening in dictatorships on the other side of the world.

Sheffield City Hall is a venue that Roy has filled to the rafters every time he's been for over thirty years. He has a great following in the city and he loves performing there as much as he loves the people who have supported him. The Chubbettes, mentioned earlier in the book, who come to gigs dressed in Chubby suits, live in Sheffield and typically show the fun side of what a night out at a Roy Chubby Brown show is all about. I'm sure you can understand the outrage of Roy's Sheffield fans when it was announced.

The decision had been made by The City Trust, who run the venue, then supported by the local Council, but I don't think neither would have been prepared for the backlash that followed, not only from Chubby fans, but also from people who would never go to

Sheffield City Hall... a full house of 2,200

watch his shows but were sick of being told what they could or couldn't do by a society that was quickly turning us into a nanny state. A petition was set up by Sheffield Chubby fans Haley Madden, Dave Johnson and Keith Butterley to get the decision reversed and to date had received in excess of 50,000 signatures with a peaceful demonstration also being arranged to take place outside the City Hall.

So far the Council have announced that they are standing by their original position of supporting The City Trust's decision... watch this space very carefully.

As a final note on this subject, and the real reason why it was originally brought up is that Roy makes it quite clear that political correctness will be left at the front door of any venue he'll be appearing at, and promises his fans that the context of his shows will never change. So even though you may never see your favourite comedian unleashed to the general public on the small screen, you can rest assured that you will still be able to 'fill yer boots' in the pleasure of his company somewhere near your home town in the foreseeable future.

When asking Roy's associates, family and friends for their memories to go in this book, everyone was only too happy to contribute. In fact, there were far more stories than we could fit in... granted, many were about Roy smacking someone over the head with his microphone in his early days, but lots more too.

There was the time Roy was interviewed on the Danny Baker Show, one of the few live TV appearances he would ever make, though Danny had to keep reminding Roy very politely that it was supposed to be an interview as Roy was playing to the audience instead of listening to what Danny was saying. 'I'm over here, Roy,' Danny would say with a laugh. 'Sorry, Danny. I'm used to pointing towards the audience.' There was also a full Roy Chubby Brown day on the channel Men & Motors, where they played ten of Roy's videos throughout the day.

We're now nearing the end of our long journey through Roy's life, having enjoyed the highest of his highs and endured the lowest of his lows. From the impoverished yet happy enough youngster who got to accept that the clouts around the head from his dad were the norm and braced himself for the inevitable whenever they happened – which was all too often – through his tearaway teenage years as Teddy Boy Roy, then into the Merchant Navy and ending up in borstal, before the life changing events of learning to play the drums, joining the band, and telling his first joke on stage, with the eventuality of becoming the much loved Roy Chubby Brown that we all know today.

Roy has no wish to glamorise his earlier notoriety, but to show that with a bit of effort anyone can turn their life around. He says, 'I'm sure everyone has a hidden talent somewhere. I've just been one of the lucky ones when I realised mine. So, whatever you think you're good at, don't be put off, give it a go. Later on in life, you'll wish you had.'

In conclusion, Roy admits that he certainly wouldn't have made it without the help of everyone who has been around him... his brilliant hardworking team, and Helen right by his side, keeping his feet firmly on the ground with the solid home life for which Roy had been searching most of his adult life.

In years to come, long after we've all shuffled off this mortal coil, our descendants will very likely sit in any of those old theatres that used to be filled with laughter and enjoyment, which will be banned by then because it might offend someone. While waiting for the nights 'entertainment', fully aware that it won't contain anything remotely funny so as not to 'hurt anyone's feelings', the lights will slowly dim, and during that deathly silence before anyone appears onstage, they'll hear whispering from the gallery, dropping into the stalls, then ghostly resonating around the auditorium, shhhhh ever so gently, 'You fat bastard... you fat bastard... you fat bastard... you fat bastard!'

It's enough to bring a tear to your eye, isn't it?

The End

The End... ???

NO FUCKING CHANCE!

LAST WORD FROM CHUBBS

I generally dedicate DVDs and books to my beautiful family, which I will also do on this occasion. Only this time, I wish to pay tribute as well as dedication to the many people who have played such an important part in my life and career.

I want you to know that everyone who told their stories holds a very important place in my heart… without you none of this could ever have taken place. You have all been a piece of my giant jigsaw puzzle and I'm humbled by the fact that you were all so willing to take the time with your contribution to my very own life story. And thanks for reminding me what a great life it has been.

Whether you have performed onstage with me, worked alongside me in a technical role, driven me about, been my personal assistant, or even just made me a cup of tea, I class you all as my friends.

Many of whom I'd like to pay tribute to are no longer with us, but are still in my thoughts, as I'm sure they are in yours. Their own stories have been eloquently transposed and included by those of us who worked alongside them and remember them today as if they were still here.

I can't finish my tributes without giving a huge thank you to my loyal fans who have supported me admirably amidst negativity from some quarters. My only way of repaying you is to continue entertaining in the way that I have done for the last fifty years. Many thanks again to you all, and I hope you have enjoyed reading about my colourful life.

I will be eternally grateful to every one of you… my fans, friends, work colleagues, associates and all of my family for helping to make this life of mine one that I could only ever have wished for in my wildest dreams.

I love you all.